)F ——————

)5   OF
)9 :TTLERS OF SPANISH TEXAS

D1245827

DONALD E. CHIPMAN AND HARRIETT DENISE JOSEPH

Explorers and Settlers of Spanish Texas

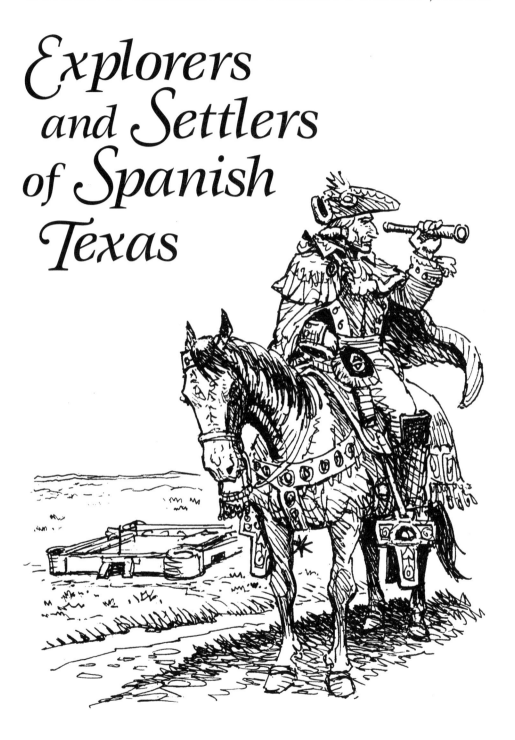

UNIVERSITY OF TEXAS PRESS, AUSTIN

Publication of this book was made possible in part by support from the Pachita Tennant Pike Fund for Latin American Studies

LIBRARY OF CONGRESS CATALOGING-IN-PUBLICATION DATA

Chipman, Donald E.
    Explorers and settlers of Spanish Texas / Donald E. Chipman and Harriett Denise Joseph.—1st ed.
        p.   cm.
Includes bibliographical references and index.
    ISBN 0-292-71231-6 (alk. paper)
        1. Explorers—Texas—Biography—Juvenile literature.
2. Pioneers—Texas—Biography—Juvenile literature.
3. Texas—Discovery and exploration—Spanish—Juvenile literature.   4. Frontier and pioneer life—Texas—Juvenile literature.   5. Spaniards—Texas—History—Juvenile literature.   6. Spaniards—Texas—Biography—Juvenile literature.   7. Texas—History—To 1846—Juvenile literature.
[1. Texas—History—To 1849.   2. Texas—Biography.
3. Explorers.   4. Pioneers—Texas.   5. Frontier and pioneer life—Texas.]   I. Joseph, Harriett Denise.   II. Title.
    F389 .C438   2001
    920.0764—dc21

00-011596

Contents

Introduction   vii

Acknowledgments   xi

ONE   *Alvar Núñez Cabeza de Vaca*
Ragged Castaway   1

TWO   *Francisco Vázquez de Coronado*
Golden Conquistador   17

THREE   *María de Agreda*
The Lady in Blue   32

FOUR   *Alonso de León*
Texas Pathfinder   46

FIVE   *Domingo Terán de los Ríos/Francisco Hidalgo*
Angry Governor and Man with a Mission   61

SIX   *Louis St. Denis/Manuela Sánchez*
Cavalier and His Bride   75

SEVEN   *Antonio Margil de Jesús*
God's Donkey   90

EIGHT   *Marqués de San Miguel de Aguayo*
Chicken War Redeemer   105

NINE   *Felipe de Rábago y Terán*
       Sinful Captain   119

TEN   *José de Escandón y Elguera*
      Father of South Texas   134

ELEVEN   *Athanase de Mézières*
         Troubled Indian Agent   149

TWELVE   *Domingo Cabello*
         Comanche Peacemaker   165

THIRTEEN   *Marqués de Rubí/Antonio Gil Ibarvo*
           Harsh Inspector and Father of East Texas   180

FOURTEEN   *Bernardo Gutiérrez de Lara/Joaquín de Arredondo*
           Rebel Captain and Vengeful Royalist   194

FIFTEEN   *Women in Colonial Texas*
          Pioneer Settlers   211

SIXTEEN   *Women and the Law*
          Rights and Responsibilities   226

Afterword   241

Bibliography   243

Index   249

Introduction

Explorers and Settlers of Spanish Texas is intended for younger readers. When the authors finished preparation of their work on *Notable Men and Women of Spanish Texas*, also published by the University of Texas Press, we were reminded of a conversation some years ago with Dr. George B. Ward. George is managing editor of the *Southwestern Historical Quarterly* and assistant director of the Texas State Historical Association. He is also a good friend. George remarked that in traveling around the state of Texas, one public school teacher after another has asked him why there was so little in print on Texas history—other than textbooks—for adolescents. Teachers who wanted to assign reports on such individuals as Coronado, Cabeza de Vaca, or the Lady in Blue could find little other than adult-level works. Even the great six-volume *New Handbook of Texas* (1996) is hardly designed for younger readers.

The authors had never tried to write for an audience other than adults. And neither of us was at all certain that we could do it successfully. We began by scanning and reading history textbooks used in the public schools to get a feel for an appropriate level of vocabulary. Next, we tried writing and then rewriting a sample chapter on Cabeza de Vaca. The task proved much more difficult than we had thought it might be. We simplified sentences, reduced the length of paragraphs, and struggled to find an acceptable style of writing.

After polishing a draft, we gave copies to several students in the Brownsville ISD. To our surprise, all of them thought the writing was "pretty good" and the subject matter "interesting." More important, those students made good suggestions, and we took them to heart. We followed by writing a second chapter on Coronado. The new chapter, together with the Cabeza de Vaca chapter, went to a friend and former student who teaches eighth-grade United States history in the Keller ISD. He made photocopies of the two chapters and had his students read them. Those students were especially complimentary of the chapters and remarked that they were well written and interesting. We also asked public school teachers in the Brownsville ISD to read sample chapters, as well as a specialist in reading in the Carrollton/Farmers Branch ISD. Once again, the comments were generally positive. Those students and teachers who were kind enough to donate their time and serve as guinea pigs for *Explorers and Settlers of Spanish Texas* are gratefully recognized by name in the Acknowledgments.

As an observation, the popularity of biography seems at present to be at an all-time high, with various outlets ranging from television to CD-ROM to the printed page. In the sixteen chapters that make up the text, we have used the biographical approach to Spanish Texas. In this manner, we have tried to humanize the past and to make our readers realize that the past was shaped by individuals who had the same strengths and weaknesses that we ourselves and our leaders have today.

In looking at personalities from Cabeza de Vaca in the early sixteenth century to Joaquín de Arredondo in the early nineteenth century, the reader is exposed to the full span of recorded history in the Spanish period. These men and women of Spanish and French ancestry are an important balance wheel of both Texas and United States history. Many of them walked the land and breathed the air that was North America well before English and Dutch nations colonized it.

The first literature that addressed parts of what later became the United States came from the pen of Alvar Núñez Cabeza de Vaca—that Great Pedestrian of both North and South America. Don Alvar was the first historian, anthropologist, and geographer of Texas and the Southwest. He was likewise the first merchant and physician-surgeon in the American Southwest. Those are a lot of firsts.

The reader will also learn about many other Spanish and French pioneers in the future Lone Star State. Herein one will find biographical sketches of sixteen men (some famous and some infamous) and of a notable Spanish nun.

The authors are especially pleased to offer adolescent readers a better understanding of women and their contributions to Texas history. Until recently, many of them have remained largely nameless and faceless. We know that they had children, washed and mended clothes, and swept their houses, but those activities are hardly the stuff of interest to readers of any age. And the importance of women as settlers in the colonial period goes far beyond bearing children and housekeeping. By reading the final two chapters in this book, one can learn about the roles, rights, and responsibilities of flesh-and-blood women in early Texas and American history.

Acknowledgments

Most authors will admit that a lot of credit for their books should go to persons whose names do not appear on the title page, and *Explorers and Settlers of Spanish Texas* is no exception to that rule. From the beginning, we knew that finding the appropriate level of vocabulary and using different sentence structure for adolescent readers would be a problem. To meet that challenge, it seemed reasonable to have students in our intended range of audience and their teachers read sample chapters. Fortunately, we had contacts through friends and former instructors of Joseph's daughter, Lindsey Nicole, who was a student at Pace High School in Brownsville, Texas.

Nicole Joseph and her younger friends, Denise Garza and Gilbert Muro (then at Stell Middle School in Brownsville), read the first chapters on Cabeza de Vaca and Coronado. Their suggestions received serious consideration and led us to rewrite sentences and recast paragraphs. Our genuine thanks are extended to Nicole, Denise, and Gilbert.

Two teachers, María Valdez and Alma Ortiz Knopp, both instructors at Stell Middle School, are also friends of the authors. They are experienced teachers with a good sense of what young people will read or will not read. Assessments of our revised chapter texts by Ms. Valdez and Ms. Knopp helped support the judgments of the three students mentioned above.

At the other end of the state, in Denton, Chipman asked Dr. Richard M. Golden, chair of the Department of History at the University of North Texas, if his son Jeremy would read the revised chapter on Cabeza de Vaca. Jeremy, then a student at Briarhill Middle School in Highland Village, Texas, gave that chapter his thumbs-up.

Rodney Hess, a former student of Chipman's and Teacher of the Year (1999) in the Keller, Texas, ISD, had students in his eighth-grade United States history classes read two chapters of the manuscript. Mr. Hess reported that his students thought the writing to be "quite good and interesting."

Finally, we called on our longtime friend Dr. Mary Doyle, chair of the Department of English at Newman Smith High School in the Carrollton–Farmers Branch ISD. Mary, a specialist in reading, applied three different formulas to determine readability. On those scales, the text of two chapters ranked at grade levels of 9.19, 8.53, and 9.50. Thus, we feel the writing is appropriate for both middle and high school students.

The authors' institutions, the University of Texas at Brownsville (UTB) and the University of North Texas (UNT), also provided valuable assistance. Joseph was aided by a reduced teaching load, and Chipman received a Faculty Research Grant to defray the cost of illustrations and maps. We wish to express our special thanks to Dean Anthony Zavaleta, Vice President for External Affairs at UTB; Dr. Farhat Iftekharuddin, Dean of the College of Liberal Arts at UTB; and Dr. Rollie R. Schafer, Vice President for Research at UNT, as well as to UNT's Faculty Research Committee, for having confidence in the scholarly content of a book intended for public school children.

At the University of Texas Press, our appreciation of its assistant director and editor in chief, Theresa J. May, knows few bounds. She encouraged this largely derivative work from our biographies in *Notable Men and Women of Spanish Texas* and supported our efforts from the very first. Thanks also to Letitia Blalock, our copyeditor, and Carolyn Wylie, our manuscript editor at the press. The authors accept the usual responsibility for errors and omissions, because our names do appear on the title page.

EXPLORERS AND SETTLERS OF SPANISH TEXAS

CHAPTER ONE

Alvar Núñez Cabeza de Vaca
RAGGED CASTAWAY

By name alone, Cabeza de Vaca (Cow's Head) sparks interest among readers of all ages. This remarkable Spaniard was born a couple of years before Columbus discovered America, and he later became the first person to write about Texas. When Cabeza de Vaca arrived on the Gulf Coast in the early winter of 1528, he was a cold and hungry victim of shipwreck on an island near present-day Galveston. For the next six years, he faced terrible hardships in Texas before fleeing south of the Río Grande into Mexico. During his time in the future Lone Star State, Cabeza de Vaca often traveled naked as the day he was born. At best, in winter he wore ragged pieces of clothing made from buffalo skins. For many of those half-dozen years, this Ragged Castaway, as he came to be known, was a slave of Texas Indians who treated him badly. Nevertheless, Cabeza de Vaca came to admire and accept Native Americans as fellow human beings. His growth from a bold Spanish conqueror to a sympathetic crusader for better treatment of Indians by other Spaniards makes his story inspiring. His personal growth also did much to convince natives that all Spaniards were not alike. As you read his story, note the remarkable change that took place in this first Spanish Texan, and remember that Cabeza de Vaca's commitment to improved conditions for Indians was permanent. In 1535, when he was finally reunited with Spaniards in Mexico, the former Ragged Castaway became a lifelong champion of Indian rights.

How did Cabeza de Vaca come to have such an unusual name? The answer lies in a centuries-long war fought in Spain between Christians in the north and Muslims in the south. Muslims invaded Spain from North Africa in 711 and, in the next few years, occupied most of the country. Around 720, Christians won their first victory and started a conflict (the Reconquest) that did not end until 1492. By the year 1212, Christian forces had pushed down from the north into southern Spain.

A shepherd and distant ancestor of Cabeza de Vaca named Martín de Alhaja was very familiar with a mountainous region known as the Sierra Morena, where he pastured sheep and where a huge battle would soon be fought. Alhaja marked a little known and unguarded mountain pass with the skull of a cow, which allowed Christian forces to mount a surprise attack on Muslim defenders and defeat them. The resulting victory so pleased the Christian king of Spain that he gave the family name of "Cow's Head" to Martín de Alhaja, who then became Martín Cabeza de Vaca. This same Martín was the grandfather of Cabeza de Vaca's mother.

It was a custom in Spain at this time for a young person to take the name of either parent's family for his own. Because his mother's name was more famous than his father's, a boy born around 1490 became Alvar Núñez Cabeza de Vaca.

When young Alvar was growing up in the south of Spain, he no doubt heard of Columbus's discovery of America and longed to cross the great Atlantic Ocean and make his fortune in what was then called the New World. But first, don Alvar decided to follow the life of a soldier in the Spanish army. When he was about twenty years of age, Cabeza de Vaca fought a battle in Italy, after which he was promoted to the rank of junior officer for his bravery. Some fifteen years later, he was selected as second in command of a large Spanish expedition that was to explore and settle what is now Florida. This well-planned undertaking left Spain in 1527 and sailed to America, where it took on supplies from Spanish-controlled islands in the Caribbean Sea.

Keep in mind that from the time of Columbus onward, Spaniards believed they would find strange and unusual creatures living in the New World. Before ever setting foot on any unexplored areas in America, they expected to find giants, dwarfs, white-haired boys, people with tails, headless men with an eye for a belly button, and apes that could play trumpets. This may sound strange, but perhaps you have seen pictures of famous historic buildings in Europe, like Notre Dame Cathedral in Paris, that sprout gargoyles and other creatures that are a mixture of humans and wild animals. The people who built these great churches in Europe during the Middle Ages also believed that unusual creatures lived in far-off lands beyond the ocean seas.

After reaching America and spending the winter months of 1527 in Cuba, the expedition that Cabeza de Vaca had joined continued on to largely unexplored Florida and arrived near present-day Tampa Bay in the following spring. First in command was a red-bearded, one-eyed captain named Pánfilo de Narváez, who soon made a really bad decision. Landing on the west coast of south Florida in April 1528, Narváez, despite the objections of second officer Cabeza de Vaca, chose to separate about three hundred men from the ships that had brought them from Cuba. The commander wanted to explore the land, believing it safe to do so since he thought Mexico was nearby. Within a matter of hours, these men were hopelessly lost in Florida and never again made contact with their supply ships.

Faced with hunger and unfriendly Indians along the coast of Florida, Narváez began a march northward in June and continued on to the region near modern-day Pensacola in northwest Florida. There the stranded Spaniards camped for about three months. Food shortages and hostile Indians forced them to think about leaving Florida by boats, which they had to build in the wilderness without proper tools.

Remember that Spaniards were the first to explore much of both North and South America, and in doing so they were often very good at dealing with unexpected problems. On this occasion in Florida, they killed their horses and lived on the meat. They melted down bridle bits and stirrups to make saws and axes so they could cut planks from trees for the bottoms of their boats. They tanned skins from the legs of their slaughtered horses to make fresh-water bags. And they used their shirts and trousers to rig sails on five very crude and leaky craft that could each hold about fifty men. Since approximately fifty of the men had already died or been killed by Indians, these five boats were enough to carry all the survivors from Florida, which they left in late September of 1528.

Because their boats were so poorly built, the Spaniards never intended to get very far from shore. Their plan was to sail along the Gulf Coast and eventually reach Mexico. But in that day and age, Spanish conquerors and explorers had a very poor knowledge of geography and few maps. They mistakenly believed Mexico to be only about ninety miles away, when the actual distance was close to fifteen hundred miles! So each day they expected to arrive at the port of Veracruz on the east coast of Mexico, only to find endless Gulf waters.

Still, the first month at sea went well, and the five small craft made good progress. As they approached the mouth of Mississippi River on their thirty-first day at sea, troubles began. A storm struck the poorly constructed boats and tossed them about like driftwood. To add to their misery, the Spaniards had run out of fresh water, because, in the words of Cabeza de Vaca, "the skins we made from the horses' legs rotted and became useless."

The five boats survived the first storm, but just barely. Then a more powerful storm hit the flimsy vessels, driving them apart until each boat had lost sight of the others. The craft carrying Cabeza de Vaca and about forty-five others survived this bad weather, but the men were so weak that they began to pass out and fall one on top of the other in the bottom of the boat. Soon fewer than five remained standing. One of those five was Cabeza de Vaca.

At about midnight on their last day at sea, Cabeza de Vaca took over the task of steering the boat through the rest of the night. Although worn out, he admitted that "sleep was the furthest thing" from his mind. Near dawn the roar of waves hitting the shore made Cabeza de Vaca aware that land was nearby. As they approached the Texas coast, a huge wave caught the vessel and lifted it "out of the water as far as a horseshoe can be tossed." The resulting jolt caused most of the men to scramble up from the bottom of the boat, where they "were almost dead." Under such awful circumstances, Cabeza de Vaca first set foot on the soil that is Texas.

Cabeza de Vaca and his companions had landed on an offshore island that he named Isla de Malhado, or Isle of Misfortune. A second boat, containing about forty-five others, had landed on the same island during the previous day. So, in all, about ninety Spaniards had reached the Texas coast near modern Galveston in November 1528.

The Isle of Misfortune was a home of Karankawa Indians, who soon appeared near the site where Cabeza de Vaca's boat had come ashore. To don Alvar and his companions, it was a frightening experience. In the words of Cabeza de Vaca, "We were so scared that they seemed to be giants, whether they were or not. . . . We could not even think of defending ourselves, since there were scarcely six men who could even get up from the ground." Fortunately for the Spaniards, the Indians were friendly. In sign language they promised to return in the morning with food, for they had none at the time. The natives, true to their word, brought fish and water on the following day.

After receiving some food and water, Cabeza de Vaca and his companions attempted to launch their boat, but the effort ended in disaster when the craft overturned and three drowned. The rest of the men were then caught by waves and cast ashore again on the same island. According to Cabeza de Vaca, "Those of us who survived were as naked as the day we were born and lost everything we had." Added to their misery was the cold of early November.

The Spaniards were in such bad shape that the Karankawas sat down among them and began to cry, weeping and wailing for the better part of half an hour. Try to imagine how upsetting this was to the Spaniards. If the Indians felt sorry for *them*, they who were Christians and thought they were far better than crude and uneducated natives, then they truly were in a lot of trouble! Over time, as we shall see, Cabeza de Vaca came to accept Indians as fellow human beings, but it would take several more years to change his attitude.

After joining up with those in the second boat, the total number of Spaniards on the Isle of Misfortune was perhaps eighty-five. But by the spring of 1529, hunger, cold weather, and various fatal illnesses had reduced their number to only fourteen or fifteen.

During the hard winter months of 1528, Cabeza de Vaca left the Isle of Misfortune and traveled to the mainland. Although he had no way to write down his impressions of the Karankawa Indians, don Alvar was blessed with a good memory. He later recorded many interesting observations about early Texas Indians in his book called *The Account*.

Don Alvar described the Karankawas as tall and well built, with bows and arrows for weapons. He believed these Indians to love their children more than any other people in the world, for when a child died, parents, relatives, and friends mourned their loss for an entire year. To our way of thinking, the Karankawas were very cruel to old people and often left them to die without any offer of help. However, food was so scarce for these Indians that they could not spare it for the elderly. Children came first, and they had to be fed. Even so, Cabeza de Vaca wrote that the Karankawas often went hungry, and that food and firewood were scarce. With a touch of humor, he added that the only thing plentiful among these people was mosquitoes.

One of the most remarkable things about Cabeza de Vaca was his skill in treating sick Indians. He had no training in medicine, and he was very reluctant to play the role of doctor. But the Indians believed him to have magical powers to cure them, and because they *thought* what Cabeza de Vaca did was helpful, they often did get well. Don Alvar's method of treating sick Indians was nothing more than saying prayers for them or blowing his breath on the part of their body that was injured.

During that first awful winter when so many Spaniards died, Cabeza de Vaca recorded that his fellow Spaniards were driven to cannibalism. They became so desperate for food that as some died, others ate their flesh. Keep in mind that many people today think of the Karankawas in Texas as having been cannibals, but those very Indians were shocked that Spaniards would eat their own.

While Cabeza de Vaca was visiting on the mainland, he himself became ill. Word spread to the Isle of Misfortune that he had died. Without bothering to check on his condition, all but two of his friends on the island decided to move down the coast toward Mexico. Luckily, don Alvar recovered his health. When he returned to the island, he learned that most of his friends were gone. Cabeza de Vaca decided that he must remain near the Isle of Misfortune, because he did not wish to leave behind the two Spaniards who had refused to leave, mostly because they could not swim.

Cabeza de Vaca spent the next four years as a merchant, and at times he moved well into the interior of Texas. On one occasion, he was captured by Indians who made him their slave. Don Alvar claimed that these natives worked him hard and treated him badly, and it took him almost a year to plan and carry out a successful escape.

During the winter months, don Alvar would usually cross over to the Isle of Misfortune and try to persuade the two Spaniards there to leave with him and move down the coast toward Mexico. But the two men always offered excuses for not leaving. What they feared most was drowning, since they could not swim.

For three more years Cabeza de Vaca waited on or near the Texas coast. During that time, he became a successful merchant, the first in Texas history. Don Alvar carried seashells into the backcountry, where he traded them for buffalo hides. The interior Indians found seashells very valuable, because the shells had edges that were sharp enough to serve as knives. Having no metals, these Indians needed tools to cut open mesquite beans for food.

Cabeza de Vaca admitted that he liked being a merchant. It gave him the freedom to travel, but it was a dangerous life. He had to avoid unfriendly Indians who would enslave him, and he was often cold and hungry. What he missed most were friends and the company of men who could speak his own language.

During the four winters that don Alvar returned to the Isle of Misfortune, one of the Spaniards there died. Finally, Cabeza de Vaca would not take no for an answer when he insisted to the sole survivor that the two of them move down the coast toward Mexico. He placed the man on a log and floated him over to the mainland. The men then began their journey toward Mexico.

As perhaps you know, moving along the Texas coast on foot is very difficult. The elevation is low, and there is a lot of standing water. Rivers enter the Gulf from Texas, and Cabeza de Vaca had to cross four streams as he made his way toward Mexico. In each case, he had to deal with a terrified companion who could not swim a single stroke. After successfully crossing the rivers, Cabeza de Vaca and his companion came to large body of water. At this point, the companion begged to go no farther. But Cabeza de Vaca took the man on his back and continued on.

After Cabeza de Vaca had swum himself and the other Spaniard across the large lagoon (body of water), he met several Indians who told him that three men were camped just ahead. The natives gave him the names of two Spaniards and a black man called Stephen. When Cabeza de Vaca asked about the fate of the others who had left the Isle of Misfortune some four years earlier, he was told that they had been killed by Indians for "sport" or because they had been the subject of bad dreams.

These same Indians told Cabeza de Vaca that the three men were the slaves of other natives who treated them badly by kicking and slapping them about. According to don Alvar, to convince him that they were telling the truth, "They slapped and beat my companion and gave me my share too." All of this was too much for Cabeza de Vaca's fainthearted friend. He turned back toward the Isle of Misfortune and disappears from our story.

Two days after the man left, Cabeza de Vaca was reunited with his former companions. The men were astonished to see him, because they believed he had died four years earlier. They were also embarrassed to admit that they should have checked out rumors of his death before leaving him behind. However, don Alvar was so happy to see them that he forgave them completely. In his words, "We thanked God very much for being together." It was one of the happiest days of their lives.

Once they were together, the three Spaniards and the African Stephen agreed that at the first opportunity they would flee toward Mexico. But again there were problems. One of the Spaniards and the black man could not swim, and they dreaded the thought of having to cross rivers. After assuring the nonswimmers that they would be helped, the four agreed to escape just as soon as possible. But it was absolutely necessary that they keep their plans secret. If the Indians learned of them, they would surely kill all four men.

The Four Ragged Castaways, as they came to be known, decided to wait six months before attempting their escape. At that time the Indians who held them as slaves would move farther south to eat the ripe fruit of the prickly pear cactus. In doing so, they would bring the four men much closer to Mexico and increase their chances for a successful getaway.

During this half year of waiting, the four learned the fate of the other men who had left Florida with them. All of the boats had made it to shore along the Texas coast, but those who had landed beyond the Galveston area had run into very hostile Indians who took the lives of some of them. Others had died of hunger and disease, while still others quarreled over food and wound up killing one another. Once again, the last to die had kept themselves alive for a time by eating the flesh of fellow Spaniards. In the end, there were only the Ragged Four—three European whites and an African black.

Once again Cabeza de Vaca found himself a slave of new masters who treated him badly. But he began to learn things about them, which he later set down in his book *The Account*. He found out that Indians along the Texas coast, known as the Mariames, regularly killed girl babies and fed their bodies to dogs. Don Alvar asked them why they would do such a terrible thing. Like those Indians you have already read about who did not take care of old people, the answer made sense.

The Mariames were a small group of Indians, and most of them were related to each other. It was not possible for their young women to marry a brother or a cousin, for this would amount to incest. Their only opportunity for marriage was to wed men of another Indian group. But all of the tribes that lived around the Mariames were their bitter enemies. If they let girl babies live to become adults and then marry outsiders, the young women would bear children for enemies and increase their numbers. The murder of female babies, although awful, was done to ensure the safety of the Mariames themselves.

Another Indian group described by Cabeza de Vaca was the Yguazes. These natives ate three kinds of roots that they had to dig and roast. The roots were hardly ideal foods, for they caused serious stomach pains, as well as swelling of the stomach. They were also bitter and tasted terrible. Still, the Yguazes were often so hungry that they would eat almost anything—including "spiders, ant eggs, worms, lizards, salamanders, and poisonous snakes." Besides these foods, the Yguazes also ate "other things" that were so bad that don Alvar could not bring himself to name them. He called these foods "unmentionables." One may well wonder what these items might have been! Cabeza de Vaca wound up saying that the Yguazes were often so hungry that he believed "they would eat stones if there were any in that land."

Despite being very disturbed by what the Yguazes ate, Cabeza de Vaca greatly admired the ability of these Indians to "run from morning to night without resting or becoming tired." The men could keep running long enough to chase down a deer on foot and kill it with their bare hands.

The Yguazes suffered terribly from swarms of mosquitoes that attacked them night and day. It was the job of slaves to keep fires burning all night so that the smoke would help drive off the insects. If you have ever gone camping, you know that the downside to this method of mosquito repellent is eyes that water all night. For Cabeza de Vaca it was even worse. When he fell asleep from exhaustion and the fire burned low, he was awakened by a sharp kick in the side and given orders to find more wood.

In describing the animals of early Texas, Cabeza de Vaca wrote the first accounts we have of buffalo. He called these animals "cows," and remarked that they were about the same size as cattle in Spain. Don Alvar admitted that he liked buffalo meat better than beef. He also commented that buffalo hides made fine blankets and that the Yguazes also used the skins of buffaloes to make shoes and shields.

Finally, six months passed, and the Indians moved to great prickly pear cactus patches of South Texas. Just as the Four Ragged Castaways planned to flee to Mexico, their masters got into a fight over a woman, which ended in blows with sticks and fistfights. Their Indian masters became so angry that they marched off in different directions, taking their slaves with them. All plans for escape had to be delayed for another year.

During this year, Cabeza de Vaca suffered terribly. He was made miserable by hunger, because when food was in short supply, slaves ate even less. Three times don Alvar tried to escape and three times he was captured. With each capture he was beaten and threatened with death.

The year passed, and once again the Indians gathered in the south of Texas to feast on the prickly pear cactus. And once again the four men were able to contact each other and lay secret plans for escape to Mexico. This time they were successful, and the four of them fled in the night. By then it was September 1534, and Cabeza de Vaca had been in Texas for almost six years.

The Four Ragged Castaways did not cross into Mexico until the following year. In South Texas, they were accepted as free men by kindly Indians known as the Avavares. The men were fed deer meat, which they had not eaten before and did not recognize. It was at this time that Cabeza de Vaca became really famous as a healer of the sick. He could cure severe headaches and other illnesses by making the sign of the cross and saying prayers. In the same manner, he also saved an Indian who had no pulse and "showed all the signs of being dead." Although free to move on if they wished, the four men thought it wise to spend the approaching winter among friendly natives, and they did so.

Cabeza de Vaca memorized things about the Avavares that are really interesting. These Indians had been terribly frightened in the past by an evil being they called Malacosa, or Bad Thing. According to the Avavares, this horrible creature was capable of pulling arms out of their sockets and cutting out pieces of intestines. The Castaways did not believe in Malacosa, but they used the Indians' fear of him to good advantage. They promised the Avavares that if they believed in the Christian God, no harm from Mr. Bad Thing would come to them.

Before his final departure from Texas, Cabeza de Vaca summed up in his mind some very general impressions of its native population. He later set them down in his book. It is sometimes claimed that Indians loved all living things before the arrival of white people in America. In truth, Indians were just like all of us. Cabeza de Vaca stated that every tribe he had met made war on almost every other Indian tribe. In short, for early Texas Indians, war was a way of life. Don Alvar himself had already concluded that Indians had the same good qualities and bad qualities that all human beings share. For example, he had come to know Indians who treated him kindly and other natives who would beat him half to death. As we said early in this chapter, it was a lesson that Cabeza de Vaca never forgot. Over the nearly seven years that he would spend in Texas, he changed his views of Native Americans and came to accept them as fellow human beings. As he changed, Indians paid him the great compliment of recognizing that all Spaniards were not alike.

In 1535 the Four Ragged Castaways said good-bye to their friends the Avavares, and crossed the lower Río Grande into Mexico. Ahead lay the most remarkable of all experiences for Cabeza de Vaca as a healer of the sick. South of the Great River, he came upon an Indian who had been shot in the chest with an arrow. The arrowhead had lodged just above the heart and was causing great pain and suffering. With a knife, don Alvar opened the Indian's chest and removed the stone point. He then closed the incision and sewed it shut with two stitches, and he stopped the bleeding by using hair scraped from an animal. The man recovered completely. So Cabeza de Vaca was the first to perform surgery in the American Southwest. This operation has earned Cabeza de Vaca a place in the *New England Journal of Medicine,* the most famous medical publication in the United States. He has also been accepted as the "patron saint" of the Texas Surgical Society.

The Castaways continued on their way across northern Mexico

*Cabeza de Vaca performs the first
surgery in the Spanish Southwest*
(DRAWING BY JACK JACKSON)

and eventually returned to Texas near the present town of Presidio.
They crossed over to the Texas side of the Río Grande and walked
upstream along its banks for seventeen days. South of modern El Paso,
they again crossed the Great River and set out for the west coast of
Mexico. Seven months after leaving their friends the Avavares, the
four men reached the Pacific Ocean.

While walking south along the coast, one of the Spaniards spotted
an Indian with a leather necklace. Tied to it was a small metal buckle
and a horseshoe nail. This meant that fellow Spaniards had to be nearby,
for the Indians had no iron. When the Ragged Castaways asked the
man where he had gotten the items, he said they had come "from some
bearded men like us." As the four men hurried on, they saw further
signs of Spaniards, such as tracks of horses and old campgrounds.

Cabeza de Vaca and Stephen were able to walk faster than their two Spanish companions, and they were the first to come upon several Spaniards riding horses. These men were so amazed by Cabeza de Vaca's appearance that could not even say a word. Having spent more than seven years in Texas and Mexico, don Alvar had a long beard and skin that was burned black by the sun, and he wore no clothing. But the mounted Spaniards knew Cabeza de Vaca was one of them, and they soon took him to meet their captain.

By then Indians who were traveling with the Four Ragged Castaways had come to accept them as friends and fellow human beings who shared things with them on an equal basis. These same natives refused to believe that Cabeza de Vaca was a Spaniard like the cruel men on horseback, who made slaves of Indians. The Indians told don Alvar that he healed the sick, while the slave raiders killed the healthy. He was naked, walked barefoot, and had no weapons, while the other men were dressed in armor, mounted on horses, and armed with swords. It is really important to note that, in the minds of the Indians, Cabeza de Vaca had become one of them. The men on horseback, on the other hand, were totally different and were dangerous enemies.

From near the Pacific Coast, the Four Ragged Castaways were taken to the house of the provincial governor, Nuño de Guzmán, who gave them clothes and horses to ride. The men then continued on to Mexico City, where they were greeted in July 1536 by the viceroy, the highest official in the colonial government. On the day after their arrival in the capital city of Mexico, the three Spaniards attended a bullfight, a spectacle brought to Mexico by Spain.

Cabeza de Vaca quickly set down his memories of spending nearly eight years in the wilderness of Texas and Mexico. When he returned to Spain a couple of years later, he used these notes to write a book about his experiences. If you find Cabeza de Vaca's story interesting, you may someday wish to read *The Account*, written in his own words.

In 1540 Cabeza de Vaca returned to the New World as the governor of a region in South America that is today the country of Paraguay. Landing on the coast of Brazil, he could not find a ship to take him by water to his destination. So Cabeza de Vaca decided to lead 250 men across one thousand miles of unexplored lands. In doing so, he lost only two men. One drowned in a river, and the second was killed by a jungle cat.

Probable route of Cabeza de Vaca across Texas and New Spain
(CENTER FOR MEDIA PRODUCTION, UNIVERSITY OF NORTH TEXAS)

As governor of this area of South America, Cabeza de Vaca insisted that the Indians be treated fairly. This was not popular with other Spaniards, who wished to work the natives hard in their search for gold. Don Alvar's kindly attitude was formed in the wilds of Texas, where he himself had often been a slave of Indians. So in a short time, Cabeza de Vaca was removed from office by Spaniards who would not accept his orders to treat Indians fairly.

Cabeza de Vaca was sent back to Spain in chains, where he faced being punished for his actions. He was accused of crimes that he did not commit, and he was charged with being a governor who took up for Indians instead of Spaniards.

For six long years, Cabeza de Vaca was tried for various crimes, and in defending himself he ran out of money to pay lawyers. He had married after returning to Spain, and his wife also used up all her personal wealth in trying to free her husband. By this time, don Alvar was about sixty years of age, and his future did not look good. Finally, a judge passed sentence on this remarkable Spaniard. Under penalty of death, he could not go back to America for the rest of life, and he would be sent to Africa for five years as punishment.

Fortunately for Cabeza de Vaca, the king of Spain decided to over-rule the judge. Don Alvar did not have to go to Africa, and he received a sum of money for his services in America. The king also gave Cabeza de Vaca a job that paid him a little money for as long as he wished to work. We do not know when Cabeza de Vaca died or where he is buried.

There are many reasons to remember Cabeza de Vaca as an important early Texan. He was the first to write about the land that would be-come the future Lone Star State. He was the first merchant in Texas. He was the first to describe the animals and plants of Texas. And he was the first to describe the Native Americans who lived in Texas. Those are a lot of firsts. Above all, Cabeza de Vaca should be remem-bered for his belief that all Spaniards should treat Indians with kind-ness and fairness. In his own words, this approach was the "only way, the road most sure, and no other." It was most unusual for a man in that day and age to have those feelings. The story of Cabeza de Vaca is also the story of a good Spaniard. As you read other chapters in this book, you will come to know explorers and settlers who had very good qualities and still others who did not.

SOURCES

Materials used in preparing this chapter are described below. You can find more information about these sources in the Bibliography at the end of the book.

Books

Any understanding of Cabeza de Vaca begins with his own account of his adventures in America. Known as *La Relación* (*The Account*), it is widely available in paperback editions. Donald E. Chipman and Harriett Denise Joseph's *Notable Men and Women of Spanish Texas* contains a more detailed treatment of Cabeza de Vaca.

Articles

For a study of his travels in Texas and Mexico, see Chipman's "In Search of Cabeza de Vaca's Route across Texas," *Southwestern Historical Quarterly* 91 (October 1987): 127–148.

Quotes

Most quotes in this chapter are taken from *The Account: Alvar Núñez Cabeza de Vaca's "Relación,"* edited by Martin A. Favata and José B. Fernández. The last quote is from Rolena Adorno's "The Negotiation of Fear in Cabeza de Vaca's *Naufragios*," *Representations* 33 (Winter 1991): 186. *Naufragios* is Spanish for *Shipwrecks*, another title for Cabeza de Vaca's *Account*.

Additional Information

A painting by a famous Texas artist named Tom Lea, which shows Cabeza de Vaca performing surgery on an Indian, is reproduced on the cover of Chipman and Joseph's *Notable Men and Women of Spanish Texas*.

CHAPTER TWO

Francisco Vázquez de Coronado
GOLDEN CONQUISTADOR

Between the years 1540 and 1542, a Spanish conquistador traveled across parts of what are today the states of New Mexico, Texas, Oklahoma, and Kansas in search of gold. This man's full name was Francisco Vázquez de Coronado. His explorations came about as a result of Cabeza de Vaca and his companions reaching Mexico City in July 1536. Once the Four Ragged Castaways were safe, they began to talk about their adventures, which had gone on for almost eight years.

As often happens when stories are repeated over and over again, with each telling a bit of truth is lost as the storyteller tries to make the adventures seem more fantastic than they really were. Also, listeners will sometimes exaggerate what they have heard when repeating it to friends or family. In a very short time, Spaniards in Mexico City came to believe that really rich cities lay to the north. Important men were eager to organize expeditions and risk lives in the hope of finding great wealth. These men believed that somewhere in America they would find fabulous cities with streets paved in gold. Since the time of Columbus, Spaniards had looked for a golden city they called El Dorado.

The most powerful of these treasure seekers was Antonio de Mendoza, the viceroy (chief royal official) of Mexico. By this time in history, Spaniards already knew about the very real wealth of the Aztecs in Mexico and the Incas in Peru. It was certainly possible that the country to the north of Mexico also contained great riches, and the viceroy was eager to check out the truth of the matter.

Mendoza chose as his scout a priest named Father Marcos de Niza.

Since Niza had never been to the north country, he needed a guide. The viceroy bought the African slave named Stephen, who had been one of the Four Ragged Castaways, and sent him back to the country he had escaped from. Keeping Niza company was another priest and several Indian helpers who carried supplies and equipment. But Stephen was to lead the way.

As the party moved up the west coast of Mexico, the priest who accompanied Father Niza fell ill and had to be sent home. Then an unfortunate decision was made. Stephen was much younger and stronger than Father Niza, and he asked to travel ahead of the main group at a faster pace. Niza gave Stephen permission to do so, and the black man was soon in front by several days.

It was agreed that Stephen would send back wooden crosses of different sizes to show how much wealth he had discovered. After several days, a huge cross arrived from the black man. He had reached villages in present western New Mexico where the Indians lived in adobe houses built like apartments that were several stories high. While among these Indians, called Zuñis, Stephen had demanded too much wealth and special privileges. The Zuñi chiefs decided that he must die because he was evil. They fell upon him with weapons and killed him.

Father Niza learned of Stephen's death as he approached the Zuñi villages, which he could see in the distance. He believed that because the chiefs had killed the African, it was too dangerous to go any closer. Without learning more about the Zuñis or their villages, Niza turned around and hurried back to Mexico City.

Along with their belief that they would find strange creatures and great treasure in America, Spaniards thought that somewhere they would discover seven towns built close together. A Spanish legend claimed that centuries ago seven Catholic bishops had fled from Muslim invaders and crossed the Atlantic Ocean. These bishops had each founded an incredibly wealthy city in the New World. The Seven Cities of Cíbola, as they were called, would be the richest of all towns in America.

When Niza met with the viceroy, he reported on the unfortunate death of Stephen. But he also had exciting news. He had been told that the Zuñis lived in seven villages. The smallest of them, according to Niza, was larger than Mexico City! Could these be the legendary Seven Cities of Cíbola?

This news created much more interest than the tales told earlier by the Four Ragged Castaways. Viceroy Mendoza quickly organized a large army of soldiers dressed in shiny armor and mounted on horses. Placed in charge of this expedition was Francisco Coronado. Father Niza would act as its guide. He would lead the army back to the place where Stephen had died. There the Spaniards believed that they would finally find the Seven Cities of Cíbola.

The viceroy made a good choice in appointing Coronado as the leader of his expedition. Don Francisco was governor of the region in western Mexico where the army would be organized. He was also the viceroy's closest friend, and Mendoza knew that his captain was wise, intelligent, and brave. Also, Coronado's wife, doña Beatriz, was a wealthy lady, and she made sure that her husband had the finest clothing and armor. To ensure that his every need was met, Beatriz provided her husband with African servants, several grooms, and extra horses and mules.

Many of Coronado's men were young, some of them being no more than sixteen or seventeen years of age. For these youngsters, marching off to find the Seven Cities of Cíbola was like a fairy tale come true. Their heads were filled with high hopes for adventure and the prospects of becoming very rich.

When Coronado set off for Cíbola, he had a total of about four hundred adults and young men in his army. More than half of them rode horses, while the rest of the troop were foot soldiers. There were also hundreds of Indians and a few black slaves who carried supplies and equipment. Coronado himself had twenty-three horses and three or four suits of horse armor. He also had a personal suit of gold-colored armor and a helmet topped with a feather plume.

Although filled with excitement, most of the soldiers had no idea of the difficulties that lay ahead on the long march to Cíbola. In late April 1540, Coronado left the town of Culiacán in western Mexico, where he had looked after last-minute details. He did not arrive at the Zuñi villages until early July. Along the way, his men suffered from a scalding sun and lack of water. They were also dirty, footsore, and often hungry, for very little food could be found on the trail. But always there was the lure of great wealth, if the cities were indeed paved with gold. That hope kept the men going.

At last Cíbola was in sight. What a shock it must have been to these treasure hunters! Instead of a great city with streets of gold and

Indians wearing sparkling jewels, Cíbola was a little town with its houses made of mud and "all crumpled together." Worse, the Zuñis were prepared to fight Coronado and his tired, hungry soldiers.

Outside the town, Coronado faced two or three hundred Indians armed with bows, arrows, and war clubs. Hiding inside the houses were even more armed natives. The Indian leaders ordered don Francisco and his soldiers to go back in the direction they had come from. They were warned not to enter the town or they would be killed.

Coronado did not want to fight the Zuñis. He told the Indians that he had come in peace and would not harm them, but they must honor his king who lived beyond the great ocean. If they failed to do so, he would use force against them. Coronado's soldiers did not wish to fight the Zuñis either. By then they were so weak and hungry that the thought of eating corn tortillas and turkeys kept their minds off the disappointment of finding nothing but mud houses.

Still, all the attempts to avoid fighting failed, and in the end Coronado led an attack on Cíbola. With his splendid golden armor and feather-decorated helmet, Francisco was so conspicuous that he quickly became the target of Indian attacks. As he entered the pueblo on foot, Indians standing on the roofs of two- and three-story buildings hurled down stones on the Spanish captain. Had he not had a good, strong helmet, Coronado would almost certainly have been seriously injured or killed. Twice he was knocked off his feet, and twice he was rescued by his men, who covered his body with their own and took the full blows of the stones.

When the town finally fell to the Spaniards, Coronado had two or three cuts on his face, an arrow in his foot, and many bruises on the rest of his body. Most important of all for the Spaniards, Cíbola contained good supplies of food. In the words of one of the soldiers, "We found something we prized more than gold or silver; namely, plentiful maize [corn] and beans, and turkeys larger than those in Mexico. And [we found] salt better and whiter than any I have ever seen in my whole life." It was clear that extreme hunger had changed Spanish values.

After the battle for Cíbola, Coronado and his men explored the other Zuñi towns and found them as poor as the first. By then his soldiers were really angry with Father Marcos de Niza and called him a liar for reporting towns larger and richer than Mexico City. Fearing that some of his soldiers might actually injure the priest, Coronado sent Niza back to Mexico City.

For several months, Coronado kept his main army at Cíbola while he decided what to do next. Thinking that other parts of this new land might contain some wealth, he sent out captains toward the west. One of these men, named García López de Cárdenas, was the first white man to see and describe the Grand Canyon of the Colorado River in present-day Arizona.

During the fall of 1540, while Coronado remained at Cíbola, he was visited by Indians from the east who were led by a handsome native that the Spaniards called Bigotes (Whiskers). Bigotes told don Francisco that there were richer towns beyond the mountains to the east. Also, beyond those same mountains were many "cattle" (buffaloes).

Coronado chose Captain Hernando de Alvarado to explore these new lands and told him to report back in eighty days. Alvarado was the first white man to see the great Sky City of Acoma. It was a town built on top of a huge column of rock several hundred feet in height, with a large flat top. The only way to get to Acoma was to use the handholds and footholds that had been carved in stone by its Indians. Alvarado thought Acoma to be the greatest stronghold that he had ever seen.

Continuing on, Alvarado reached the eastern edge of the Pueblo towns. At Pecos he found two Indians from the Great Plains, which lay even farther east. One of these natives was called the Turk, because Alvarado thought he looked like a man from Turkey. This man was an Indian from present-day Kansas, and he was important later on in drawing Coronado toward Texas.

Alvarado then continued his march beyond Pecos across the plains of eastern New Mexico and toward the Texas Panhandle. There he saw thousands of buffalo, which had first been seen and described by Cabeza de Vaca. Captain Alvarado thought those great animals to number more than fish in the sea. As he approached Texas, the Turk began to talk of a land still farther to the northeast that was called Quivira. There the Spanish would finally discover the rich towns of gold and silver they were looking for.

To prove the richness of the land, the Turk claimed that he had brought a gold bracelet from Quivira. It had been stolen from him by

Bigotes and another Indian chief called Cacique at the pueblo of Pecos. Bigotes had supposedly hidden the bracelet from the Spaniards, and the Turk suggested that Alvarado should question the two Indians on its whereabouts.

Alvarado was so excited by the Turk's story that he cut short his exploration and hurried back to Pecos. There he questioned Bigotes and Cacique about the bracelet. Both denied its existence and accused the Turk of lying. Alvarado, however, did not believe their denials. He arrested the two chiefs and placed them in irons. He then resumed his march toward Cíbola.

While Alvarado had been on the buffalo plains, other Spaniards sent out by Coronado had found land along the Río Grande near present-day Albuquerque that was occupied by Pueblo Indians. This area seemed to be a good place to camp during the winter of 1540–1541. With this news, Coronado decided to move his army there. So Alvarado, the captive chiefs, and the Turk did not have to travel all the way to Cíbola. Instead, they waited on the Río Grande for don Francisco's arrival there.

At first, the Río Grande Indians were friendly. In trying not to upset them, Coronado's scouts camped outside their pueblos. But when cold weather and snow came, the Spaniards asked the Indians to move out of one of their twelve villages. This the Indians agreed to do but were unhappy about it.

In the dead of winter, Coronado's entire army moved from Cíbola to the Río Grande. On his first night there, don Francisco heard the report of Alvarado and met the Turk. Again, the Indian repeated his story about a land called Quivira, which was near his homeland. In Quivira the Spaniards would find a river flowing through the plains with fish as big as horses. The great chief of this land used pitchers, bowls, and dishes that were made of pure gold. To determine whether the Turk knew gold and silver when he saw them, the Spaniards tested him by handing him trinkets made of tin. The Indian quickly said that those items were not made of valuable metal.

Next, Coronado tried to find out if the story about the stolen bracelet was true. When don Francisco asked Bigotes about the gold jewelry, he again claimed that the Turk was lying. It did not exist. To get to the bottom of the matter, Coronado took Bigotes into a courtyard where he set dogs upon the poor Indian in a form of torture called "dog baiting." Despite being bitten by the animals, Bigotes insisted that there was no bracelet.

Although he failed to find evidence of gold from Quivira, Coronado was wildly excited. He wanted to believe the Turk's story and he did. The Seven Cities of Cíbola had proved worthless, but here was another chance to make his expedition a great success. So the Spaniards waited for winter to pass. In the spring they could leave for the Great Plains, where they would find Gran Quivira.

That winter of 1540–1541 was especially cold. Most of Coronado's men had marched through hot weather on their way to New Mexico, and they had little or no warm clothing. The shivering soldiers began to demand cotton blankets and animal skins from the Pueblo Indians. When the natives refused to give them up, armed soldiers took these very items off the backs of the Pueblos. They also demanded turkeys, corn, and beans.

Finally, the Pueblos could not bear any more of this harsh treatment. They began a revolt by stealing several horses and amused themselves by killing the animals with bows and arrows. The Indians then fortified themselves within the walls of one of the other villages. There they refused to surrender and waved the cut-off tails of horses in the faces of the Spaniards. To defeat them, the Spanish battered down an outside wall and built a fire inside it. Heavy smoke drove the Indians from their houses, and many of them were killed by Coronado's soldiers.

A second revolt, in another village, also ended with victory for Coronado's men after some hard fighting. In this case, the Spaniards used horses, crossbows, lances, and muskets to attack the Indians. When these weapons failed to bring victory, the Spaniards cut off all outside water to the pueblo. Finally, in March, the siege ended. The Indians at this pueblo surrendered more from lack of food and water than from Spanish arms. Since it was spring, the natives had to plant crops or their families would starve the next winter.

Having put down two revolts, Coronado was glad to leave the Río Grande for the plains. By then he had received more horses and men from the viceroy in Mexico. When he crossed the Río Grande on April 23, 1541, Coronado led more than fifteen hundred persons, one thousand horses, five hundred cattle, and about five thousand sheep. It was a huge departure for the land described by the Turk, with the Turk himself acting as guide.

On his march to the plains, Coronado's first problem came as he attempted to cross the Pecos River. Because it was spring, the stream was swollen with water from melting snow. If he tried to swim the animals across the river, the sheep with water-soaked wool would struggle and then drown. There was nothing to do but wait for the stream to go down or build a bridge. Coronado called on his carpenters, and in a short time a wooden bridge spanned the Pecos.

After safely crossing the Pecos River, Coronado continued on toward the Texas Panhandle. The Spaniards soon came across enormous herds of buffalo. One of the soldiers, Pedro de Castañeda, later remembered how these strange animals had stirred interest among the Spaniards. The animals were so fearsome in appearance that "at first there was not a horse that did not run away on seeing them." Castañeda described buffaloes as having large eyes that "bulge out on the side, so that when they run they see anyone who follows them." He thought their beards and horns made them look like huge goats with a hump larger than a camel.

After seeing so many bison, the Spaniards met the first Indians who lived on the plains. These were nomadic Apaches, who followed the movement of buffalo herds from one place to another. They lived in little tents (tepees) made of buffalo hides and depended almost entirely on bison for food. Coronado noted that these natives, because they could not find water on the plains, drank the buffalo's blood and stomach juices and carried extra liquid in gut containers. These Apaches also used almost every part of the buffalo—meat for food, hides for clothing and tepees, and bones and horns for tools.

The large dogs kept by the Apaches were especially interesting to the Spaniards. These animals were used to pull things from one campsite to another on wooden poles called a travois. The Apache dogs were half-wild, and they barked and snarled at being harnessed and put to work.

While crossing part of the Texas Panhandle, Coronado's men camped near a large canyon that the Turk had led them to. While there, the Spaniards encountered harsh West Texas weather for the first time. They lived through a violent thunderstorm and hailstorm they would not soon forget.

The storm began in the afternoon with high winds and dark clouds that soon brought hail. In a very short time, the hailstones were "as big as bowls, or larger," and fell "as thick as raindrops," so that in places they covered the ground a foot or more in depth. The hailstones were so large that they dented Spanish helmets and caused the soldiers to take cover under their shields. Almost all the horses broke loose from their tethers and dashed madly into the canyon as they tried to escape the painful stones.

Perhaps worst of all, the hailstones broke all the clay pots and plates used by Coronado's army. These could not be replaced. On the plains of New Mexico and Texas, the natives did not use any kind of dishes. They simply snatched up raw or half-cooked buffalo meat with their hands and ate it.

After the hailstorm, Coronado decided to send most of his army back to the Río Grande. There were simply too many men and animals to move very fast, and he intended to strike out for Gran Quivira with about thirty mounted soldiers and six or seven soldiers on foot.

To make sure that the army had plenty of food for the return trip to the land of the Pueblos, the Spaniards began to hunt and kill hundreds of buffaloes. They cut up the meat and dried it to make jerky. The daily hunts proved especially dangerous, because of the endless plains that surrounded the canyons.

Spaniards compared these lands, which they called the Llano Estacado (Stockaded Plain), to the ocean. There was not a single point on the horizon that could serve as a landmark. The grass was as tall as a horse's belly, and it rolled and tossed in the wind like waves at sea. In the excitement of following and killing buffaloes on the hunt, Coronado's soldiers often lost their bearings. This was easy to do, because all around them the sky seemed like a small dome set over a "sea of grass."

It might seem that the Spaniards needed only to follow the tracks of their horses back to camp, but that did not work. According to Pedro de Castañeda, the grass would straighten up again as soon as they went across it. And once the sun reached its high point around midday, it was not possible to determine any direction by it.

Once lost, a hunter needed to stay quietly in one place until the sun began to set. Only then could he determine which direction was west. Not everyone had this much discipline. Those who lacked patience, "had to put themselves under the guidance of others." Unfortunately, some hunters became hopelessly lost and continued on as if they were crazy.

Back at camp, Spaniards fired off guns and blew bugles, hoping

Coronado and the Turk
crossing the Llano Estacado
(DRAWING BY JACK JACKSON)

to help lost hunters find their way. Depending on the direction of the wind, sound might not carry very far. Coronado may have lost more soldiers to the landscape of the Great Plains than to battles with Indians.

As the main army headed back to the Río Grande and the land of Pueblos, Coronado marched off in a different direction, toward Gran Quivira. Now it was time for the Turk to make good on his promise that he could lead Coronado to a country where gold was so plentiful that Indians used it for tableware.

Once again, Coronado had never seen anything like the seemingly endless plains that he had to cross. There was not a single tree, shrub, or rock to mark the way. Don Francisco had to use a compass to keep him on course for much of the trek to Kansas. Even so, he became so concerned about getting lost that he made a poor foot soldier count every step taken by his horse over the course of an entire day! Only in this manner could the Spanish commander keep track of the distance he had traveled through a land described as containing "nothing but cattle and sky."

As he approached land along the Arkansas River in present-day Kansas, Coronado became increasingly concerned that the Turk had lied to him about the wealth of Grand Quivira. He kept the native in chains and questioned him daily about his truthfulness. When at last the Spaniards came to what the Turk called Grand Quivira, they found only Wichita Indians who lived in grass huts with large fields of corn nearby. These same Indians would later move southward toward Oklahoma and Texas, with most of them living along the Red River.

Under torture, the Turk finally admitted that he had told gross lies to the Spaniards. There had never been a gold bracelet taken from him by Bigotes. He had led the Spaniards onto the Great Plains, drawing them closer to his homeland. In doing so, he planned to gain his freedom by urging the Quivirans to slaughter the Spaniards and their horses. But nothing had worked out as the Turk had hoped.

Coronado was not a bloodthirsty captain and did not like seeing anyone die. But it was now clear that his last hope of finding wealth in Grand Quivira for his friend the viceroy and for the king of Spain had failed. Partly out of anger and frustration, and partly to satisfy the desire of his soldiers for revenge, don Francisco reluctantly agreed that the Turk must die. His lies had brought great danger to the lives of Spaniards on the plains of New Mexico, Texas, Oklahoma, and Kansas. And not a single ounce of gold had been found. Before heading back to the Río Grande to join the main army, Coronado ordered that the Turk be strangled. The execution was carried out, and the Indian's body was left in the land that he led the Spaniards to.

Not every Spaniard was in a hurry to leave the land of the Wichitas, even though there was no gold. Juan Padilla, the only priest on the march to Gran Quivira, wanted to expose these natives to the Christian God. He would later choose present-day Kansas as his mission field.

But for Coronado there was nothing to do except admit failure and march back to the Río Grande as quickly as possible. The return march followed a more direct route along the course of the Arkansas River

Likely route of Coronado's travels to and from Quivira in present-day Kansas
(CENTER FOR MEDIA PRODUCTION, UNIVERSITY OF NORTH TEXAS, ADAPTED FROM
HERBERT E. BOLTON'S *Coronado: Knight of Pueblos and Plains*)

and eventually across the extreme northwest corner of the Texas Panhandle. Once he reached present New Mexico, don Francisco followed
the proven trail that crossed the Pecos River. He arrived at the Río
Grande during the fall and chose to remain among the Pueblo Indians
for a second winter.

While he waited for spring and warmer weather to begin the march
back to Mexico, Coronado suffered a serious injury. He decided for
fun to race his favorite horse against an animal owned by one of his
soldiers. At full gallop, the saddle girth on Coronado's horse broke

and spilled him under the hooves of his own mount. In the accident, Coronado received a severe blow to the head. Although the injury was not life-threatening, his friends admitted that the handsome and dashing captain was never again "quite the same."

Perhaps the accident, along with a sense of failure, changed the personality of Coronado. His good cheer and positive attitude were replaced by gloominess that lasted for the rest of his life. It was a sad turn of events for a man who seemed to have everything—a rich and beautiful wife, as well as the respect and admiration of his soldiers.

Coronado's return march, from the Río Grande to Culiacán and then on to Mexico City, was uneventful. It was completed in the spring of 1542. Don Francisco must have felt especially bad as he explained to his friend, Viceroy Antonio de Mendoza, that he could not find any wealth in the north country.

While still in New Mexico, Coronado had written to his king, Charles V, to inform him of the expedition and his leadership of it. In this letter, he described something no Spaniard, other than those in his army, had ever seen: the Great Plains. Don Francisco told his king, "[I] reached some plains, so vast that I did not find their limit anywhere that I went, although I traveled over them for more than 300 leagues [900 miles]." He also reported that he had seen so many "cows" that it was "impossible to number them."

In this same letter, Coronado wrote, "I have done all that I could possibly could do to serve Your Majesty and to discover a country where God Our Lord might be served and the wealth of Your Majesty increased." I have done this "as your loyal servant and vassal [subject]."

Despite Coronado's inability to find gold, in many respects his expedition of 1540–1542 was not a failure. Someone had to explore the land before the Spaniards could try to settle it. Don Francisco was the first to realize that a great land mass separated Florida and California. Maps up to this time showed very little territory between the Atlantic and Pacific Oceans. So Coronado contributed importantly to our early knowledge of North American geography.

It has been suggested that horses may have strayed away from the Coronado expedition and become the ancestors of the wild mustangs that later roamed the United States. This notion is false. There were almost no female horses (mares) among the hundreds of horses that accompanied Coronado and his army. Indians did not acquire large numbers of horses in North America until around 1650. This was more than one hundred years after Coronado had crossed the plains. These animals were most likely descendants of horses that had strayed from Spanish ranches and farms in northern Mexico.

Finally, what about the leadership qualities of Francisco Coronado? Had he not been a good leader, would his men have risked their lives to save him when he fell under a shower of stones at Cíbola? Had he not enjoyed the confidence of his men, they might well have turned on him after the disappointment of finding nothing but a "huddle of mud huts" at Cíbola, when they had hoped for golden cities. When they had to cross the endless sea of grass, guided only by a compass on their way to Gran Quivira in Kansas, would not these men have lost confidence in don Francisco?

Perhaps most important, Viceroy Antonio de Mendoza never regarded his Golden Conquistador as a failure, despite losing so much money on the expedition. After all, how could one be blamed for not finding gold where there was none to be found? Mendoza remained a friend of Coronado until the viceroy left Mexico in 1550 for a new post in Peru. Four years later, Francisco Vázquez de Coronado died in Mexico. Buried with his wife, Beatriz, in Mexico City, he remains one of the best examples of Spanish leadership in America.

SOURCES

Materials used in preparing this chapter are described below. You can find more information about these sources in the Bibliography at the end of the book.

Books

The most widely read biography of Coronado is Herbert E. Bolton's *Coronado: Knight of Pueblos and Plains*. Also useful are A. Grove Day's *Coronado's Quest: The Discovery of the Southwestern States* and John M. Morris's prize-winning *El Llano Estacado: Exploration and Imagination on the High Plains of Texas and New Mexico, 1536–1860*. Morris's book is the source for the description of the hailstorm in the Texas Panhandle.

Quotes

Most quotes in this chapter are from Herbert E. Bolton's *Coronado: Knight of Pueblos and Plains*. Coronado's letter to the king of Spain

(October 20, 1541) is quoted from *Texas History Documents: Volume 1 to 1877*, edited by Randolph B. Campbell.

Additional Information

Today one can drive to Acoma Pueblo. It is situated on top of a great column of rock to the west of Albuquerque, New Mexico.

"Llano Estacado" is often translated as "Staked Plain." But in traveling Interstate 40 between Tucumcari, New Mexico, and Amarillo, Texas, one sees the caprock in the distance. It seems to mark one side of the Llano like a stockade or fortress. *Estacada* in Spanish is best translated as "stockade," not "stake." Beside, how could Coronado have found wooden stakes on treeless plains?

Father Padilla returned to present-day Kansas in 1542. He was killed by unidentified Indians to the east of Quivira. Padilla was the first Spanish priest to die in the American West.

CHAPTER THREE

María de Agreda
THE LADY IN BLUE

In July 1629 about fifty Jumano Indians arrived at the Franciscan convent of Saint Anthony at old Isleta in New Mexico. The Indians had traveled a great distance from West Texas. These natives said that they came at the urging of a beautiful young woman who had appeared to them out of thin air. This Lady in Blue had taught the Jumanos about Christianity. The priests were amazed. Who was this mysterious image? How could a Spanish woman appear to the natives on a distant frontier, talk to them in a language they could understand, and influence them to seek Catholic missionaries? To answer these questions requires a belief in miracles.

In the 1600s María de Jesús, a nun in Spain, reported that her spirit often went to America to introduce Christianity to the natives. This separation of the spirit from the body so that they are in two different places at the same time is called bilocation. An investigation by the Catholic Church at the time supported María's claims of bilocation, as did the tales told by the Indians.

To this day, many Catholics are inspired by the life of María de Agreda. These faithful believe in miracles. Other people, however, deny that bilocation is possible. They believe that the Lady in Blue is only a legend. After reading about Sister María's life, you may decide for yourself.

María Coronel was born on April 2, 1602, in Agreda, a small village in northeastern Spain. She was the oldest daughter of very religious parents, Francisco Coronel and Catalina de Arana. The family owned a small castle but had little else by way of wealth. From the time of the baby's baptism on April 11, the Catholic Church was an important part of María's life.

Although not strong or healthy, María was an unusual child with an excellent memory. She seems to have had a supernatural vision when she was two. Then, at age twelve, María declared that she wanted to become a nun. Despite her deep religious feelings, however, the young woman was tempted to commit improper acts. She feared that this was an insult to God and felt a sense of loss when the Lord was "silent" to her. Her teenage years were full of "sickness, sadness, and despair." Later in life, she concluded that this youthful suffering cleaned her spirit so that she could receive special grace (favor) from God.

María's ties to the Catholic faith were strengthened by her upbringing. Catalina de Arana, who eventually had eleven children, provided her eldest daughter with a Christian education. Both parents "made their children pray in constant devotions and . . . engage in mental prayer."

According to Catholic sources, Catalina had a dream in which God told her to make the Coronel castle into a home for a new order of nuns. Following these heavenly directions, she founded the Convent of Discalced (Barefooted) Franciscan Nuns of the Immaculate Conception. Along with her mother, María entered the new religious order in January 1619. María's father entered a nearby Franciscan monastery, which already housed two of his sons. The young woman later wrote: "The Almighty [God] favored our family so much, that all of us were [pledged] to him in the religious state." It is interesting that María's strong faith did not permit her to complain that eight of her brothers and sisters had died while still young. She simply accepted this as God's will.

On February 2, 1620, María Coronel took her formal vows to become a nun and accepted the name of María de Jesús. At that time, she was not yet eighteen years old. Unfortunately, this young woman was almost always in bad health, and she suffered emotionally as well. Fearing the temptation to sin, she worried that she might not be able to resist evil. María punished herself in attempts to achieve purity, and in doing so she often lost a great deal of blood. Her religious superiors became so concerned for her health that they ordered her to stop this practice. She then fasted for long periods of time by living on only bread and water. And in her own words, her life became one long "act of prayer . . . and complete self-denial."

The Order of Discalced Nuns, also called the Poor Clares, wore brown habits with an outer cloak of coarse blue cloth. The group grew in numbers until the Coronel castle was too small to house all of them. The nuns, including Sister María, then moved to new and larger quarters, the Convent of the Immaculate Conception in Agreda.

After taking her vows as a nun, María began to have hundreds of out-of-body experiences during the 1620s and early 1630s. Kneeling in prayer, she would become pale, sway unsteadily, and pass out. At these times, no one was able to wake her. In those trances, the young nun had visions in which God sent her spirit to distant lands to teach Christianity.

The bilocations supposedly took María to New Mexico and Texas, where the Indians understood her preaching, even though she spoke in Spanish. The nun's spirit also saw the Franciscan clergy who were working in New Mexico. María knew that the natives needed priests to baptize them. She advised the Indians to seek out these missionaries and ask them to come to Texas.

María told her confessor, Father Sebastián Mancilla, about her supernatural experiences. He truly believed that the miracle of bilocation was occurring and informed his superiors of the miraculous events. In turn, they asked Archbishop Francisco Manso y Zúñiga of New Spain (Mexico) to determine whether there was any truth to María's stories. In 1628 the archbishop wrote to Father Esteban de Perea, head of the missionaries in New Mexico. Perea was asked to provide any information that could prove the claims of the Spanish nun in Agreda, Spain.

Just over a year later, in July 1629, the Jumanos arrived at Saint Anthony in New Mexico, as described at the beginning of this chapter. The natives wanted to be baptized. When asked why, they talked of a woman dressed in blue who came among them preaching. This was especially amazing because the Poor Clares in Spain wore blue cloaks. The Jumanos also said that this lady, who appeared out of the sky, had sent them to seek priests in New Mexico. This account by the Indians supported María's claims of bilocation.

The timely arrival of the Jumanos caused Father Esteban to send a follow-up party into their land. With a Jumano chief as their guide, Fathers Juan Salas and Diego López marched over one hundred leagues

The Lady in Blue descends from the sky
(DRAWING BY JACK JACKSON)

(about three hundred miles) eastward. The trip was dangerous, be-cause they had to pass through Apache country.

In Southwest Texas the two missionaries were welcomed by a large parade of Indians with tall crosses covered with flowers. The natives asked the Franciscan priests for baptism. Women with small babies at their breasts even asked that their infants be baptized.

The Indians said that the Lady in Blue had told them that the missionaries were coming. She also explained to them how they should properly welcome the priests. When asked about her, the Jumanos described the woman as young and beautiful, wearing a brown dress with a rough blue, sky-colored cloak. She always came softly before them like "light at sunset." Kind and gentle, she spoke "sweet" words to them. She also taught them to respect the cross.

Fathers Salas and López were affected deeply by their experiences among the Jumanos and by the natives' stories of their spiritlike visitor. When they returned to old Isleta, the two clergymen convinced Father Alonso de Benavides that he should go to Mexico City to report on the situation.

After spending some time in the Mexican capital, Father Alonso decided to go to Europe and seek out the Lady in Blue. He reached Spain in August 1630. Father Alonso then arranged a meeting with Fray Bernardino de Siena, the head of the Franciscan Order.

Fray Bernardino told Father Alonso that he had long known about María de Jesús's bilocations. In fact, years earlier he had gone to her convent to hear the story from her own lips. More recently, Fray Bernardino had received a report from the archbishop of Mexico about the nun's appearances in the New World. Fray Bernardino wanted to visit Sister María at Agreda again, but he had too many other duties. Instead, he urged Father Alonso de Benavides to meet this remarkable woman for himself.

Father Alonso reached the village of Agreda in late April 1631 and went directly to the convent. By this time, María was the mother superior (abbess) of her convent. She had been elected abbess a few years earlier at the unusually young age of twenty-five.

According to Father Alonso, Mother María de Jesús was a woman "of beautiful face, of white skin . . . and large black eyes. The form of her habit . . . is of brown sackcloth, very coarse . . . and over this brown habit is worn the white sackcloth habit. . . . The cloak is of blue sackcloth, very coarse, and the veil is black."

María told Father Alonso that she recognized him. Her spirit had seen him baptizing Indians in New Mexico. She also accurately spoke of another missionary in New Mexico, whom she could not have seen in person. This priest, who was well known to Father Alonso de Benavides, was described as an old man who did not look his age because he had no gray hair. María also reported on the complexion and shape of this missionary's face.

The abbess claimed that she had guided Juan de Salas and Diego López on their trip to the land of the Jumanos in West Texas. She described the main Jumano chief, whom the Spanish called Capitán Tuerto (Captain Squint-Eye), as well as other Indian leaders. Father Alonso asked why the nun had not allowed him and the missionaries to see her during her bilocations to America. She answered that the Indians "had a greater need" to observe her.

At the end of his interview with María de Jesús, Father Alonso asked the abbess to write down all that she had told him. She did as instructed. In this document, Mother María declared that God had chosen her, "his most unworthy subject, imperfect and incompetent," to take the Catholic faith to all nations. She wrote that she was carried to the lands of the Jumanos and others "by the will of God, and by the hand . . . of the Angels." Mother María said that the events being described had happened from 1620 to "this present year of 1631, in the region of Quivira and Jumanas." Both of these names were used by Spaniards at that time to refer to lands occupied by Indians.

In her statement, the abbess begged the missionaries to carry on the work of converting the Indians with whom she had made contact through her spirit. Although hardships would be encountered, the rewards in the "harvest" of souls for the Roman Catholic Church would be great. María informed Father Alonso that she knew the Lord was pleased with the missionaries' efforts in America. She claimed that she had learned this from God and his holy angels.

After his interview with Mother Superior María de Agreda, Father Alonso wrote from Spain in 1631 to his fellow missionaries in New Mexico. He explained that the nun felt sorry for those who did not know about "our Lord." She believed that these poor souls were condemned to Hell unless someone brought Christianity to them. It had been her privilege to be chosen by God to preach the holy faith, especially to Native Americans.

Father Alonso stated that María's spiritual trances sometimes happened as often as three or four times in a single day. In each case, her breathing became very slow and her body temperature dropped so that her skin felt cold to those who tried without success to wake her.

In his letter to the missionaries of New Mexico, Father Alonso also wrote about the "great uplift" of his soul when María had recognized him. He reported that the nun had described the aging but still dark-haired Father Cristóbal Quivoz exactly. She also provided familiar details about other missionaries, specific natives, and the frontier of New Mexico.

Father Alonso explained that he had begged Mother María to let the missionaries in New Mexico see her during her bilocations. She promised to do so, if God allowed it. Father Alonso also wrote his fellow Franciscans that they should feel comforted by having such a "companion and saint" in their labors.

In a formal statement presented to King Philip IV of Spain, Father Alonso wrote about the work of the Catholic Church in New Mexico and about María de Agreda's "travels" to America. This account was in such demand that hundreds of copies were made. Some were even sent to the pope in Rome. Father Alonso de Benavides also spoke in person to the king. He begged continued support for the missionary efforts on the New Mexico/Texas frontier.

According to María de Jesús, she had no further bilocations after 1632. But in a letter written in 1634, Father Alonso declared that the Lady in Blue continued to have a positive influence on Native Americans. He wrote that five thousand "barbarian" natives had been converted at that time. Father Alonso again stressed the miraculous manner in which Christianity was introduced to the Jumano Indians. Before Spaniards came to their land, these natives had no priests to minister to them. And when asked why they chose to accept the Catholic religion, the Jumanos pointed to a portrait of an older Franciscan nun. Although younger in appearance, "a woman dressed like this passed among us always preaching," the Indians stated.

After her period of bilocations, Sister María devoted herself to writing. Believing it to be a holy mission, she wrote a biography that told about the life of the Virgin Mary. This book, *The Mystical City of God*, caused many problems for the abbess. Some of the ideas that Mother María presented went against the accepted teachings of the Catholic Church at that time. A local priest ordered her to destroy the work, and she did.

The abbess, however, still felt herself to be under divine orders to tell of the life of Jesus' mother. Since no one had forbidden the Lady in Blue to write the book a second time, that is exactly what she did! The task took five years to finish.

María's writings also caused her to get into trouble with the Holy Inquisition. This was a powerful court within the Catholic Church that worked to keep the faith pure. Since the Spanish Inquisition often stirs interest among young readers, it seems appropriate here to tell how a person came to its attention and why María de Agreda was in trouble.

The Spanish Inquisition had been set up in 1478, at the time that Queen Isabella ruled the country. She, of course, would later sponsor the voyages of Christopher Columbus. The purpose of the Inquisition was to make sure that the Catholic faith was not undermined by the religious beliefs of Spanish Jews who had converted to Christianity.

During the 1400s, Christian rulers made it especially difficult for Jews, who had lived in Spain for centuries, to remain true to their faith. If a man was a Jew, he could not teach at any Spanish university, because it was feared that a Jewish professor might teach about his religion, rather than about Christian Catholicism. Likewise, Jews could not practice some professions, such as law or medicine.

If a Jew accepted baptism in the Catholic Church, however, and converted to that faith, then the restrictions that applied to universities, law, and medicine were removed. Although many Jews remained true to their faith and were denied employment because of it, thousands of others accepted Christian baptism. These recent converts were called New Christians, and they began attending services in the Catholic Church. But they were often viewed suspiciously by long-time Catholics, who were called Old Christians.

Some of that suspicion was justified. Many New Christians missed the practices of Judaism, which they had known all their lives. They also missed going to their own synagogues (religious temples) with old friends and relatives. So these recent converts to Catholicism sometimes observed the Jewish faith in secret, usually within their own homes. This was a dangerous practice, because it made them guilty of a serious crime known as apostasy (going back to one's earlier faith).

Remember that religious freedom, which means having the right to follow any religion or none at all, did not exist at this time in history. The Christian kings of Spain wanted all Spaniards to share their faith. They used religion to unify their subjects and believed Catholics would be more loyal to them. So the Spanish Inquisition tried to find people who were regarded as "false Christians," meaning those who appeared to be Christians in public but were secretly still Jews at heart.

Beginning in the 1480s, people suspected of being false Christians were arrested and brought before courts of the Inquisition. Such people had to prove that they were not guilty of apostasy. If they failed to do so, they could be tortured and even put to death on orders of Inquisition judges. The goal was for Spain to have only one religion. That faith was Catholicism and no other.

The Spanish Inquisition did not try cases involving Jews who had never converted to Catholicism. But this was not as fair at it sounds. In the spring of 1492, all Jews in Spain were given 120 days to convert to Catholicism. If they would not do so within four months, then they had to leave their homeland.

Thousands of Jews fled from Spain in 1492, with most of them going to North Africa. When the 120 days had expired, which came at the very time Columbus sailed from Spain, all Jews who stayed in Spain had to accept Christian baptism. At that time, they could no longer practice their old religion. If they did, they were likely to be arrested and severely punished on orders of the Inquisition.

At the time María de Agreda began writing her book, *The Mystical City of God*, Jewish apostates were no longer a serious problem in Christian Spain. But the Spanish Inquisition remained a powerful court to ensure that Catholicism was kept pure and sinners were punished. Other offenses tried by the Inquisition included sorcery (witchcraft), bigamy (being married to more than one person), and major heresy (denying the teachings of the Catholic Church).

The Catholic Church was especially suspicious of persons who believed that God had spoken to them directly, such as María de Agreda. This, in the mind of church leaders, was dangerous, because the voice that people heard might well be that of the devil. The Catholic Church wanted its faith to be taught by its priests and missionaries, who were trained in religion and took orders from the pope in Rome. This control ensured that all Catholics would receive the same message in matters of religion.

After María de Agreda died in 1665, the Spanish Inquisition examined her book "word for word" before it would agree to its publication. Finally, after five years, the Inquisition decided that the Lady in Blue's work was acceptable for all Catholics to read. But that changed in a few years.

In 1681 María de Agreda's book was judged not suitable reading for Catholics. The problem was that Mother María's book placed too much emphasis on Jesus' mother, Mary, and not enough on Jesus rising from the dead. Even so, within a few months, Pope Innocent XI decided that *The Mystical City of God* was a fine work that could be read by all Catholics. Later popes agreed, and the Lady in Blue's book came to be popular with priests working in America.

Problems with the Inquisition during her lifetime did not stop María de Agreda from becoming a close friend of King Philip IV. In fact, she played an important role in his life for more than twenty years.

Although a Catholic, King Philip was also a worldly man. Despite the teachings of his religion, he committed adultery and fathered several illegitimate children. He also enjoyed hunting with friends, taking part in theatrical productions, and posing for portraits. At times these activities occupied more of his time than the duties of ruling an empire.

Many challenges faced Philip, and the demands of being king proved difficult for him. Both the Portuguese and the French were threatening his kingdoms. In the summer of 1643, the king headed to Aragon to take part in a war against France. While making the journey, he decided to visit the Convent of the Immaculate Conception and meet its famous abbess.

On July 10, 1643, the king met María de Agreda. He asked about the bilocation experiences that had been reported. In a convincing manner, she described to him her spiritual travels among the natives of America.

During their long conversation, Philip was deeply impressed with the nun's wisdom. He was sorely in need of "unselfish" advice. Unlike others who attempted to influence him, this wise woman did not seek power or wealth. Instead, she cared only about Philip's welfare and that of his kingdoms.

Sister María spoke critically to the monarch about those in the royal government who had committed harsh acts and used "ungodly methods." She urged Philip to have faith in God and in himself, rather than rely on such men. As he prepared to leave Agreda, the king felt renewed hope. He asked the abbess to write him and give him her private advice. She should also pray for him with her "saintly soul."

A strong spiritual link was formed between the king and the abbess. In Mother María, Philip IV found a trusted adviser, as well as a special friend. The two wrote to each other regularly. For more than two dozen years, he would confess his sins and weaknesses to her on paper. Understandably, Philip ordered the mother superior never to speak about the contents of the letters to anyone.

In his first letter to María on October 4, 1644, Philip wrote on only one-half of a sheet of paper (the left side of the page). María was instructed to write her reply on the right side of the same page and return it to the king. Whenever the king received a reply from the Lady in Blue, he always burned the letter after reading it. This method was meant to help keep the contents of their letters a secret, and they used it regularly.

In the letter of October 4, the king said that he was sorry for having sinned and offended God. Writing of the many problems facing his empire, Philip IV declared that he had very little trust in himself. He feared that he was to blame for the punishments falling upon his kingdoms. The monarch needed María's help to "do right." He asked the Lady in Blue to "speak with all frankness." She should also pray for God to guide his actions and his arms.

In her reply, the abbess advised her monarch to trust in the Lord. She would pray for him. But she also warned that his kingdoms were in danger because he was at war with other Catholic countries. This was against God's will. María assured Philip that things would improve "as soon as Your Majesty has abandoned the old evil ways and been delivered from sin." The Lady in Blue also warned Philip IV to beware of those around him who cared more for their own welfare than his.

During the twenty-two years that the king wrote to Mother María, he told her not only about matters of state but also about personal affairs. Because he believed that no one else would ever see the letters, Philip wrote honestly about his concerns, his actions, and his associates. For example, he confessed to María that he continued to commit serious sins, such as adultery. In her replies to these letters, the abbess expressed a strong sense of justice and concern for her country. That she also cared greatly about her king was never in doubt.

When Philip IV died in 1665, he did not know that María de Agreda had made a copy of his letters and her replies before returning them to him. Although she disobeyed her king's orders, we are lucky that she did. These copies give us valuable information about the nun, the king, and their times.

María de Jesús died at Agreda on May 24, 1665, in the same year as her king. Because she had led such an unusual life, the Lady in Blue stirred a lot of interest in the Catholic Church. After all, here was a person who could perhaps send her spirit across the Atlantic Ocean to Texas and New Mexico. If true, this was a miracle.

Here was a nun who had founded a new religious order in Spain, known as the Discalced Nuns. In a short time, while she was still in her twenties, she became an abbess because her leadership qualities were so unusual. Later in life, she wrote a book that got her in trouble with the Spanish Inquisition. In fact, as we noted, she had to write it twice! After her death, the book was regarded as a great work on religion.

All of this was highly unusual for a young woman who never left northeastern Spain. Yet she was even visited by the king of Spain at her monastery. As mentioned, Philip IV was so impressed by the Lady in Blue that he wrote letters to her for twenty-two years, sharing with her his personal weaknesses and thoughts.

It is little wonder that many high officials in the Catholic Church thought María de Agreda's life to be so special that she deserved to be considered for sainthood. After her death, a bishop in eastern Spain began to take a careful look at the nun's life and her special qualities.

The work of this bishop impressed Pope Clement X in Rome. In January 1673, the pope decided that María de Agreda was so unusual and special that she should be declared "Venerable." This means that he thought the former abbess was worthy of becoming a saint in the Roman Catholic Church. Thus began a long process that has continued for more than three hundred years. As recently as the 1970s, the Spanish government actively supported the hope that the Lady in Blue might become a Catholic saint.

Sainted or not, María Coronel played an important role in American and European history. Certainly, Father Alonso de Benavides, who once headed the Franciscans in New Mexico, believed that the souls of many Indians were saved through her efforts.

Today, the fame of the Lady in Blue lives on, especially in Texas history. According to one Indian legend, when Mother María last appeared to the natives, she blessed them and then slowly faded away into the hills. The next morning the area was covered with a blanket of strange flowers that were a deep blue color, like her cloak—the first Texas bluebonnets. She has been given credit for creating the first chili recipe, aiding malaria victims along the Sabine River in the 1840s, and appearing as a spirit during World War II.

The story of María de Agreda reminds us that a sickly child who spent her entire adult life in a convent in northeastern Spain could still make a difference in many lives and on two continents. She definitely influenced her king, Philip IV. Others insist that her bilocations brought a Christian message across the Atlantic Ocean to Indians in Texas and New Mexico. Studying her life helps us believe in miracles.

SOURCES

Materials used in preparing this chapter are described below. You can find more information about these sources in the Bibliography at the end of the book.

Books

Books dealing with the Lady in Blue are Clark Colahan's *The Visions of Sor María de Agreda: Writing Knowledge and Power* and T. D. Kendrick's *Mary of Agreda: The Life and Legend of a Spanish Nun.*

Quotes

Quotes in this chapter are from Clark Colahan, *The Visions of Sor María de Agreda;* Frances Parkinson Keyes, *I, the King;* and the following articles: Cuthbert Gumbinger, "The Tercentenary of Mother Agreda's *Mystical City of God," Age of Mary* (January–February 1958): 16; Joseph Mary Madden, "A Brief Biography of Venerable Mary of Agreda," *Age of Mary* (January–February 1998): 91–92. Also quoted are the following published documents: Alonso de Benavides's Letter from Spain, 1631, in *Age of Mary* (January–February 1958): 126–127; Letter of Venerable María de Agreda, 1631, in *Age of Mary* (January–February 1958): 127–128. An additional quote came from an unpublished work: Memorial of Father Alonso de Benavides Regarding the Conversions of New Mexico, February 12, 1634, Catholic Archives of Texas, Austin.

Additional Information

For general works on the Spanish and Mexican Inquisitions, see *The Spanish Inquisition,* by Henry Kamen, and *The Mexican Inquisition of the Sixteenth Century,* by Richard E. Greenleaf.

Correspondence between María de Agreda and Philip IV is discussed in *I, the King*, by Frances Parkinson Keyes.

A single-issue journal, *The Age of Mary: An Exclusively Marian Magazine* (January–February 1958), contains valuable articles and documents on María de Agreda.

A good reference source for the Lady in Blue is the six-volume *New Handbook of Texas*, published by the Texas State Historical Association, as well as its online version at <www.tsha.utexas.edu>. You can also check out a María de Agreda website at <www.withmary.com/agreda/agreda.html>.

CHAPTER FOUR

Alonso de León
TEXAS PATHFINDER

Alonso de León was one of Texas's great explorers and pathfinders. By traveling across much of what became Spanish Texas in the late 1680s and early 1690s, he helped establish a road that ran from the Río Grande near today's Eagle Pass to Louisiana. This route was called the Camino Real (King's Highway). Part of it later became the course of a modern Texas highway.

León is famous for reasons other than just laying out the Camino Real. In 1690 he helped set up San Francisco de los Tejas, the first Spanish mission in East Texas. He also looked for and found several French children who had been kidnapped by Karankawa Indians. All were orphans. Their mothers and fathers had died in a colony set up on the Texas coast in the 1680s by the Frenchman René-Robert Cavelier, Sieur de La Salle.

León also served the king of Spain as governor of Nuevo León and Coahuila, two areas that became states in modern Mexico. He was a very able military man who held the rank of general at the time of his death in 1691. As you read about don Alonso, notice that he was lucky enough to get a good education in Spain. His parents sent him across the Atlantic Ocean to Spain when he was only ten years old. These must have been very lonely years for a boy separated from his mother and father by five thousand miles of ocean. But education helped make young León a successful and important man in Texas history.

In 1639 or 1640, Alonso was born as the third son of Alonso de León, who gave his full name to this child. The older Alonso had grown up in

Mexico City, where he attended school, and he placed great value on education. When the father moved from the capital to the northern frontier as a rancher in 1635, he worried because there were no schools there for his children. As soon as young Alonso was able to live away from home, he was sent to Spain, where he entered a military academy as a cadet.

Alonso planned a career in the Spanish navy, and he studied toward that goal for five or six years. When he was a fifteen-year-old student, he helped defend Spain when it was attacked by a squadron of English ships in 1655. But it seems the young cadet did not like his prospects in the Spanish navy, because he soon returned to Nuevo León, where he married and began a family. For the rest of his life, Alonso de León lived on the northern frontier of Mexico, close to Texas.

For about twenty years, Alonso de León led groups of men from Nuevo León to search for wealth in nearby unexplored lands. These expeditions discovered some rich salt mines and located two seaports on the northeast coast of Mexico. As he became a more experienced military captain, León also learned about land in Mexico that lay along the south bank of the Río Grande. His successes even led to his appointment as governor of Nuevo León.

By the mid-1680s, León was no longer governor of Nuevo León but was highly respected in the province. At that time, the Spanish believed La Salle had probably established a colony somewhere along the northern Gulf Coast. Spain became very alarmed, and this concern would eventually bring León onto the Texas scene.

The French threat turned out to be a very real one. La Salle had first traveled down the Mississippi River from Canada in 1682. At the mouth of the great river, he claimed the entire area for France. The explorer named it Louisiana to honor his king, Louis XIV. La Salle then returned to Canada and sailed to France. He suggested to his monarch that the French establish a colony at or near the mouth of the Mississippi River. The king liked the idea, for France and Spain were then at war. A French outpost on the Gulf Coast would bring his subjects close to rich Spanish silver mines in northern Mexico.

Louis XIV provided generous support for La Salle's plans. He gave the French explorer ships that were loaded with supplies, equipment, and cannons for his colony. When the four vessels reached the islands of the Caribbean Sea, one of them was lost to Spanish pirates. The other three ships sailed on toward the mouth of the Mississippi but missed it by four hundred miles. By mistake they landed on the Texas coast at Matagorda Bay.

Perhaps two hundred colonists were unloaded there, and that number included a few women and girls. One of the three remaining vessels was wrecked during the landing, and a second sailed back to France. The remaining ship was named the *Belle*, but it was soon lost when it ran aground in Matagorda Bay during a storm.

The Spanish were especially concerned about La Salle's colony, for if successful it would give the French a claim to Texas. To meet this threat, in 1686 the new governor of Nuevo León called on Alonso de León. Don Alonso must find the French outpost and arrest or kill all the colonists. But no Spaniard was familiar with lands along the Gulf Coast, and of course no one knew the exact location of La Salle's colony. As a result, it would take four expeditions and three years for don Alonso to find it.

The first definite clue that there were French colonists on the Gulf Coast came in June 1686. At that time, an Indian brought news to Monterrey in Nuevo León that white men lived in a settlement to the north. León's first attempt to locate those foreigners did not include crossing the Río Grande. He marched along its right bank to the Gulf and then turned south. Along the coast, don Alonso found items from a wrecked vessel and a bottle containing a little spoiled wine, but he found nothing else.

A second effort by León came in February 1687, and on this occasion he did cross the Río Grande into Texas. He traveled along the river's left bank to the Gulf and then turned north and went perhaps as far as the coast near modern Kingsville. On this march, he found absolutely nothing to indicate that there were Frenchmen in the area. His second expedition was as unsuccessful as the first.

While León was leading overland marches in search of the French, Spanish officials in Mexico also sent out two searches by sea. These efforts likewise found no evidence of La Salle or his colony. Then came news from Europe that was really encouraging. Spaniards learned from secret information picked up by a Spanish official in England that the French colony had probably failed. The report indicated that La Salle's followers suffered from diseases and were threatened by hostile Karankawa Indians. This optimistic news was soon shattered, however, by clear evidence that Frenchmen were living among the Indian tribes of Texas.

This bad news for the Spanish came from two Indians who traveled from Texas to Coahuila. One of these natives claimed to have been "in the very houses of the French." At about the same time, León had assumed the governorship of Coahuila. So he faced more responsibilities than just checking out the presence of unwelcome foreigners to the north of the Río Grande.

As governor of Coahuila, don Alonso had to deal with one Indian revolt after another. In fighting Indians he came to distrust even those natives who had accepted mission life under Spanish control. León believed that these mission neophytes were guilty of "bad faith," because they were in constant communication with those who had rebelled against the Spanish. In November 1687, his own son had been wounded in Indian wars, and this incident also hardened don Alonso's attitude toward Native Americans.

During Indian wars in Coahuila, León captured a famous rebel chieftain named Little Geronimo. Don Alonso sentenced the chief to death, placed a rope around his neck, and hanged him until he "died naturally." León justified the execution because it "served as an example to other Indians of these parts." It is clear that don Alonso viewed Native Americans like most military men. He did not trust them under any circumstances. As we shall see, his suspicious view of all Indians would soon place him at odds with missionaries in Texas.

When he was finally able to investigate the presence of foreigners north of the Río Grande, León led a small group of soldiers on a difficult march. At the end of it, he found a large settlement of Indians who honored a naked and tattooed Frenchman named Jean Jarry as their great chief. Don Alonso arrested Jarry, returned him to Coahuila, and then sent him to Mexico City to be questioned by high officials in the government.

The fact that a Frenchman had been found among the Indians of Texas was cause for alarm in the capital. The leaders of government there sent Jarry under guard back to Coahuila. They also ordered Alonso de León to carry out a fourth expedition, with Jarry acting as his guide.

This time the Spanish were determined to find the French colony. In early April 1689, don Alonso led a huge expedition containing 114

*Alonso de León crosses the Guadalupe
River in search of La Salle's colony*
(DRAWING BY JACK JACKSON)

men, including Father Damián Massanet, soldiers, servants, and the Frenchman Jarry. Father Massanet, a Franciscan priest, would become the first important missionary in Spanish Texas.

León kept an official diary that contains information about his search for La Salle's colony, as do letters written by Father Massanet. From these accounts, we have interesting details about South Texas— the first since Cabeza de Vaca's *The Account*, written 150 years before.

Don Alonso commented on great patches of prickly pear cactus that extended as far as the eye could see and on thick groves of mesquite trees. Two weeks into the march, León and his men came upon the first buffalo they had seen and killed six of them for food.

The León expedition of 1689 crossed several major rivers in Texas before it came to the Guadalupe, near present-day Victoria, Texas. From this location, don Alonso began a march down Garcitas Creek toward the Gulf Coast. On April 20 he and his men finally found the object of a search that had gone on by land and sea for three years. At the remains of La Salle's fort, they saw the terrible results of a Karankawa Indian attack that had taken place at Christmastime in the previous year.

León and Massanet recorded these words: "We found six houses, not very large, built with poles plastered with mud, and roofed with buffalo hides, another house where pigs were fattened, and a wooden fort built from the hulk [wood] of a wrecked vessel." All of the houses had been robbed and the furniture broken into pieces. More than two hundred books had been ripped apart and their "rotten leaves scattered through the patios." Among this devastation were the remains of three bodies, one with a dress clinging to the bones. All of the supplies had been spilled from kegs, with other items such as nails and tools thrown here and there. According to don Alonso, La Salle's fort contained absolutely nothing of value.

What León and Father Massanet did not know is that La Salle himself had been murdered in East Texas some two years earlier by his own men. In fact, the French commander had died at the very time don Alonso was exploring the Texas coast in 1687. But the task at hand in 1689 was to say Mass over the three bodies and bury them.

León then began to explore the region around the ruined fort and look for possible French survivors. On his march toward the French colony, don Alonso had left a letter with Indians, who were told to deliver it to any white people they found living in the wilds of Texas. The letter contained an invitation for foreigners to surrender and return to a life among Christians. When León returned to the French fort, he found waiting there a reply from two Frenchmen.

The two men agreed to surrender and expressed their desire to return to the world of Christians. Two years earlier, these same Frenchmen had written a pitiful message, which they gave to Indians. Their hope was that the natives could somehow find white people and give it to them. León, however, never saw this first letter. But the words of one of the Frenchmen, who had played a major part in La Salle's murder, show how much he hated living away from other Europeans. "I do not know what sort of people you are. We are French. We are among the savages. We would very much like to be among Christians such as we are. We know well that you are Spaniards. We do not know whether you will attack us. [But we are unhappy] to be among the beasts like these [Indians] who believe neither in God nor in anything. Gentlemen, if you are willing to take us away . . . we will deliver ourselves up to you."

Traveling to the north for about sixty-five miles, León came upon the two Frenchmen and arrested them. Eight Tejas Indians from East Texas and a chieftain were also present. In talking to these natives and learning about their homeland, Father Massanet became excited about the possibility of establishing a mission among them. He told the chief and his followers that they should accept Christianity and that he would visit their land in the following spring when they would be planting corn.

The two Frenchmen were questioned by León and provided news of what had happened at the French colony. Disease, Karankawa arrows, and rattlesnake bites had caused the death of some colonists. Others simply wandered away and were lost in the woods. On three occasions, La Salle had led expeditions in search of the Mississippi River, while leaving several colonists behind to guard the fort.

As time passed, many at the French colony began to dislike their commander, because La Salle was not a easy person to get along with. He was a suspicious leader who never trusted anyone or shared his thoughts with them. People who do not respect others or are unable to admit mistakes can expect very little consideration in return. Anger over La Salle's leadership on the part of some of his followers turned to hatred. Somewhere in East Texas on his third attempt to find the Mississippi River, La Salle was shot in the head by one of the colonists. His body was left in tall weeds for coyotes and vultures.

In the meantime, word spread from one Indian tribe to another that the great French commander was dead. This news eventually reached the Karankawas. Those natives realized that the French colonists were without a strong leader and began to plan their murder.

At Christmastime in 1688, five Indians approached the colony and pretended to be friends. Other natives soon appeared, and they too were friendly. As these Karankawas hugged the French, a large war party armed with sharp sticks and clubs crawled forward. With a shout, the Indians turned on the colonists and killed all of the adults, including several women and three priests. A three-month-old infant, the first European child born in Texas, died when a Karankawa warrior "held it by a foot and bashed its head against a tree." But seven older children were saved from death by the kindness of Karankawa women, who grabbed them and took them to their village. Five of the French children were later rescued by Alonso de León. Two more were later freed by a lieutenant of don Alonso.

When León and Massanet returned to Coahuila, they brought news of the disaster at La Salle's colony. They also carried information about the Tejas Indians in East Texas, although they had not visited the villages of these natives. Don Alonso and Father Massanet reported that the Tejas lived in nine settlements with wooden houses. These natives in East Texas also farmed fields of corn, beans, pumpkins, watermelons, and cantaloupe.

Because the Tejas were much more advanced than the hunting and gathering tribes of northern Mexico, they were looked upon as ideal subjects for conversion to Christianity. Father Massanet was especially enthusiastic about setting up missions for these Native Americans. He traveled all the way to Mexico City, where he presented his plans to Spanish officials there. The viceroy, who was the head of government, gave his support to the project.

At this point, important differences between León and Massanet began to appear. Those disagreements would only get worse as time went by. As mentioned earlier, León's long experience as a military captain and governor made him distrust all Indians. Don Alonso wanted army outposts, called presidios, to be set up in East Texas.

This, he said, must be done before there was any attempt to convert the Tejas to Christianity. Presenting a different view, Father Massanet believed that the missions would be more successful if no soldiers were stationed nearby. He argued that armed soldiers would frighten the natives and make them less likely to trust the priests.

Government officials in Mexico City agreed with Massanet. Peaceful approaches to the natives were better. It was also less expensive if soldiers did not have to be stationed in East Texas. As we shall see, it was Alonso de León who was correct, and it was Father Damián Massanet who was wrong.

In the immediate future, the French threat in Texas could not be ignored. Officials in the capital told León to recruit just enough soldiers to help the priests set up a mission and protect them from Indians and the French. Don Alonso believed that one hundred soldiers were necessary for the task. Father Massanet objected to such a large number. León had his way, although Massanet continued to question the need for so many soldiers.

The Franciscans decided to send six missionaries to Texas. This number included Father Francisco Hidalgo, who would make conversion of the Tejas Indians to Christianity his lifelong interest. Hidalgo, however, did not go to Texas at this time. He remained at a mission in northern Mexico.

On April 6, 1690, the León-Massanet expedition crossed the Río Grande and set out for East Texas. Along the way, León met Indians who told him that they knew of Frenchmen in the area. León wisely gave gifts of tobacco and biscuits to these natives, who promised to keep him informed of any foreigners living in the woods.

Near the end of April, León and Massanet again visited the remains of La Salle's colony. They looked through the crude buildings to see if anything had changed. Finding things the same as before, they then burned the French fort.

Continuing on toward their destination in East Texas, León learned that there were French children living as captives among the Indians. Don Alonso chose eight soldiers and passed through "a forest of oaks and grapevines." After marching about fifteen miles, the Spaniards found Pierre Talon, who was fourteen years of age. They gave some gifts to the natives in exchange for young Pierre, who was covered with tattoos in the manner of most Texas Indians. Two days later,

León recovered Pierre Meunier, another French youth who had been tattooed.

The full expedition then continued on to East Texas. León was much impressed with the Tejas Indians' cultivated fields, which contained corn and beans. Their villages "had very clean houses and high beds in which to sleep." On this occasion, León met the governor, or high chief, of the Tejas. The governor took don Alonso to his home, gave him a bench to sit on, and fed him "a luncheon of corn tamales . . . all very clean."

Over the next several days, León and Massanet looked for an ideal location for the first Spanish mission in East Texas. They chose a site on May 27, and spent the next five days building a residence for the priests and a chapel for the Indians.

Before leaving on the return march to Coahuila, León offered to leave fifty soldiers at the mission. Massanet insisted that only a few troops be left as guards for Mission San Francisco de los Tejas. Despite León's protests, the Franciscan priest would not change his mind. So when Father Massanet and General León headed home on June 1, only three soldiers remained behind. Massanet said he felt no need to have more soldiers because the high chief of the Tejas had promised not to mistreat the missionaries. Unfortunately, as we shall see in the next chapter, his promise was not kept for very long.

As León and Massanet marched homeward toward Coahuila, they learned near the Guadalupe River of still more French youths living among the Indians. Once again, don Alonso separated a few men from his command and set out to find the kidnapped children. The thought of Christian boys and girls held captive by Native Americans greatly troubled León, and he was determined to rescue them at any cost.

After three days of searching, don Alonso came upon Indians who held a sister and a brother of Pierre Talon. Both children were covered with tattoos and painted from head to foot. Marie-Madeleine Talon was then sixteen. Her brother, Robert, was only five years old. León had to arrange ransom for the Talons, and he quickly agreed to the price asked by the Indians.

The natives noticed that León had not argued over the terms of freedom for the children, which led them to think that they had not asked a high enough price. So the Indians changed their minds and refused to release the Talons unless they were given all of don Alonso's horses. In León's words, the Indians wanted to collect "even the clothing which we wore upon on backs." As a military man, don Alonso's distrust and anger toward Indians rose to a dangerous level.

At that moment, other Indians showed up with still another Talon child named Lucien. He, like his sister and brother, was covered with tattoos and paint. Once again, León and the Indians had to settle on a ransom. And, in arguing, both sides became angrier and angrier. Finally, according to don Alonso, the Indians began waving bows and arrows and screaming that they "would have to shoot and kill us all."

Almost immediately, León ordered his soldiers to open fire with their muskets. In a short time, four Indians lay dead and several others were wounded. Don Alonso felt justified in his actions. Father Massanet did not see the incident that way. The priest claimed that León was too hot-headed, that he did not have good control over his soldiers, and that Indian lives were needlessly lost.

The Talon children, four boys and a girl, were returned to life among Christians. Many years later they told of what had happened to them as a family. When they first arrived in Texas with La Salle, they were a family of eight. There were six children, ranging in age from a few months to twelve years. The youngest, Robert, had been born at sea on one of La Salle's ships as it sailed from France to the Texas coast.

Shortly after the Talons landed at Matagorda Bay, the father had wandered into the woods. Perhaps he was looking for food, but he never returned and the children never knew what happened to him. Then one of the two Talon girls died of an illness. She was probably thirteen years of age. In a short time, Mrs. Talon had lost her husband and a daughter. Soon, she would also experience the loss of a son.

When La Salle left on his third and final attempt to find the Mississippi River, he forced young Pierre Talon to go with him. Against the wishes of his mother, the boy was to be left with the Tejas Indians to learn their language and help the French deal with them. La Salle's plans ended abruptly when he was murdered by his own men. The French boy witnessed that bloody event just one day before his eleventh birthday. Pierre then found himself abandoned by his countrymen and adopted by Indians.

But the worst was yet to happen. When the Karankawas attacked the French colony at Christmastime in 1688, the remaining four Talon children lost their mother. She was clubbed to death by a Karankawa warrior.

León and Massanet never heard or read the awful story that was later told by the Talon children. After the rescue of Marie-Madeleine, Robert, and Lucien from the wilds of Texas, there is again clear evidence that Massanet and León did not look on Indians in the same way. As a priest, Massanet could not accept shedding human blood. He thought if León had been more patient, he could have won the cooperation of Native Americans through peaceful means.

Later, León and Massanet would both be called upon to report to the viceroy what had happened on the 1690 expedition. Yes, it had resulted in the founding of Mission San Francisco de los Tejas, the first Spanish mission in East Texas. Yes, it had located five French children held by Indians, and they had been set free. Yes, it had resulted in the death of four Indians. Yes, Spanish knowledge of Texas and its Indian population had been increased. The two agreed on these facts but on little else.

Father Massanet believed that the Tejas were glad to have a Spanish mission among them and become Christians. He saw no need to keep more than three soldiers to protect the Franciscan missionaries. Massanet also believed that a fair price could have been arranged for the three children, and that no one needed to be killed in setting them free.

León, on the other hand, was much more experienced in dealing with Indians. Again, he had fought a long series of Indian wars in Nuevo León and Coahuila. His view that all Native Americans were alike and not to be trusted was wrong—just as all Spaniards were not the same. In this case, León came closer to being right about the problems of unprotected missions in Texas than did Massanet.

In his letters to the viceroy, don Alonso gave a highly favorable report on some aspects of the Tejas Indians. He pointed out that they lived in clean houses and slept in bunk beds above the ground. They raised good crops of beans, corn, watermelons, and cantaloupe. The Tejas were such good planners that they always kept seeds for the next year's planting. In fact, they were so careful that they kept enough seed to see them through two crop failures in a row.

Father Massanet assured the viceroy that no more soldiers were needed to guard the one mission for the Tejas. Instead, he urged that carpenters be sent to build living quarters for the priests and their helpers. He also suggested that Indian children from Mexico who had been baptized as Christians be sent to Texas. These youngsters were to serve as good role models for Tejas children.

Massanet did request fourteen more priests and seven religious helpers for East Texas. He believed all the Indians there to be good prospects for conversion to Christianity. In all, the Franciscan priest asked the Spanish crown to set up eight new missions. And the viceroy agreed to this request.

As plans went forward in Mexico City, the viceroy decided that he did not want Alonso de León to return to Texas. He was to stay in Coahuila and give his attention to Indian wars there. In truth, don Alonso had greatly irritated the viceroy and his advisers in the capital. He had not told high officials the kind of news they wanted to hear. His recommendations, if carried out, required spending a lot of money to set up presidios and station soldiers in Texas. León was also the target of bitter complaints by Father Massanet, who accused him of being too harsh in dealing with Indians.

A new governor for Texas was appointed at this time. His name was Domingo Terán de los Ríos. We will learn more about Terán in the following chapter. Note that the new governor was not nearly as able or dedicated as Alonso de León. Note also that León was absolutely correct in his belief that Spanish missions without nearby presidios were bound to fail in Texas.

In all, from 1686 to 1690, Alonso de León carried out five land expeditions, four of which entered Texas. He learned new information about the land and gave names to many Texas rivers, such as the Guadalupe. León also gathered much new information on the native population of Texas. He established a good part of what would become the famous Camino Real that ran from the Río Grande to East Texas. That road was so well traveled in early Texas history that it became the route of modern Texas Highway 21, which starts at San Marcos, south of Austin. It runs through College Station, where Texas A&M University is located, and then on to Nacogdoches and the border of Louisiana.

Alonso de León was of course more than just an early pathfinder in Texas history. His concern for the Talon children, who had seen their mother murdered before their very eyes, is touching. He was absolutely determined that these children be set free and brought

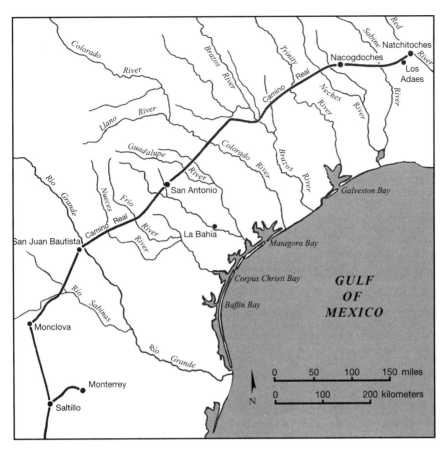

The Camino Real (King's Road) running from San Juan Bautista to Los Adaes
(CENTER FOR MEDIA PRODUCTION, UNIVERSITY OF NORTH TEXAS, ADAPTED FROM
WILLIAM C. FOSTER's Spanish Expeditions into Texas, 1689–1768)

up as Christians. In rescuing them, he may have been too short-tempered. Father Massanet always insisted that León's actions had needlessly cost the lives of four Indians. To readers today, León's treatment of Native Americans probably seems heavy-handed. His approach to Indians at this time in history, however, was very similar to that of every other military person who entered Texas.

Alonso de León appears to have been a good man in most respects. True, he made mistakes like all human beings. But one should remember that he helped found the first Spanish mission in East Texas. Also, the fact that he became a general and governor of two provinces in northern Mexico speaks to his talent and loyalty to king and country.

Within two months after he was passed over as governor of Texas in favor of Domingo Terán, Alonso de León died in Monclova, Coahuila. At death, he was only slightly more than fifty years of age.

Robert S. Weddle, a historian who has studied the life of don Alonso, believes that his health was ruined by "Coahuila Indian wars and the long marches into Texas." He was certainly an important man in early Texas history. Unfortunately, his contributions to the future Lone Star State have not always been fully appreciated.

SOURCES

Materials used in preparing this chapter are described below. You can find more information about these sources in the Bibliography at the end of the book.

Books

The best book dealing with Alonso de León is Robert S. Weddle's *The French Thorn: Rival Explorers in the Spanish Sea, 1682–1762*. For León's route across Texas in 1689, see William C. Foster's *Spanish Expeditions into Texas, 1689–1768*. See also Donald E. Chipman and Harriett Denise Joseph's *Notable Men and Women of Spanish Texas* for a more detailed biographical sketch of León.

Quotes

Quotes in this chapter are from the following sources: Letter of Fray Damián Massanet to Don Carlos de Sigüenza, 1690, in *Spanish Exploration in the Southwest, 1542–1706*, edited and translated by Herbert E. Bolton; Vito Alessio Robles, *Coahuila y Texas en la época colonial*; Letter of Fray Damián Massanet and Itinerary of the De León Expedition of 1689, in *Spanish Exploration in the Southwest, 1542–1706*, edited and translated by Herbert E. Bolton; Robert S. Weddle, *Wilderness Manhunt: The Spanish Search for La Salle*; and Robert S. Weddle, Mary Christine Morkovsky, and Patricia Galloway, translators and editors, *Three Primary Documents: La Salle, the Mississippi, and the Gulf*.

Additional Information

The *Belle* is the sunken vessel that was excavated from a cofferdam in 1996 and 1997. It has yielded thousands of artifacts that are like a time capsule from the late 1600s.

In the following chapter, you will read about the release of the fourth Talon boy, named Jean-Baptiste.

CHAPTER FIVE

Domingo Terán de los Ríos/ Francisco Hidalgo

ANGRY GOVERNOR AND MAN WITH A MISSION

The year 1691 marked the death of Alonso de León and the appointment of Domingo Terán de los Ríos as the first governor of Texas. One of the most dedicated soldiers in the early history of Texas would be replaced by a man who was far less able. Not many people in the present Lone Star State can name our first governor, and probably with good reason. Terán did not like Texas any better than most readers will like him. In fact, Terán came to hate Texas and everything about it. At the earliest opportunity, he headed back to Mexico. On the other hand, Father Francisco Hidalgo was a priest who truly loved Texas and its Indian population. This dedicated missionary made work among the Tejas of East Texas his passionate interest for most of his adult life. In looking at these early Texans, we see two men who could not have been much more different.

On January 23, 1691, Domingo Terán was chosen as the first governor of the province then known as Tejas. Terán should have been well suited for the job, because he already had experience as a frontier governor. Before accepting the Texas assignment, he had served as the chief executive of both Sinaloa and Sonora.

As governor of these provinces in northern Mexico, Terán had fought a number of Indian wars, and he showed a talent for discovering rich silver mines. Success had made him a very arrogant and bad-tempered man. Terán saw governing Texas, which was much poorer than Sinaloa and Sonora, as beneath his abilities.

Terán's instructions as governor of Texas ordered him to set up eight missions among the Tejas natives and their neighbors. He was to resupply Mission San Francisco de los Tejas; he was to make sure there were no Frenchmen to the east of the mission; and he was to explore the country as thoroughly as possible.

The new governor was particularly upset that he had to share leadership of the expedition with Father Damián Massanet, who had founded Mission San Francisco in the previous year. Terán had command of the soldiers, but Massanet was in charge of the missionaries. When it came to setting up the eight missions, the governor could do nothing without the full approval of the priest. This restriction greatly irritated Terán, and he wrote the viceroy in protest. Still, Terán promised to do his best to make the expedition of 1691 a success.

Because Terán had orders to explore rivers and bays along the coast, he was to be supported by two ships. Those vessels were to sail from the port of Veracruz to Matagorda Bay, where the governor would make contact with them. The ships would also bring extra supplies, as well as fifty soldiers under the command of Captain Gregorio de Salinas Varona.

Terán himself left Coahuila on the march to Texas on May 16, 1691. In his party were fifty soldiers, ten priests, and three religious helpers for the missionaries. Terán's second in command was Captain Francisco Martínez. Like all of Spain's early expeditions into Texas, this one drove great herds of cattle, sheep, and goats. The animals would provide livestock for the new missions, and they could be butchered as needed if the Spaniards could not kill buffaloes for meat.

The plan was for the two ships to arrive at Matagorda Bay toward the end of April, and Francisco Martínez was to meet them at the bay with twenty soldiers. But in this day and age it was impossible to have good communication between the northern frontier of Mexico and the port of Veracruz. Terán ran into unexpected delays in Coahuila and did not leave for Texas until mid-May. So already timing was a problem.

Terán did not cross the Río Grande and reach Texas soil until late May. By 1691 the earlier expeditions of Alonso de León had named many of the rivers, as well as the province of Tejas itself. Terán was so filled with self-importance that he decided to rename every river and creek he crossed, as well as the province itself. He began by calling the Río Grande the Río del Norte (River of the North). The Nueces River became the San Diego, and so it went.

Early on, the 1691 expedition came to the site of present-day San Antonio. There Terán stopped on the banks of a small stream that was lined with cypress and oak trees. Peaceful Indians camped nearby, and the governor remarked that the location would be an ideal place to set up a mission. So Terán deserves credit for discovering this important spot in Texas, which he named San Antonio de Padua.

The Spaniards then continued on to the Guadalupe River near present-day New Braunfels, where they encountered some two thousand Indians on horseback. These natives, mostly Jumanos and Cíbolos, had recently visited East Texas. They carried news from Mission San Francisco de los Tejas, and much of it was bad.

Smallpox raged at the mission, and one of the three Franciscan priests had died of a fever during the previous winter. The Jumanos and Cíbolos seemed to be familiar with Christianity, because many of them wore religious items such as the images of saints and crosses. Nevertheless, in the middle of the night there was a stampede resulting in the loss of fifty Spanish horses. In the morning, the Indians were suspiciously gone. Terán blamed the Jumanos and Cíbolos for the loss of his mounts, and the incident did not improve his attitude toward Indians.

Near present-day Austin, Terán camped on the Colorado River for more than two weeks. During that time, Francisco Martínez took a troop of twenty soldiers and marched off to Matagorda Bay to meet the two supply ships. But the ships, which were supposed to have been there by late April, had not arrived.

Martínez waited at the bay for five days. During that time, he found two French children, Jean-Baptiste Talon and Eustache Bréman, who had been kidnapped from La Salle's colony by Karankawa Indians. Both of the children, like those found by Alonso de León, were covered with tattoos and had to be ransomed for horses and tobacco.

By this time, it was near mid-July, and the ships were still not in view. On July 12 Martínez gathered up the two children and began the march back to the Colorado River. On the afternoon of that very day, the two ships dropped anchor at Matagorda Bay. Missing the connection with the supply vessels by a matter of hours would cause no end of trouble and worry for Domingo Terán.

When Captain Martínez reached the main camp on the Colorado, he asked permission to return to the bay immediately. His request sparked a heated argument between Terán and Massanet. The priest insisted that there be no more delays in setting out for East Texas. This was especially important, since bad conditions were known to exist at Mission San Francisco de los Tejas.

Massanet reminded the governor that in matters relating to the missions he held the upper hand. So Terán was forced to break camp and continue the march toward East Texas. The pace was too slow, however, to suit the missionaries, and they complained bitterly about it. On this portion of the journey, it is important to remember that the Terán-Massanet expedition did not follow the Camino Real, the King's Highway established by Alonso de León. Instead, it traveled to the north of the old road.

Because of the delays caused by the unsuccessful march to Matagorda Bay, it was late July into early August, and the weather was hot and dry. Nevertheless, the expedition faced swarms of mosquitoes night and day. As it approached East Texas, the weeds and trees were loaded with bloodsucking ticks and itchy chiggers. It was so dry that even a river as large as the Brazos had almost no water, and what still ran was "more salty than the sea."

In the drought and heat of the Texas summer, the large herds of sheep and goats that accompanied the expedition began to die of thirst and exhaustion. Terán slowed the pace to try to save as many animals as possible, but this decision greatly irritated Father Massanet.

When the expedition reached the Trinity River, the priests refused to stop and camp there. Instead, the padres pushed on without permission toward Mission San Francisco de los Tejas. Among the nine missionaries recruited by Massanet was a young and enthusiastic priest named Francisco Hidalgo. For Hidalgo, his true calling as a missionary to the Indians of East Texas was about to begin. Needless to say, the lonely padres at Mission San Francisco were delighted at the arrival of their Franciscan brothers.

The priests who stayed at San Francisco de los Tejas in 1690 had set up a second religious outpost named Santísimo Nombre de María, about five miles east of the original mission. But the Tejas Indians did not respond well to either of the missions. At no time would the natives agree to live away from their own houses and villages.

In a short time, Terán and the full expedition arrived at the location of the first Spanish mission in East Texas. The governor camped in one of the few open areas among the pines of East Texas, but the undergrowth and nearby trees were again loaded with bothersome insects. In the heat of August, Terán came to hate this primitive campsite, and he was determined to leave the province as quickly as possible.

Terán's best hope of a quick retreat from Texas lay at Matagorda Bay. Surely, he reasoned, the supply ships must be there by now. But ever since the Río Grande crossing back in May, almost no rain had fallen during the Texas summer. Because there was little grass for the horses, almost all of the animals were too weak to ride.

When the expedition finally reached its destination in East Texas, Terán had planned to rest the horses and let them graze to regain their strength. Unfortunately, the summer drought was so severe that the countryside had been stripped of vegetation by vast herds of buffaloes. So when the governor left for the coast, most of his soldiers either walked or rode more hardy mules. Accordingly, it was a sorry-looking group of men who set out for Matagorda Bay.

Terán traveled west to the Guadalupe River on the Camino Real, established in the late 1680s by Alonso de León. Still, he complained about everything. The old route was so crooked, in his words, that "only a sleepwalker could have opened such a road." Upon reaching the Guadalupe, the governor left the trail and began the final leg of the march toward Matagorda Bay.

As he marched toward the Texas coast, Terán began to think of a way to get out of Texas, quickly and for good. If the ships were not in the bay, he intended to follow the coast back to Mexico. Should the ships be there, he would get aboard one of the vessels and sail to Mexico.

The ships were indeed anchored in Matagorda Bay, where they had been since narrowly missing contact with Francisco Martínez back in mid-July. Far from being able to board one of the ships, Terán had orders from the viceroy to return to East Texas. Once there, he was to explore lands northward to the Red River.

Terán added the fifty men brought aboard the two ships to his command and began the march back to East Texas, which he had hoped never to lay eyes on again. He left the bay on September 27,

*Texas's first governor is
caught in an East Texas snowstorm*
(DRAWING BY JACK JACKSON)

and the drought continued for several more days. And then rain came in torrents, as it often does in October.

Beyond the Brazos River, Terán and his men had to slog through a sea of mud. They waited days for streams to go down, so the men and animals could cross safely. Everywhere what had recently been dry and dusty soil had been replaced by what seemed like endless marshes.

When the governor finally reached the second mission in East Texas, he was in a black mood. His best hope was to carry out the viceroy's orders as quickly as possible and then leave Texas. So Terán hastily organized an expedition to the Red River, and it left on November 6.

Father Massanet accompanied the Red River outing, and he had high hopes of setting up several missions along the banks of the river. This, however, was a troubled march, hampered by freezing rain and more than a foot of snow. Within a week, both horses and mules began to play out, and Terán was afraid that his entire army would soon be on foot.

There was so much rain and melting snow that the Sabine River ran at flood stage. When he reached this stream, Terán had to build a wooden bridge to cross it. Two days later he had to construct a second bridge to cross open water. This was followed by three straight days of freezing rain that brought the expedition to a standstill.

Leaving most of his men in a makeshift camp, Terán chose a few of the strongest and pushed on to the Red River. There he found Kadohadacho villages and determined that these natives were willing to become Christians. However, the weather was so bad that even Father Massanet agreed that he could not set up a single mission.

The return march to the encampment began on December 8. Because of melting snow, Terán recorded even worse conditions than on the outward trek. Twenty of the mules died, and the rest were too weak to ride. So the proud Spaniards were forced to travel on foot through rain, mud, and snow. Bridges they had already built on the outward march were covered with water, and new ones had to be built. Then the expedition was hit by a new batch of freezing rain and snow. It finally staggered into Mission Santísimo Nombre de María on December 30, 1691. This entire march makes one tired just reading about it.

In early January 1692, Terán made preparations for another march to Matagorda Bay. He had formed such negative impressions of East Texas that he believed the area was not fit for human habitation.

After resting a few days, Terán demanded fresh mounts from the horse herd at Mission San Francisco. When the padres refused to hand them over, the governor rounded up the animals and took them anyway. His actions sparked terrible arguments with Father Massanet and worsened already bad relations. However, when Terán set out for Matagorda Bay on January 9, 1692, six of the Franciscans left with him. These missionaries had found life in East Texas too discouraging.

This second march to the bay was much worse than the earlier trek. The ice and snow of the previous December had melted and flooded streams. It took the governor and his party ten days just to cross the Trinity River. There followed days of slogging through mud and standing water. Meanwhile, Terán's scouts brought back reports that the "country ahead resembled an immense sea."

Terán's army encountered such heavy rains that the men could not find dry wood to build campfires or warm themselves. Soldiers had to eat cold food and sleep in wet clothing, and then the fresh horses taken from the mission began to play out. So the footsore soldiers had to walk. Terán himself became increasingly angry and declared the country so bad that "no rational [sane] person has ever seen a worse one."

Terán's attitude hardly improved upon reaching the Navasota River. The stream was so swollen that he had to build rafts. Then, in attempting a crossing, Terán's craft overturned, dumping him and his baggage into icy water. The expedition finally reached its goal, arriving at Matagorda Bay on March 5.

Terán had seen quite enough of Texas. He boarded one of the two ships for a quick return to Mexico, but his troubles were far from over. While waiting in the bay for favorable winds and tides, six men drowned in a boating accident. When the ships finally tried to get underway, the men on board found the vessels trapped in mud. To free them, it was necessary to lighten the cargo by throwing sea chests, barrels of powder, and gun carriages overboard. This worked, and after a brief voyage to the mouth of the Mississippi River, the ships ran with the wind toward Mexico. On April 15, 1692, Texas's first governor arrived at the port of Veracruz and once again set foot on the soil of Mexico.

Francisco Martínez did not have the good luck to return home by ship. He had to march the soldiers and priests back to Coahuila by land, which he successfully did. Because Martínez had been with León on two of his marches into Texas, he probably used the Guadalupe River crossing near present-day Victoria and then continued on to Monclova, Coahuila. He arrived there well after Terán had stepped ashore at Veracruz.

Domingo Terán de los Ríos did very little to earn recognition for himself in Texas history. He was ordered to found eight new missions but established none. In fact, he weakened Mission San Francisco de los Tejas by forcibly taking many of its healthy horses. Don Domingo also did not investigate lands to the east to see if Frenchmen were there, as he was likewise ordered to do. Worse, his impressions of Texas were so negative that they helped keep Spaniards out of the province for years to come.

As mentioned early in this chapter, Terán applied new names to almost every creek, river, and campsite he encountered in Texas. He even suggested a new name for the province. Tejas, named after Indians in East Texas, was not good enough for a self-important governor. Instead, don Domingo suggested that Texas be named Nueva Montaña de Santander y Santillana.

Fortunately Terán's suggestion was ignored, for if accepted it would have messed up Texas legends and songs beyond repair. Can you imagine Big John Wayne in a western movie having to say, "Now you listen up, pilgrim! I'm from Nueva Montaña de Santander y Santillana, and we don't tolerate that down there"? Or how about having to sing "The eyes of Nueva Montaña de Santander y Santillana are upon you," or, even worse, "The stars at night are big and bright, deep in the heart of N.M. de S. y S."? In the end, Spanish officials displayed good sense. They stayed with "Tejas," which eventually came to be spelled "Texas."

Let us now turn our attention from Domingo Terán to a good man who truly loved Texas and its native population. In Texas history, he is far more important than our ill-tempered first governor. This "man with a mission" remained at San Francisco de los Tejas in 1692. He, perhaps more than anyone else, would make certain that Texas remained Spanish, not French.

Although Francisco Hidalgo is Texas's most dedicated missionary, we know very little about his early life. He was born in Spain, most likely in 1659, and probably was an orphan. At fifteen he chose to enter the Franciscan Order and later became a priest.

In 1683 Father Hidalgo crossed the Atlantic to help set up a college of Franciscans at Querétaro, a town located about ninety miles to the northwest of Mexico City. The college, named Santa Cruz (Holy Cross), was founded to help spread the Catholic faith among Indians in the New World.

Using Querétaro as his base, Hidalgo began to preach in the raw mining towns that were nearby. He evidently had great skills as a speaker, and at times he attracted enthusiastic listeners numbering more than three thousand. Father Francisco also had great success in

*Father Hidalgo preaches
to the Indians of East Texas*
(DRAWING BY JACK JACKSON)

getting sinners to change their evil ways. One of his fellow priests remarked that Hidalgo was so skilled as a preacher that he could settle long-standing feuds between individuals and their families. Wherever he went to preach, he brought forth "general confessions . . . on every hand."

In his sermons, Father Francisco revealed the talents of a gifted teacher. He told appropriate stories and used simple illustrations that were easily understood by his audiences. His sermons, nonetheless, were so moving and powerful that those seeking forgiveness were often reduced to floods of tears.

Some five years after his arrival in Mexico, Hidalgo decided to carry his Christian message to the northern frontier town of Monclova in Coahuila. Along the way, he learned to live off the land and toughen his body by sleeping on the ground when it became dark.

From Monclova, Hidalgo moved on to a mining camp called Boca de Leones (Mouth of Lions) in Nuevo León. Most of the men at Boca de Leones worked in nearby silver mines, but Father Hidalgo "sought a different kind of wealth." His goal, simply stated, was to convert all Indians to the Catholic faith.

While at Boca de Leones, Hidalgo was joined on the frontier by his fellow Franciscan, Damián Massanet. Father Damián soon founded a new mission about halfway between the mining camp and Monclova. This religious outpost was called Mission San Bernardino de Caldera, and it was from here that Massanet was called upon to join Alonso de León in the search for La Salle's colony in 1689.

Francisco Hidalgo was not permitted to join the León-Massanet expedition of the following year, which established the first Spanish mission in East Texas. Instead, his Franciscan superiors assigned him to a new outpost that was an offshoot of Mission Caldera. However, when Domingo Terán led ten priests into Texas in 1691, Father Hidalgo was one of that number. Once he reached East Texas, Hidalgo knew he had found his calling among the Tejas Indians, and he would not think of leaving the mission in 1692. When Domingo Terán left on his second march to Matagorda Bay, Hidalgo was not one of the six Franciscans who departed with him.

When Terán and Francisco Martínez reached Mexico, the Spanish knew they would have to quickly resupply the four priests who had remained in East Texas. By then, however, only San Francisco de los Tejas remained. The same floods in early 1692 that made travel so unpleasant for don Domingo and his army had washed away the second religious outpost.

Chosen to lead the supply expedition was Gregorio de Salinas Varona, the newly appointed governor of Coahuila. Salinas was a good choice for the job, because he had served under Alonso de León in 1690 and Terán after Salinas's arrival at Matagorda Bay with the two ships in 1691. His journey to East Texas was along the Camino Real marked by León, because that was the only route he knew.

The Salinas party reached Mission San Francisco on June 8, 1693, and made a quick turnabout. After just six days, Salinas headed home along the same road. Half of the priests in East Texas had become completely discouraged by the reluctance of the Tejas Indians to accept the Christian message. The natives would not attend Mass, and they had come to believe that the baptismal waters were fatal. This mistaken belief was rooted in the Indian observation that when missionaries applied holy water to the heads of critically ill Indians (called last rites), the natives almost always died soon thereafter.

Since the Indians understandably refused to live at the missions or give up their old ways of life, religious work among them required lots of patience and faith on the part of the Franciscan padres. Fathers Hidalgo and Massanet had those qualities, but two of their fellow missionaries did not. When Salinas took the road back to Mexico, two of the four Franciscans departed with him. That left only Hidalgo, Massanet, and a few soldiers to carry on the work of the mission and keep a Spanish presence in East Texas.

The two priests knew their situation was shaky, and Father Massanet quickly wrote the viceroy, asking for help. In his letter, Massanet stated that unless certain conditions were met and met soon, the entire mission project would have to be abandoned. He called for a presidio to be built near the mission and staffed with enough soldiers to protect the priests and enforce discipline on the Indians.

On August 31, 1693, the viceroy and his advisers decided that it would be too expensive to build a presidio in far-off Texas and staff it with soldiers. Since all efforts to bring the Christian message to the Tejas had so far failed, Salinas must make still another march to East Texas. The purpose of this expedition would be to close down Mission San Francisco and bring the two missionaries safely back to Mexico.

The rescue effort, however, never reached Texas. Salinas was delayed by bad weather, and at the same time relations with the Tejas became dangerous. Led by their chief, named Bernardino by the Spanish, the Indians threatened bloody rebellion if the Spanish did not leave.

Even Hidalgo and Massanet had to admit failure. Secretly, they and the soldiers packed sacred objects and buried military cannons. On the night of October 25, 1693, Mission San Francisco de los Tejas was set on fire by the priests themselves. Burning the mission may seem strange, but it ensured that the Christian chapel would not be profaned (misused) by the natives.

As flames consumed the mission, Hidalgo, Massanet, and a few companions fled in the night toward the safety of the coast. Unfortunately, this small group of Spaniards did not have an experienced guide. They wandered in the wilds of Texas for forty days before one of the group finally got his bearings and led them to safety in Mexico. Spain's first missionary effort in East Texas had ended on a very bad note.

Hidalgo and Massanet did not reach Monclova in Coahuila until February 17, 1694. Both priests were soon sent to their missionary college at Querétaro, and Texas was not occupied by Spaniards for the next twenty-two years. Part of the reason for this were the negative impressions of the province that were formed in the minds of men such as Texas's first governor, Domingo Terán de los Ríos. Captain Gregorio de Salinas Varona shared that view. His experiences in Texas led him to remark that East Texas would not be a fit place for Spaniards to live, because in going there one would suffer "a thousand discomforts."

This unfavorable view of Texas was not shared by Francisco Hidalgo. From the moment he left Texas in October 1693 until he returned in 1716, Father Hidalgo was truly a "man with a mission." That "mission" was twofold—it was a goal and it was a commitment to work in his own mission among the Tejas Indians.

It took Hidalgo the better part of twenty-five years to accomplish those objectives. During that time, he never lost sight of bringing a Christian message back to the Tejas. In finally accomplishing that goal in 1716, Father Hidalgo's actions bordered on treasonous relations with the French. That story and later years in the life of this dedicated missionary are best related in the following chapter on a French cavalier, Louis St. Denis, and his Spanish bride, Manuela Sánchez.

SOURCES

Materials used in preparing this chapter are described below. You can find more information about these sources in the Bibliography at the end of the book.

Books

The best information on Domingo Terán may be found in Robert S. Weddle's *The French Thorn: Rival Explorers in the Spanish Sea, 1682–*

1762. Carlos E. Castañeda's *Our Catholic Heritage in Texas, 1519–1936* contains admiring words about Father Francisco Hidalgo. For Terán's route across Texas, see William C. Foster's *Spanish Expeditions into Texas, 1689–1768.* Donald E. Chipman and Harriett Denise Joseph's *Notable Men and Women of Spanish Texas* has a more detailed biographical sketch of Hidalgo.

Quotes

Quotes in this chapter are from the following sources: Robert S. Weddle, *The French Thorn: Rival Explorers in the Spanish Sea, 1682–1762;* Lino Gómez Canedo, editor, *Primeras exploraciones y poblamiento de Texas (1686–1694);* Juan Domingo Arricivita, *Crónica seráfica y apostólica del colegio de propaganda fide de la Santa Cruz de Querétaro en la Nueva España,* Part 2; and Robert S. Weddle, *San Juan Bautista: Gateway to Spanish Texas.*

CHAPTER SIX

Louis St. Denis/Manuela Sánchez
CAVALIER AND HIS BRIDE

In the late 1600s, the unfavorable reports on Texas of Domingo Terán de los Ríos and Gregorio de Salinas Varona, combined with the dismal failure of the first two missions in East Texas, dampened the spirits of almost everyone. This included nearly a dozen Franciscans who at one time or another had served in Texas.

These missionaries belonged to a religious order that demanded sacrifices from its members that seem unbelievable in today's world. Franciscans had to beg for every scrap of food and could not own any personal property. They were required to dress in a coarse-cloth habit (outer one-piece garment), tied at the waist with a cord. They were supposed to walk, not ride animals, and at best wear sandals for foot gear. In fact, many members of the order chose to walk barefooted, despite rough ground and the cold of winter. So it was hard to discourage a Franciscan who did not even know the meaning of luxury.

With this in mind, it seems unusual for so many Franciscans to have given up on Texas. One notable exception turned out to be Francisco Hidalgo, the Man with a Mission. Even though his religious order sent him far away from Texas to its college at Querétaro, Father Hidalgo never lost sight of his life's work. This was nothing less than to save the souls of Texas Indians for his Christian God.

As he had done when he first arrived in Mexico, Hidalgo again took up the job of preaching against sin in the rough mining camps and towns near Querétaro. Once again he showed great skills as a religious teacher. The good Franciscan could move audiences to tears with his sermons, and he showed the same patience and understanding that marked his work among the Tejas Indians of East Texas.

After several years of preaching, things changed for Father Hidalgo. In 1697 Father Antonio Margil, whom we will meet in the next chapter, returned to Querétaro from Central America. Margil became head of the college of Santa Cruz, and he soon looked to the northern frontier province of Coahuila for renewed work among its Indians.

Other than the early efforts of Fathers Hidalgo and Massanet, there had been little progress in winning the souls of Indians in Coahuila. Margil was determined to change that, and Hidalgo leaped at the opportunity to go northward toward Texas.

One year after Margil returned to Querétaro, he sent Francisco Hidalgo and a priest named Diego de Salazar to Coahuila with orders to set up a mission there. For Hidalgo it was the first step in a long and difficult journey back to his calling among the Tejas.

Hidalgo and Salazar set up their first mission, called Santa María de los Dolores. This outpost attracted a few neophytes (mission Indians), and the eager Franciscans then founded another mission to the north of it on the Río Sabinas. The second establishment was named San Juan Bautista, and it brought Father Hidalgo even closer to Texas.

Letters from the two Franciscans to Father Margil soon carried enthusiastic reports on their successes among the local Indians. Much encouraged, Margil then sent two additional priests to Coahuila. The more famous of the two was Father Antonio de Olivares, the future founder of Mission San Antonio de Valero, later known as the Alamo.

Things were going reasonably well at Mission San Juan Bautista when a tragic event happened. A Christianized Indian who served as an interpreter was killed by Indians who lived outside the mission. The padres were fearful that the man's relatives, who were residents at the mission, would blame them for this death.

Because of their concern that some of the neophytes would seek bloody revenge and because it was difficult to draw irrigation water from the Sabinas River, the Franciscans decided to relocate the mission. They kept the name San Juan Bautista but moved the outpost to just south of the Río Grande. This greatly pleased Father Hidalgo, for Texas was now near at hand.

Aiding in the construction of the second and more famous Mission San Juan Bautista was Captain Diego Ramón, one of the great names in early Texas history. Ramón and Father Hidalgo laid the foundation of this mission on January 1, 1700. Soon built close by was a presidio with the same name—San Juan Bautista. The combined mission and presidio would become known as the Gateway to Texas.

In short order, two more missions were built in the same vicinity. This location had roots in the nearby Río Grande crossing used by Alonso de León, Domingo Terán, and Salinas Varona. Spaniards named favorable river crossings *pasos* (passes). Today a major Texas city gets its name by having served for many years as El Paso del Río Grande.

Oddly enough, the pass near San Juan Bautista was known as Paso de Francia (French Pass). Its name came from the numerous Río Grande crossings made in search of Frenchmen who had come to Texas with La Salle.

Although Father Hidalgo had finally reached the very threshold of Texas, there was still not a single Spaniard living north of the Great River. This would remain the case for the next sixteen years. The three existing missions did serve the native population along the Río Grande. They also ministered to hunting and gathering tribes that ranged north of the river.

Nine long years passed before a single Spanish expedition ventured into the interior of Texas. However, in the spring of 1709, Captain Pedro de Aguirre led a march to the site of present-day San Antonio. There he noted the same favorable surroundings for a mission, remarked on by Domingo Terán in 1691. And like Terán, Aguirre called the site San Antonio de Padua.

This *entrada* (entrance) was made in part to check out rumors that the Tejas were willing to accept the return of Spaniards to East Texas. Instead, it was learned that the old chieftain Bernardino was still angry at the Spanish and would not accept their religion.

Two priests accompanied the Aguirre expedition, and they were much disappointed by this news. One of them, Father Olivares, left the Río Grande and made the long and dangerous trip to Spain. There he made special pleas for new and better financed missions in Texas. The second priest, Father Félix de Espinosa, likewise left the Río Grande and returned to the Franciscan's college at Querétaro.

This left only Francisco Hidalgo at San Juan Bautista. He was so stubborn and determined to return to work among the Tejas that he had to find a way to do it. Father Hidalgo's plan would eventually bring Louis St. Denis, known as the French Cavalier, to San Juan Bautista. That proved to be the key, the trigger, that would send Spaniards back into Texas. This was a dangerous tactic on the part of Hidalgo, but it led to Spain's permanent occupation of the future Lone Star State, a presence that would last for the next 105 years.

As mentioned, Texas was abandoned by the Spanish in 1693. They did not return until 1716—and only then because of the combined scheming of Father Hidalgo and St. Denis.

To understand how this came about, we must shift our attention to Louisiana. After the death of the Frenchman La Salle, his close and faithful friend Henri Tonti traveled from Canada to France. That European country was then ruled by the great Sun King, Louis XIV.

Tonti urged his king to pick up the pieces of La Salle's shattered dream and establish a French colony on the Gulf Coast. Instead of planting the colony in Texas, where one had failed in the 1680s, France should set up towns and military garrisons near the mouth of the Mississippi River.

La Salle's old friend also explained the advantages of controlling the Mississippi River and its mouth to Louis XIV's advisers. The French colony in New France (Canada) would have an outlet to the sea by way of the river. French outposts on the lower end of the Father of Waters, as the Mississippi was occasionally known, would keep this vital region out of the hands of Spanish and English enemies. It would also bring France close to the rich silver mines of northern Mexico.

The king and his ministers liked Tonti's proposal. For their colonizer, they chose Sieur d'Iberville, a French explorer born in Canada. Iberville enlisted four of his brothers for the venture, the most famous of them being Sieur Bienville. (For his part in the founding of New Orleans later on, in 1718, this brother would be called the Father of Louisiana.)

On this occasion, the French were successful in finding the mouth of the Mississippi. In April 1699, Iberville set up a temporary fort near present-day Ocean Springs, Mississippi, before sailing back to France. There he picked up fresh supplies and more colonists. One of the recruits was a Canadian-born relative named Louis St. Denis.

St. Denis, the eleventh of twelve children, was born near Quebec on September 17, 1674. His parents had enjoyed some success in Canada and were able to send their son to France for schooling. At age twenty-five the young adventurer signed on with Iberville at the port of La Rochelle.

St. Denis headed a company of Canadians, and attached to his command were two familiar names, Pierre and Jean-Baptiste Talon. These brothers, as perhaps you remember, were survivors of La Salle's colony near Matagorda Bay. They had been rescued and ransomed by Alonso de León and Francisco Martínez, and both bore tattoos in the manner of Texas Indians.

It seems likely that St. Denis was able to become a leader at such an early age because of his family ties to Iberville and his brothers. In any event, by 1700 Louis St. Denis in the company of Bienville, twenty-two Canadians, and seven Indian guides moved across northern Louisiana toward Texas.

St. Denis and Bienville were ordered to renew French contacts with Texas Indians and check on the Spanish. Their expedition, however, had to face incredible hardships. It rained almost constantly, creating swamps with waist-deep water. The men had to build rafts to protect their supplies, which they pushed or pulled through cold water. As Bienville remarked, "Never in all our lives have my men or I been so tired. This is fine business for cooling the fires of youth."

At last the exhausted men contacted Kadohadacho Indians to the east of their villages. From these natives they learned that mounted Spaniards had reached the Red River. But relying on sign language and figures drawn in the dirt can lead to serious misunderstandings. What the French explorers failed to comprehend was that the natives were reporting on Spaniards who had been to the Red River *nine years earlier*. This was the ill-fated Domingo Terán expedition of 1691.

The Kadohadachos also reported that Spaniards lived in missions and worked among Indians in present-day East Texas. Again the natives did not mention, or perhaps the French misunderstood, that no Spaniards had been in Texas since 1693, seven years earlier.

So when St. Denis and Bienville returned to Louisiana, they had the mistaken impression that Spaniards were then in Texas. In history, as in life, what people believe can sometimes be as important as the facts themselves.

Shortly after his return from the Red River expedition, St. Denis was sent on a second march toward the same location. He was to gather information on how many Spaniards lived to the west of Louisiana and how far it was to the Spanish mines in Mexico. This effort by St. Denis failed because of serious illnesses among his men, which forced a return to Louisiana. And later, another march ended with the same results. By then, eleven years had passed, and the French in Louisiana still believed there were Spaniards in Texas. Thanks to Francisco Hidalgo, that was about to change.

For Hidalgo, the years were slipping by and he was still no closer to achieving his goal of returning to East Texas. He knew of French settlements along the Mississippi River, and he was determined to put that knowledge to good use. In January 1711, Hidalgo wrote a famous letter to the governor of Louisiana.

Father Hidalgo asked if there were French missionaries working among Indians along the Mississippi River. If that was the case, would the governor consider sending a few Catholic priests westward to Christianize the Tejas? This amounted to inviting a foreign nation onto lands claimed by the king of Spain. Some have regarded this letter as an act of treason. But one could also argue that Hidalgo had a higher commitment to saving the souls of Texas Indians than to serving the interests of Spain.

The Hidalgo letter of 1711 took almost two years to reach the governor of Louisiana. It passed from one Indian group to another, until it was finally delivered to a French mission on the Mississippi. Catholic priests then passed the letter on to the governor of Louisiana, who received it in early May 1713.

From the letter, it was clear that there were no Spaniards in Texas, otherwise Hidalgo would not have had to ask the French for help in setting up a mission. For the first time, the governor realized that he and others in Louisiana had been operating for many years on bad information. Again, this stemmed from what was poorly reported by Indians or badly misunderstood by the expedition of 1700.

The governor of Louisiana soon called on St. Denis, who on at least three occasions had approached Texas. At that time, Louis St. Denis was thirty-nine years of age and unmarried. He was eager to try Texas one more time and perhaps make his fortune as a trader.

St. Denis quickly organized a company of Canadians, and, led by Indians scouts, the group moved westward toward Tejas communities between the Neches and Angelina Rivers in East Texas. Two members of the group must have had serious doubts about going back among Texas Indians. They were the Talon brothers, Pierre and Robert, returning to a land that had claimed the lives of their parents and a sister.

The Talons were vital to the success of the French expedition. They knew the land and could serve as interpreters. Traveling by canoe, the party paddled up the Mississippi and Red Rivers to the villages of Natchitoches Indians. St. Denis left some trade goods at Natchitoches, perhaps little realizing that much of his later life would be spent there. He and his party then set out on foot for the land of the Tejas.

On reaching his destination, St. Denis established good relations with the Tejas Indians. The tattooed faces of the Talons were reminders of their years among the Tejas and Karankawas, and their appearance won them easy acceptance by the natives. When Louis St. Denis asked the whereabouts of Father Francisco Hidalgo, he was told that the Tejas had not seen him for more than twenty years.

The Tejas did offer to take the Frenchmen to where they could find the Franciscan priest. So a party of eight set out for the Río Grande and San Juan Bautista. This group included St. Denis, the two Talon brothers, another Frenchman, and four Tejas Indian guides. On July 19, 1714, the men crossed the Great River and traveled a short distance beyond it to the presidio.

In charge of the garrison was the distinguished commander Diego Ramón. Don Diego had been present at the founding of the mission on January 1, 1700, and in the meantime he had assembled much of his extended family at the Gateway to Texas.

On the day after finding Spaniards at San Juan Bautista, St. Denis penned a letter to Father Hidalgo, who had just recently been recalled to his college at Querétaro. The Frenchman admitted that he was in a bad way. In his words, "We have been living on the road by what we could hunt. And up to the present we are [without] supplies and other things necessary for life."

A few days later, Diego Ramón likewise wrote Hidalgo at his college. Note his words: "There are in this presidio four Frenchmen, a captain named Luis de Sn. Dionisio, and another Pedro Talon, and the other Roberto, who were among those rescued by General Alonso de León." According to don Diego, all four Frenchmen were unable to speak Spanish.

Father Hidalgo's heart must have skipped a beat as he read the next lines from Captain Ramón. "I say that if His Majesty [the king] does not take warning and the Natchitoches villages are not settled, the French will be masters of all this land." It seems that by writing his letter to the governor of Louisiana, things could not have worked out better for the Man with a Mission.

Hidalgo probably counted on the threat of Frenchmen coming into Texas and influencing Indians there to stir his king and viceroy into action. This had been the case earlier, when Alonso de León had looked for La Salle's fort until he found it. A similar concern had prompted the founding of Mission San Francisco de los Tejas in 1690. Later, when the Spanish learned that La Salle was dead and the French threat had ended, they decided to give up on the expense of building presidios and missions in East Texas.

Now the ball was set in motion by the appearance of the French Cavalier at San Juan Bautista in July 1714, and the Spanish would never again lose interest in Texas. For the moment, however, Captain Diego Ramón did not know what to do with St. Denis.

Ramón informed Louis St. Denis that he could not leave the presidio. Instead, he was put under pleasant house arrest in the home of Ramón. The Frenchman had to remain there until word arrived from the viceroy in Mexico City, telling Captain Ramón what to do about the foreigners.

It took several weeks for a letter to travel from San Juan Bautista to the capital. Then the viceroy had to meet with his advisers and get their input. Once a decision was made, a letter had to travel from Mexico City to the Río Grande presidio. Weeks went by.

Meanwhile, Captain Ramón's beautiful seventeen-year-old granddaughter, Manuela Sánchez Navarro, caught the roving eye of the dashing French Cavalier. And since Manuela Sánchez did not object, romance was soon in the air. However, Louis St. Denis had plans that involved both love *and* money.

As time passed at San Juan Bautista, the Spanish relaxed their guard over the Talon brothers. One night they escaped across the Río Grande and headed for Louisiana. With them went a secret letter from St. Denis to Sieur de Cadillac, his governor at Mobile.

Fearing that the Talons might be captured and the contents of his letter revealed, St. Denis carefully stated that he was unable to "write

you fully of all that has happened here." He informed the French governor that he himself could not return to Louisiana, because "the
captain [Ramón] dares not allow me to depart without order from the
viceroy." In truth, St. Denis had no intention of leaving. There were
the obvious charms of señorita Sánchez, and he had begun to think of
himself as a successful trader between French Louisiana and Spanish
Texas.

When the Talons reached Mobile, they gave a full report of their
Texas experiences to Governor Cadillac. They informed him that
Spanish mines at Boca de Leones were only about 150 miles from the
Río Grande. The Talons also reported that St. Denis planned to marry
Commandant Ramón's granddaughter, and in doing so would make
himself a part of the most powerful Spanish family in northern Mexico.

All of this aroused the suspicions of Governor Cadillac, who expressed the view that his "agent was not tending strictly to business."
He further stated in a report to France that since "he must marry a
Spanish girl, one may believe his journey [in Mexico] will be very
long." In conclusion, Cadillac described St. Denis as having "some
good qualities but some bad ones also—he loves his comforts, and is
not sufficiently [devoted to] the king's service."

Back at San Juan Bautista, word finally arrived from the viceroy
in Mexico City. St. Denis must be sent to the capital. There he would
be questioned by the viceroy and his advisers. Domingo Ramón, one
of Commandant Ramón's sons, would escort the French Cavalier to
Mexico City. Before leaving, Louis St. Denis won a promise of marriage from the teenage beauty Manuela Sánchez.

Once in the capital, St. Denis was very well treated, for the Spanish had much to learn from him. The Frenchman described every
mile of his journey from Mobile to San Juan Bautista. He commented
on the Tejas Indians and told the viceroy that the Indians in East
Texas would welcome back the Franciscan missionaries.

It seems likely that St. Denis wanted to draw the Spanish closer
to Louisiana by urging the reoccupation of Texas. In this manner, he
could possibly carry on profitable trade between the French and Spanish empires in America. St. Denis had many friends and relatives in
Louisiana, while he himself would become a Spanish citizen by marrying into the Ramón family.

In planning a career as a merchant between French Louisiana and

Spanish Texas, St. Denis made a serious mistake. Spain followed a policy (mercantilism) that did not permit its colonies to trade with anyone but Spain itself. This was especially important if European powers, such as Spain and France, were at war, as was often the case.

The Spanish viceroy and his advisers were quick to figure out St. Denis's goals. They sent orders to the northern frontier that all trade with the French in Louisiana was strictly forbidden. To avoid French influence over the Indians of East Texas, Father Hidalgo and other members of the Franciscan order must set up new missions in East Texas.

Still, St. Denis was a clever man and made a very good impression on the viceroy and other officials in Mexico City. They liked the French Cavalier and were impressed that he intended to take a Spanish bride. So in a major expedition intended to reoccupy East Texas, St. Denis would be permitted to act as supply officer. The military commander of the expedition would be Domingo Ramón.

Meanwhile, Governor Cadillac had his own reasons for distrusting St. Denis. He worried about his "bad qualities." Those weaknesses might make the French Cavalier loyal to Spain, not to his governor in Louisiana or the king in France.

But for St. Denis, these were exciting times. As soon as he was made supply officer for the planned expedition into Texas, he left Mexico City and hurried back to San Juan Bautista. In late 1715 or early 1716, a great social event took place at the Gateway to Texas. Louis St. Denis married Manuela Sánchez Navarro.

At the time of her marriage, Manuela was eighteen. Her husband was more than twice that age. But marriage opportunities for a young woman at San Juan Bautista were limited. For one thing, the Ramóns were a powerful family, and not just anyone would do as a husband for the commandant's lovely granddaughter.

Manuela Sánchez was perhaps the most famous woman in the early history of Texas, yet until recently she has been mistakenly called a niece or a even daughter of Commandant Diego Ramón. History is a constantly changing subject as scholars find new information in archives and libraries, and we now know much more about this Spanish woman. However, if you do not find genealogy (family history) interesting, just skip the next paragraph.

Born at Monclova, Coahuila, in 1697, Manuela Sánchez was not a blood relative of the Ramón family. Her father was Diego Sánchez

Navarro, and her mother was Mariana Gomes Mascorro. Manuela's grandmother, the mother of Diego Sánchez Navarro, was a widow with small children when she married Commandant Ramón. The future commander at Presidio San Juan Bautista then became a stepfather and guardian of his wife's children, including her son Diego. After the son married and his wife gave birth to Manuela, their daughter became the stepgranddaughter of Commandant Diego Ramón.

By the spring of 1716, Domingo Ramón had assembled a large expedition at San Juan Bautista, which was to occupy Texas for Spain. It included Father Hidalgo and eight other priests, three religious assistants, twenty-six soldiers, several dozen settlers, and livestock numbering in the thousands. The very size of this undertaking clearly shows that Spain intended more than just setting up mission outposts. The expedition of Domingo Ramón and Louis St. Denis would establish a permanent Spanish presence in Texas. As further evidence of Spain's intent, seven of the soldiers were married and brought along their wives. These are the first Spanish women on record in Texas.

The departure from San Juan Bautista of this large company of men and women in April interrupted the honeymoon of St. Denis and his bride. As he crossed the Río Grande, the French Cavalier left behind a young bride who had just turned nineteen. She was also pregnant.

With the assistance of Domingo Ramón and Louis St. Denis, Mission San Francisco was again set up in East Texas. Its location was near the original mission founded in 1690 by Damián Massanet and Alonso de León. Considering Father Francisco Hidalgo's role in bringing about this expedition, it was certainly appropriate that he was named missionary at this site.

By early 1717, there were six new missions and one presidio in East Texas. These outposts were set up in the very locale where two had failed in the 1690s. They were also far removed (more than four hundred miles) from the nearest Spanish community, San Juan Bautista on the Río Grande.

While the Spanish were spending their first winter in East Texas, St. Denis visited French settlements at Natchitoches and then traveled on to Mobile. He was still on reasonably good terms with Governor Cadillac, who badly needed trade with Spanish Texas and Mexico. Louis St. Denis's marriage into the Ramón family might be the key to business ventures that would increase the wealth of Louisiana.

Louis passed through East Texas on his way back to San Juan Bautista, where Manuela waited with their infant daughter. Traveling with him were dozens of mules loaded with goods that were his, as well as other things belonging to Governor Cadillac.

At the Gateway to Texas, Louis's happy reunion with his wife and their daughter was soon spoiled by his arrest. Commandant Ramón, his stepgrandfather by marriage, had been warned by the viceroy to be very suspicious of the French Cavalier. To Spanish officials it seemed certain that Louis St. Denis was about to violate trade restrictions with French Louisiana.

For his part, Louis reacted angrily. By his marriage to Manuela, he was now a Spaniard known as don Luis, not a suspicious French agent. Unfortunately, his protests were of no use. Under orders of the viceroy, St. Denis and all forbidden merchandise from Louisiana must be brought to Mexico City.

Two years had passed since St. Denis's first visit to the capital. That occasion had worked out well for him—so well that the viceroy had appointed him as an important official in the Spanish expedition to reoccupy Texas. Things had changed, however, both in Europe and in Mexico.

France and Spain were no longer allies in Europe, and a new viceroy headed the government in Mexico City. None of this was good news for St. Denis. For a time, he was thrown in jail, and the trade goods from Louisiana were taken from his control. However, a kindly official in the capital felt sorry for the French Cavalier. He was able to get St. Denis released and return some of his merchandise.

But the Frenchman was ordered not to leave the capital, and he could never return to Texas or to his wife. For more than a year, St. Denis scraped by on little food and less money. Fearing that he might again be thrown in jail for his angry remarks about Spanish officials, Louis fled Mexico City on the night of September 5, 1718.

Somehow, Louis made his way to Natchitoches without being arrested, but he dared not pass through San Juan Bautista. Once he was on French soil in Louisiana, Louis begged Spanish officials to let his wife, Manuela, join him. And they agreed to this reasonable request. In the early 1720s, the French Cavalier became military commander at Natchitoches, where he lived with his Spanish wife and a growing family for more than twenty years. Until his death in 1744,

Louis St. Denis and
Manuela Sánchez at Natchitoches
(DRAWING BY JACK JACKSON)

Louis was never far from the minds of Spanish officials. They did not trust him and feared his influence over Texas Indians.

By a strange turn of events, a man born in Canada and educated in France wound up bringing Spaniards into Texas to stay in 1716. His appearance at San Juan Bautista, thanks to the letter of Father Francisco Hidalgo, caused genuine concern on the part of Spanish officials in Mexico City. In their view, East Texas had to be occupied and defended against French designs from Louisiana.

Louis St. Denis always insisted that by marrying Manuela Sánchez he intended to become a Spanish citizen. But he failed to convince everyone of his sincerity. It would seem that the Spanish viceroy and his advisers were correct in their evaluation of the French Cavalier. One historian who has carefully studied the life of Louis St. Denis believes that he seemed "to have had difficulty in balancing his greed with his devotion to family." If offered "a finger, he would have taken an arm." Simply stated, he could not "turn his back on the opportunities he saw in contraband [illegal] trade."

In the following chapters, where you can read more about the life of Louis St. Denis, you can decide what you think of him. He and his wife were a constant worry to Spanish officials. They feared Louis's motives, and they worried about his influence over Texas Indians. Living at Natchitoches in Louisiana, the French Cavalier and his bride were only twenty miles from Spanish outposts in East Texas.

SOURCES

Materials used in preparing this chapter are described below. You can find more information about these sources in the Bibliography at the end of the book.

Books

Robert S. Weddle's *The French Thorn: Rival Explorers in the Spanish Sea, 1682–1762* is the best single source on Louis St. Denis. Donald E. Chipman and Harriett Denise Joseph's *Notable Men and Women of Spanish Texas* has biographical sketches of both Louis St. Denis and Manuela Sánchez.

Articles

Patricia R. Lemée's recent articles are fresh looks at the cavalier and his bride. See Patricia R. Lemée, "Manuela Sánchez Navarro," *Natchitoches Genealogist* 20 (October 1995): 17–21, and Patricia R. Lemée, "Tios and Tantes: Familial and Political Relationships of Natchitoches and the Spanish Colonial Frontier," *Southwestern Historical Quarterly* 101 (January 1998): 341–358.

Quotes

Quotes in this chapter are from the following sources: Robert S. Weddle's *The French Thorn: Rival Explorers in the Spanish Sea, 1682–1762;* Letter from St. Denis to Francisco Hidalgo, July 20, 1714, Catholic Archives of Texas, Austin; and Letter from Diego Ramón to Francisco Hidalgo, July 22, 1714, Catholic Archives of Texas, Austin. Commandant Ramón used Spanish spellings for the first names of the three Frenchmen.

CHAPTER SEVEN

Antonio Margil de Jesús
GOD'S DONKEY

Without doubt, the most famous Franciscan missionary to serve in Spanish Texas was a saintly, balding man who did not enter the future Lone Star State until late in life. Father Antonio Margil's stay in Texas was brief, especially when compared with that of his friend Father Francisco Hidalgo, whom you read about in previous chapters. Margil's work in Mexico, as well as his contributions in Texas, were so remarkable that he is a candidate for sainthood in the Catholic Church. This good man has many admirers in Mexico and Texas who firmly believe that he performed miracles on both sides of the Río Grande.

On August 18, 1657, a son was born in Valencia, Spain, to Juan Margil and his wife, Esperanza Ros. Valencia is near the eastern coast of Spain, and it is one of that nation's largest and most beautiful cities. It is famous for its great cathedral and its huge market, where one can buy anything from live eels to fresh flowers. Valencia is also remembered as the birthplace of the remarkable Antonio Margil de Jesús.

As a boy, Antonio showed unusual devotion to the Catholic faith. Instead of playing with other children, he built toy altars at home and prayed in front of them to the best of his ability. When not at home, Antonio walked to nearby churches and prayed before real altars in the afternoons and evenings. When custodians finally locked the doors of those churches at night, young Antonio was forced into the streets of Valencia and sent toward home.

The parents of this devout boy became increasingly concerned about his constant prayer and failure to eat regular meals. They begged him to have fun like other youngsters and not follow such a harsh routine. But Antonio replied that time seemed to fly while he prayed, and he assured his mother and father that he was not injuring his health.

Antonio followed this pattern year after year, until he became a teenager. When not quite sixteen, he asked for and received permission from his parents to enter the Franciscan Order as a novice (beginner). Novices had one year to decide whether or not they were cut out to be a religious person, and during that time Antonio passed all tests with flying colors. He prayed constantly, ate little, and wore an itchy hair shirt (made from cloth containing horsehair) to test his willingness to serve God for the rest of his life. On the afternoon of April 25, 1674, Antonio made his final decision. He would someday become a Franciscan priest.

While still a novice, a curious thing had happened that tells us much about Antonio Margil. Thinking that he was not being watched, he slipped away from his teachers one day and went to a church. Inside was a tomb (burial chamber) containing a person who had died some weeks before. Margil opened the tomb and stuck his head into the awful-smelling grave. Unknown to him, his supervisor had followed him into the church and now demanded to know what he was doing. Margil replied that he wanted to remind his "body of what it is now and what it will one day become."

By this time in his life, Antonio Margil had already labeled himself as "Nothingness Itself." This meant that he must never think of himself as having any value. If he accepted that he had no worth as a human being and nothing to fear in life, including his own death and rotting flesh, he could then do exactly what God wanted him to do.

As he continued his studies, Margil proved to be an excellent student, and he was especially good at theology (religious studies). More and more his teachers became convinced that this young man's future lay as a teacher in one of Spain's universities. Antonio would not hear of that. He already knew that he would find his calling among unschooled Indians in the New World (America), rather than in the company of learned men in the Old World (Europe).

While completing his studies for the priesthood, Margil continued to punish himself by wearing a hair shirt, and he often carried a heavy wooden cross for many hours. On one occasion, to test his will and obedience to God, he decided to let a swarm of mosquitoes bite him throughout the evening. However, he never again attempted this form of self-punishment. Margil appears to have had a severe reaction to the mosquito bites, for on the following morning "his face was so swollen and puffed up that he was hardly recognizable."

Shortly after his twenty-fifth birthday, Margil was ordained with full powers as a priest in the Catholic Church. At that time, he took advantage of an opportunity to go to America and work among Indians. Franciscans were being recruited in Spain for a new missionary college that would be set up in the Mexican town of Querétaro, located about ninety miles northwest of Mexico City.

The ships that would transport two dozen Franciscans across the Atlantic left the port of Cádiz on March 4, 1683. En route to the Indies, as the Spanish called America, the twenty-four priests traveled on different vessels in a large fleet. This permitted them to preach to the passengers and offer comfort to the sick. The voyage turned out to be a long one, lasting for ninety-three days.

When the fleet arrived at Veracruz harbor in Mexico, pirates had just carried out a daring raid on the port city. The attackers had been interested in bars of gold and silver stacked like bricks on the docks of Veracruz. These precious metals from Mexico were to have been sent to Spain on the very ships that had carried the two dozen Franciscans across the Atlantic Ocean. Instead, Spaniards found the docks empty. The pirates had quickly placed the treasure on board their smaller, swifter ships and escaped without punishment. During their short stay in Veracruz, these vicious seamen had also robbed the people of their gold chains, jewels, and pearls. Anyone who resisted or refused to hand over their valuables was shot or stabbed on the spot.

When the Franciscan missionaries finally came ashore after more than three months at sea, they found the port of Veracruz filled with dead and dying people. Their first task was to say prayers over the dead and give what comfort they could to the wounded. For Father Margil this was a such a sad experience that he burst into tears.

After several days in Veracruz, the Franciscans were ordered to divide themselves into groups of two or three and take different roads toward Mexico City. This would permit them to preach to more people along the way. Margil and his fellow priests traveled light, carrying only a staff (walking stick), crucifix, and prayer book. As mentioned in an earlier chapter, Franciscans had to beg for their food. Their religious order instructed them to enter towns and "eat what is set before you."

Margil and three of his companions were the first of their group to travel on to Querétaro from Mexico City. When they reached their destination, the four Franciscans began making preparations for the arrival of their companions. Once the priests were all present at their new college, named Santa Cruz de Querétaro, they began mission work among nearby Indians.

Father Antonio Margil was more devout than any of his fellow Franciscans. His self-punishment certainly seems extreme to us in our world of today. He often carried a heavy wooden cross and wore a crown of thorns. While other priests slept, he prayed through much of the night and beat himself with a whip, because he believed suffering brought him closer to God.

The young priest believed that it was also his duty to change the evil ways of sinners in Querétaro. Father Antonio walked its streets and visited the slum districts of the city. His message was always the same—it was a sin to enjoy bullfights, feasting, and dancing. It seems that Margil had some success. One traveler left the city complaining that "Querétaro is no longer Querétaro," meaning there were not as many amusements as before.

Margil remained at his missionary college for about six months and then left for Veracruz. At the port city, he boarded a ship that took him to his new assignment in Yucatán, the land of the Maya Indians. He would spend the next thirteen years in that part of Mexico and in Central America. Margil and an older priest, who was also from Valencia, became close companions. They traveled together, preaching along the way to Indians in Guatemala, Nicaragua, Honduras, and Costa Rica.

While in the Chiapas region of Mexico, Margil and his friend were taken prisoner by hostile Mayas. These Indians beat the two priests and tore their garments into shreds. For five days they were given no food, and throughout that time the Mayas threatened to kill them and eat them at any moment. Each day the Mayas would examine their intended victims by feeling Margil and declaring him "all right," but they regarded the flesh of the older priest as "spoiled." Margil and his companion never showed any fear of death. They were so brave that the Indians finally decided to spare them. For Margil, it was one of his few religious failures. The Mayas refused to listen to his Christian message, and even he was forced to admit that "God's hour had not yet arrived" for those Indians.

During his years in Mexico and Central America, Margil's fame as a saintly man with unusual powers began to spread. Sick people became well by simply touching his robe. He gave cornmeal to the poor from a small cup that never seemed to be empty. In rainstorms, water would not soak through his habit (outer garment).

Perhaps equally astonishing, Margil could cover great distances in a day, although he would never ride a horse or donkey. It was at this time that Father Antonio took to calling himself "God's donkey." He did not believe that he deserved to ride any animal. Instead, he would always carry God's message on foot. Margil also amazed people by never having trouble crossing rivers. When asked how he could cover such great distances without being seen on the road or getting wet crossing streams, he would smile and reply, "I have my shortcuts and God also helps me."

After being away from Querétaro for many years, Margil returned there in 1697 to assume the position of guardian (head) of the missionary college. During his absence, his fellow Franciscans had carried the Christian message as far north as New Mexico. But little had been done in Coahuila, a province just to the south of Texas. Father Antonio intended to change that. He soon sent Father Francisco Hidalgo to that region, as well as other missionaries from the college. Their story was related in previous chapters.

Margil himself again took up God's work in Querétaro. He built a new room at the college that was stocked with medicines to treat the sick. No one, regardless of their condition of health, was ever turned away. Also, without actually being present, Father Antonio seemed to know about the slightest misdeeds of his fellow Franciscans. To many people he seemed all-knowing.

At this time Margil began reading out loud from the writings of the mysterious Lady in Blue, whom you read about in Chapter 3. Her works and miracles in New Mexico and Texas were particularly inspiring to him. Because Father Antonio needed only about three hours of sleep at night, he had much time to read, pray, and look after the affairs of the college.

As usual, the saintly Franciscan ate little. He skipped breakfast and limited his other meals to broth and salad greens. On rare occasions when he allowed himself the pleasure of a dessert, he would always put salt on it. This was to remind him that life often includes bitter as well as sweet things.

Upon completing his three-year term as guardian, Margil again returned to take up God's work in Central America. This time he was sent by his religious order to found another missionary college in Guatemala. He covered the long distance to that location in just six weeks, with all of the journey made on foot. When intent on getting to his destination, it seems that Father Antonio could cover about forty-five miles every day. Not only did he walk every step of the way, he always insisted on going barefoot, even over the roughest of ground. One can imagine how tough his feet became. He had calluses as thick as shoe leather, which at times had to be trimmed with a coarse wood file!

Back in Guatemala, Margil took on his role there as guardian of the new college. He helped build the church with his own hands. He assisted in the construction of living quarters for his fellow Franciscans, again with his own hands. There was no job too hard for him to perform. While he was helping workers with a heavy stone for the foundation of a building, it slipped out of the hands of workmen and appeared certain to crush a man beneath it. Margil reached down with one hand and held the stone long enough for the man to scramble to safety. Those present could not believe their eyes. The skinny Franciscan seemed to have powers that defied the laws of gravity.

One day while crossing a courtyard, ten oxen fell to their knees as if to honor Father Antonio. This embarrassed the good priest, and he quickly used his cloak to shoo the animals back to a standing position.

When the buildings of this missionary college were finished, Margil left immediately to take up work once again among the Indians of Central America. Even while away from his college, Margil followed a strict schedule of three hours of sleep at night, one hour for an afternoon siesta (nap), no breakfast, and nothing but broth and salad greens for his other meals. On this occasion he traveled to Nicaragua. When walking, Margil was seldom silent—he preferred to recite prayers and sing religious songs along the way.

In Nicaragua, Margil faced a new problem. He had to deal with witches who killed adults as well as young children and ate their flesh seasoned with chili peppers. Once again he failed, just as he had among the Mayas of Chiapas. He could not find the witches or change their evil ways.

Father Antonio returned to his college from Nicaragua in July 1703. By this time, living out of doors, walking great distances, sleeping little, and eating less had taken a heavy toll on him. He was then forty-six years of age, and his appearance was not good. People remarked that his robe was dirty and had more patches than original cloth. To those who were critical of his looks, Father Antonio replied that "everyone goes to God, some in shoes and others barefoot. There are many ways to heaven."

Three years later, after having failed to root out still another colony of witches, Margil left Central America for the last time. By then he was almost completely bald, his feet were horribly deformed, and he walked in a stooped position.

Father Antonio was called back to Mexico to set up still another missionary college in the western part of the region. This religious house was located at the rich mining town of Zacatecas. Named Nuestra Señora de Guadalupe, this Franciscan institution would later supply missionaries for Texas, including Margil himself. However, his Texas days were still many years down the road. Ahead lay the most serious failure of all, and it would nearly cost him his life.

Some Indians in the mountains of western Mexico had never been exposed to the Christian message. These Native Americans lived among spectacular gorges in rugged country and had never seen a Spaniard. Margil and a Franciscan companion accepted the challenge of bringing God's word to these pagan (non-Christian) peoples, but they were determined to enter those lands without the protection of armed soldiers.

When he reached the region of these natives in 1711, Margil sent two Indian guides ahead of him. One of them spoke the language of these Native Americans, and it was hoped that he could pave the way for the Franciscans. Father Antonio sent a message with the guides: "No human interest brings us to preach the good news in your land, but only the desire to snatch your souls from the hands of the devil and from hell. [We will] give our lives if necessary to save your souls."

The Indian guides were not permitted to travel far before they were stopped by hostile natives and told to turn back. So Margil's message did not reach their chief. But the chief sent a message of his own for the two priests. "[The] Fathers should not tire themselves out. We are quite happy without any Father or Spanish officials. If you want to kill us, go ahead and kill us, but we are not going to give ourselves up so that you can make Christians of us."

Margil did not easily accept failure, nor did he fear for his life. He and his Franciscan companion chose four Indian guides and headed into an area they had been told to stay away from. The six men had traveled only a few hours when an Indian suddenly appeared before them. He was covered with black and red paint, and he demanded to know if the Christians were armed. When the priests assured the warrior that they did not have any weapons on them, he permitted them to go forward.

Near sundown they were surrounded by more than thirty Indians, all screaming and waving arrows and knives. Margil and his companion immediately fell to their knees and spread their arms wide, thereby inviting the Native Americans to pierce them with arrows. This behavior apparently confused the warriors. They decided to spare the priests' lives but told them that they could go no farther.

Margil returned to his college at Zacatecas and remained there for another two years. At that time, he was replaced as guardian of the missionary college. The new head of the school informed Father Antonio that he could preach in any part of Mexico that suited him. His choice was Coahuila, which would bring him to very doorstep of Texas. In January 1714, Father Antonio took the long road to the north. As usual, he traveled on foot.

By then, Margil was almost sixty years of age. He could still cover many miles in a day, but every step must have been painful. He had almost no hair, his feet were horribly deformed, and his body was permanently bent forward.

On the northern frontier, Margil arrived at the rough mining camp known as Boca de Leones (Mouth of Lions). From there he was to travel on to San Juan Bautista. At the gateway presidio near the Río Grande, he would be joined by three other priests from the college at

*God's Donkey walking
barefoot across Texas*
(DRAWING BY JACK JACKSON)

Zacatecas. But first, Father Antonio helped round up goats, oxen,
cattle, and horses that would be a part of the Domingo Ramón and
Louis St. Denis expedition of 1716. Margil planned to join other Spaniards in the permanent occupation of Texas. He would be in charge of
setting up missions run by priests from his college at Zacatecas.

Perhaps because he needed to take care of some last-minute business, Margil remained at Boca de Leones when Ramón left for San
Juan Bautista. Despite his having to travel slowly out of consideration for eight women and two children riding in ox carts, Ramón
arrived at the Río Grande settlements well before Margil.

Meanwhile, Father Antonio began to make his way alone through the desert by following the tracks of the Ramón party and the more than one thousand head of livestock that accompanied it. However, the good Franciscan soon fell ill with a fever, and for the first time in his life he could not make his way across a small stream.

Stranded without food or assistance, Margil somehow got word of his situation to friends at San Juan Bautista. Three priests and two soldiers rushed to his assistance, and with difficulty they carried the seriously ill man to the Río Grande. By then, all preparations had been completed for the occupation of Texas. On April 20, 1716, Ramón crossed the Great River and waited six days for Father Antonio to recover his strength.

Far from getting better, Margil's condition went from bad to worse. His fever was dangerously high and he appeared close to death. On the seventh day, Ramón set out for East Texas, leaving behind what all believed to be a dying priest. Instead, Margil began to get better. His recovery was slow, and it was the middle of June before he could leave San Juan Bautista for the land of the Tejas Indians.

Father Antonio arrived in East Texas in mid-July. By then, four missions had already been set up. It was agreed that the Franciscans from the colleges at Querétaro and Zacatecas would each have three religious outposts among the Indians. The priests, however, had run into unexpected problems. Although the Tejas were friendly, they would not give up their own religion and move into the missions. And the Spanish did not have the military strength to make the Indians do as they wished. So any attempts to set up two more missions seemed unwise.

The first winter in East Texas came without a single Indian living among the Franciscans, and it seemed that their effort might fail, just like the first missions in the 1690s. Renewed hope came when St. Denis returned from Louisiana with fresh supplies in late 1716. In the following spring, Father Margil and his fellow priests from Zacatecas set up two more missions.

After St. Denis left for San Juan Bautista in March 1717, Father Antonio again faced problems in East Texas. The summer of that year saw almost no rain. There were disappointing harvests of corn and beans because of the drought. The following winter was another bad one, and the Tejas simply would not enter any of the six missions.

The summer of 1718 was perhaps even drier than the previous

one. Food became so short in supply that the Franciscans were forced to eat the meat of crows, which were shot from their roosts with muskets in the early mornings. The crow meat was particularly bad-tasting because the priests did not have any salt.

It was at this time that Margil performed what many in East Texas still regard as a miracle. There had been almost no rain. Crops dried up and creeks ran dry. Father Antonio prayed night and day that rain might fall, and then he received a vision and knew what to do about the drought. He walked to the banks of La Nana Creek and struck a rock twice with his staff. Two natural springs poured forth and continued to flow for years. These were called Los Ojos de Padre Margil (The Springs of Father Margil).

Throughout the hard winters and dry summers of East Texas, Margil seems to have suffered less than the other Franciscans and complained not at all. He had faced far worse during his many years in Central America. He remarked that if God was still with them in times of trouble, then it was no longer trouble but glory. Those who observed Father Antonio remarked that "he spent the days, weeks, and months absorbed in God, growing old gently."

Meanwhile, San Antonio had been founded in 1718. In the following year, the Chicken War, which you will read about in the next chapter, swept every Spaniard out of East Texas. The six missions there were all abandoned, and Margil found himself at San Antonio by October 1719.

It occurred to the good Franciscan that San Antonio needed more than just one mission. San Antonio de Valero, later known as the Alamo, had been founded by a priest from the college at Querétaro. The Zacatecan fathers had no halfway mission between the Río Grande and East Texas, and Margil intended to change that.

Father Antonio had to have the approval of Texas's new governor, the Marqués de San Miguel de Aguayo, to set up his new mission. He wrote a friendly letter to Aguayo, congratulating him on his appointment as governor. Margil also asked permission to name the second religious outpost at San Antonio after him. This pleased Aguayo, and he gave his full approval.

Margil quickly chose a site for his mission. It had good land nearby that could be watered by building an irrigation ditch to the San Antonio River. With the aid of the military captain at Béxar, Mission San

José y San Miguel de Aguayo soon took shape. Remember that Father Antonio himself had a lot of experience in constructing new buildings, for he had done this in Guatemala, Mexico, and East Texas.

If you visit San Antonio's five missions today, the most beautiful of them is the one founded by Margil. It would also become the most successful in terms of attracting Indian neophytes and keeping them. Over the years, Mission San José has changed a lot in appearance, as stones replaced the original structure. It first began to serve the religious needs of Indians in the area on February 23, 1720, and it stands today as perhaps the best reminder of Margil's years in Texas.

When East Texas was again occupied by Spaniards, in 1721, Margil returned there to take up his work among the Native American population. On this occasion, he chose to live near Los Adaes presidio, which served as the capital of Texas. He regularly walked the banks of the Red River and often visited the French fort commanded by St. Denis at present-day Natchitoches, Louisiana.

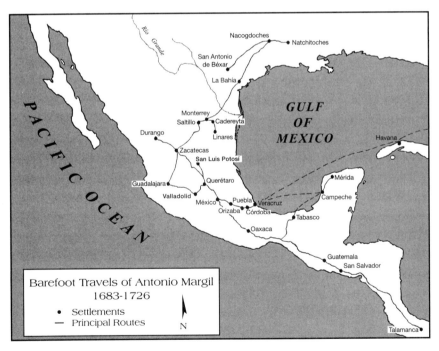

The many travels of Father Antonio Margil from Central America to Texas
(CENTER FOR MEDIA PRODUCTION, UNIVERSITY OF NORTH TEXAS)

As it turned out, Father Antonio's days in Texas were soon to end. In late 1722 he learned that he had once again been appointed guardian of the college at Zacatecas. It was not the good Franciscan's wish to return to Mexico—he had made it clear that he wished to remain in Texas for the rest of his life. But as always, Margil set aside his own desires and did what his religious superiors told him to do.

Walking barefoot every step of the way, God's Donkey left East Texas for the last time in January 1722 and took the long road to Zacatecas in western Mexico. This journey required almost six months to complete.

In Mexico, Margil joined with his friend Félix de Espinosa of the Franciscan college at Querétaro in trying to convince the viceroy that he should give more support to the Texas missions. The viceroy listened politely to the two priests but told them that he would not spend one additional peso (dollar) on Texas. In Europe there was peace between Spain and France, so missions on the border between Spanish Texas and French Louisiana seemed less important than in earlier years.

Father Antonio served out his three-year term as guardian, although his health was failing. At times he ran a high fever, and it seemed certain he would die. But on each occasion, the good priest would recover. When he was no longer head of the college at Zacatecas, Margil continued to carry a heavy wooden cross throughout part of the day and wear a crown of thorns like Jesus.

Near the end of his life, Father Antonio went to visit old friends at the missionary college in Querétaro, which he had helped set up when he first arrived in Mexico. While there he lost consciousness and appeared certain to die. He recovered a little, only to be hit by chills and pneumonia.

Although his friends begged him not to travel alone, Margil set out for Mexico City in the summer of 1726, on foot. When it was pointed out to him that there were no doctors along the way and that he might die with no one to bury him, Father Antonio replied that he was not worried. He said, "That is what I deserve; I am not entitled to Christian burial; I ought to die out in the wild, where the beasts can devour me."

Margil did arrive in the capital, although he was at death's door. He asked to make a final confession before a priest, as Catholics still do today. Father Antonio was hardly guilty of sins of any importance, but he remained humble to the end. He admitted that, like all men, he had been tempted by the devil to do evil things, but God had always come to his rescue and had guided him along the right path. Otherwise, he said, he did not know what would have become of him.

Father Antonio Margil died on August 6, 1726, between one and two o'clock in the afternoon. He final words were: "It is time now to go and see God." Two days later, his funeral was attended by the viceroy and other important officials in Mexico City.

After Margil's death, Franciscans in Guatemala, Mexico, and Texas began to study the life and accomplishments of this good man. They believed he had performed miracles that made him a candidate for sainthood in the Catholic Church. And so began a long and difficult process that has gone on for close to three hundred years.

First of all, one must be judged to be worthy of sainthood, which is called venerable. Margil did not receive the title of "venerable" until he had been dead for 110 years. Until very recently, his body lay within a small chapel of the great cathedral of Mexico City, but members of the Franciscan Order in Zacatecas wanted his remains to be located there. His coffin was moved from the capital and now lies in the Guadalupe Friary of Zacatecas, Mexico.

Many people in Texas and Mexico continue to work to this day in an attempt to advance Margil toward sainthood. The Margil House of Studies in Houston, Texas, is very active in this effort, as are Franciscans elsewhere in the United States, in Mexico, in Guatemala, and in Rome.

It is true that only a small part of Antonio Margil's long life was spent in Texas, but look at his accomplishments there. He set up two missions in East Texas and Mission San José in San Antonio. There are still Texans living in Nacogdoches who can take you to the banks of La Nana Creek and point out the exact location of the two springs of fresh water that poured from the rock struck with Father Antonio's staff back in the summer of 1718. In 1999 at the annual meeting of the Texas State Historical Association in Dallas, historians discussed their research into Margil's old mission near the East Texas town of San Augustine.

Many Texans are still determined to honor the memory of Father Antonio Margil. Whether or not he becomes a saint in the twenty-first century, his story is certainly worth studying and knowing, for Margil lived an entire life of sacrifice in the service of God.

SOURCES

Materials used in preparing this chapter are described below. You can find more information about these sources in the Bibliography at the end of the book.

Books

See Donald E. Chipman and Harriett Denise Joseph's *Notable Men and Women of Spanish Texas* for a more detailed biographical sketch of Margil. The most readable and accurate full-length biography of Margil is Eduardo Enrique Ríos's *Life of Fray Antonio Margil, O.F.M.,* translated by Benedict Leutenegger. Also of value is William H. Oberste's *The Restless Friar: Venerable Fray Antonio Margil de Jesús.*

Articles

Peter P. Forrestal, translator, "The Venerable Padre Fray Antonio Margil de Jesús," *Preliminary Studies of the Catholic Historical Society* 2 (April 1932): 5–34.

Quotes

Quotes in this chapter are from the following sources: Peter P. Forrestal, translator, "The Venerable Padre Fray Antonio Margil de Jesús," *Preliminary Studies of the Catholic Historical Society* 2 (April 1932): 6–7; Eduardo Enrique Ríos's *Life of Fray Antonio Margil, O.F.M.,* translated by Benedict Leutenegger; Isidro Félix de Espinosa, *El peregrino septentrional atlante: Delineado en la exemplaríssima vida del Venerable Padre F. Antonio Margil de Jesús;* and Letter from Margil to Huei Tacat and Other Chiefs of the Nayarit, May 9, 1711, in *Nothingness Itself: Selected Writings of Ven. Fr. Antonio Margil, 1690–1724,* translated by Benedict Leutenegger and edited by Marion A. Habig.

CHAPTER EIGHT

Marqués de San Miguel de Aguayo

CHICKEN WAR REDEEMER

The most eastern of the Spanish missions set up by the Domingo Ramón–St. Denis expedition of 1716–1717 was actually in present-day Louisiana. Known as San Miguel de los Adaes, this outpost was founded by Father Antonio Margil. Two years later, in mid-June 1719, Los Adaes was unguarded and unoccupied except for a half-naked soldier and a religious helper. The mission did not have a single Indian living there.

Los Adaes was only twenty miles from St. Denis's fort at Natchitoches. This placed it in a dangerous position. Spain and France were often rivals in Europe. If war broke out between the two nations, the mission would likely be the first target of French attacks on Spanish Texas.

Today we live in age where things happening all around the world are known about immediately and seen on evening television news programs. But in the 1700s it was common for several months to pass before anyone in America knew of events happening in Europe. A ship bearing news had to cross the Atlantic Ocean. If it was a French ship, then French colonists were the first to be informed. The exact opposite was true if it was a Spanish vessel.

A war between France and Spain broke out in January 1719. The French at St. Denis's fort were the first to get the news, but not until June of that year. Philippe Blondel, a military officer, gathered up half a dozen soldiers and marched on Los Adaes. There Blondel captured the unarmed Spanish soldier and arrested the religious person.

The French soldiers took the few things worth having at the mission. Next, Blondel turned his attention to the mission henhouse that contained a number of chickens. Without doubt, thoughts of a tasty dinner back at Natchitoches crossed the mind of the French captain. His men caught the hens, tied their legs together, and put them across the back of Blondel's horse.

When excited, chickens often flap their wings and make squawking sounds. This is exactly what happened, and it frightened Blondel's horse. It suddenly shied (jumped sideways) and dumped its rider in the dirt. In the confusion, the Spanish religious person escaped and ran into the woods, and the French soldiers could not catch him. Blondel and his half-dozen soldiers then brought the captured soldier and fowl back to Natchitoches. It is likely that the chickens were claimed as "prisoners of war" and did not last long before they wound up in a French cooking pot.

Because the French soldiers had been more interested in raiding the mission henhouse at Los Adaes than in guarding the two prisoners, the Spanish later made fun of them. They said that this incident started the "Chicken War." So in Texas history, the war between France and Spain that began in 1719 on the American frontier has this unusual name. To frightened Spaniards in East Texas, who were several hundred miles from San Antonio, this war was not funny at the time.

The religious person who had escaped from the French quickly made his way to another of Antonio Margil's missions. In telling of the events at Los Adaes, the escaped prisoner probably made the story very dramatic and scary. Father Antonio also soon picked up a rumor spread by Indians that one hundred French soldiers were marching on Texas from Louisiana. Unsure if this were true or not, the Spaniards panicked and decided to abandon their mission.

Margil quickly buried valuable tools to keep the enemy from getting them. He also packed religious objects and took them when he and a few companions fled. They made their way to the only Spanish garrison in East Texas, called Presidio de los Tejas.

The Spanish commander at the presidio was Domingo Ramón, who had helped set up the missions in the first place. Don Domingo faced a serious problem. If one hundred French soldiers were indeed on their way to Texas, then he was in big trouble. Many of his soldiers were only boys with almost no clothes, muskets, or horses. Eight of the older soldiers were married, and their wives were already unhappy with life on the frontier. These women joined the men in demanding that everyone flee to the safety of San Antonio. Panic followed, and it soon turned into a Spanish version of the old story about Chicken Little, who thought the sky was falling.

The Chicken War of 1719 actually had serious results. It led to the total withdrawal of all Spaniards from their six missions and one presidio in East Texas and western Louisiana. When he attacked Los Adaes with only six soldiers, Blondel surely did not imagine that he would accomplish so much with so few men!

The Spaniards who fled to San Antonio camped along the way and did not arrive until the fall of 1719. Once there, the priests found only slightly better conditions than at their crude campsites. They had to live in straw huts with dirt floors.

It was at this time that Father Antonio Margil got the idea of setting up a second mission at San Antonio. As you will remember from the previous chapter, this required him to get permission from the new governor of Texas, the Marqués de San Miguel de Aguayo. Governor Aguayo liked the idea, and he was pleased that the mission would be partly named after him.

Thanks to his wife, who was one of the largest landowners in all of Mexico, the Marqués de Aguayo was truly wealthy. It is interesting that women could own as much or more than a man in the early history of Mexico, for this was not the case in the English colonies that became the United States. Spanish women could inherit land, and it was theirs to keep. Since almost no one had any money or hard cash in those times, wealth was measured in how much land or livestock a person owned.

The Marquesa de San Miguel de Aguayo, whose given name was Ignacia, had inherited lands and titles from both her mother and father, the first Marqués de San Miguel de Aguayo. After her parents died, doña Ignacia moved to Spain, hoping to find a suitable husband among Spanish royal families. Her first husband died young, as did the second. On her third attempt, the marquesa married a Spanish nobleman with an impressive name—José Ramón de Azlor y Virto de Vera. She and her husband sailed to Mexico, where they could better look after doña Ignacia's vast lands. Once there, don José took the title of second Marqués de San Miguel de Aguayo, which actually came from his wife.

The marqués and marquesa settled in Coahuila at a hacienda (great house) called San Francisco de los Patos. Aguayo used his wife's money to put together a private army that did not cost the Spanish crown a single peso. He used these armed men to put down Native American revolts in the province of Coahuila.

When the marqués learned that the war of 1719 had caused the Spanish to leave their missions and presidio in East Texas, he offered to fight the French with his private army. He would do this as a favor for his monarch, the king of Spain. Thus, Aguayo can be called the Chicken War Redeemer, because he offered to recover, or redeem, something that had been taken from Spain.

The viceroy of Mexico accepted Aguayo's offer and gave him permission to raise an even bigger private army, as long as the marqués and his wife paid for it. Aguayo lost little time in making preparations and recruiting soldiers. By June 1720, he was ready to leave for East Texas, but bad luck delayed him for several months. First, the marqués stayed in Coahuila to put down another Native American revolt. Then, in the summer of 1720, a severe drought killed grass and dried up creeks, as well as other sources of water. Aguayo had bought four thousand horses, but without enough grass or water thirty-five hundred had died. The dead animals had to be replaced, which took time. Then the drought was broken by heavy rains. Repeated downpours brought things to a near standstill, as men and animals struggled through a sea of mud. The marqués had run into such bad luck that it seem as if "all hell" was working against him.

By late 1720, Aguayo had again gathered thousands of livestock, several tons of supplies, and five hundred men. If his preparations seem overdone, we need to remember that Spain and France were at war. It was a long march from Coahuila to East Texas, and Aguayo could not count on much help from Mexico once he got there.

Just as he was finally ready to leave Coahuila, news from the viceroy changed the very nature of the Aguayo expedition. Spain and France were discussing a way to end the war in Europe. If peace came, then the marqués could not carry out attacks on the French in East Texas or Louisiana. He could only redeem what Spain had already claimed and defend himself if attacked by Frenchmen. Delays caused by Indian revolts and bad weather had likely robbed him of the opportunity to become a military hero in Texas.

The march to the Río Grande crossing at San Juan Bautista began in mid-November. It was slowed by having to drive thousands of horses, cattle, sheep, and goats. The main body of Aguayo's army did not arrive at the river until December 20. It found the stream swollen with flood waters and more than a musket shot in width. Indians more familiar than Spaniards with the Great River told Aguayo that it would take a long time for it to return to a normal flow.

Because he was anxious to get on with the march, the marqués tried different means of getting his livestock and supplies across the Río Grande. He attempted to swim some of the animals across the current, but that did not work with the smaller ones. Sheep with their heavy winter wool are not good swimmers, and they sank like stones in a pond.

Aguayo finally settled on a large wooden raft made of ten *vigas* (beams). Empty barrels were tied beneath the *vigas* so that the float could carry more weight. To pull the craft across the current, fifty Nadador Indians with ropes tied to the raft took turns in the cold water. Although these Native Americans were given extra rations of hot chocolate and liquor to help keep them warm, all but four of the fifty became sick.

Still, the crossing worked. Six hundred mule-loads of supplies, more than four thousand horses, six hundred cattle, nine hundred sheep, and eight hundred mules safely reached the north bank of the Great River.

While waiting for his supplies and livestock to cross the Río Grande, Aguayo sent forty soldiers under Domingo Ramón to occupy Matagorda Bay. Ramón easily accomplished this because no Frenchmen were found at the location of La Salle's old fort.

Meanwhile, Aguayo marched toward San Antonio. With him went thousands of horses, cattle, and sheep. Most of us have heard or read about the great cattle drives in Texas history, which came after the United States Civil War in the 1860s. But the Marqués de Aguayo was the first to trail livestock in large numbers across the future Lone Star State.

When the marqués reached San Antonio, he was welcomed with open arms by the East Texans. These people had come to San Antonio during the Chicken War because they wanted to, but they had found life difficult there. So they were eager to join Aguayo and help him redeem their homeland.

In mid-May, the march to East Texas continued. Like many Texans today, the travelers admired the beauty of spring wildflowers such as bluebonnets and Indian paintbrush. The Franciscan priests, happy over returning to their missions among the Tejas Indians, left crosses of wood at each campsite to mark their progress.

This was a slow-moving band of Spaniards, because they had to drive large herds of livestock. It was delayed even more as stray animals had to be brought back to the main herd, and soldiers often got lost trying to recover them.

After crossing the Guadalupe River, the Aguayo *entrada* (expedition) saw its first buffalo. Because many in the party had never seen this animal before, they considered it strange and described it as follows: "Its back is humped like a camel's. Its flanks are lean. Its tail, with the exception of the tip, is short and hairless like the pig's. It has a beard like a goat." But when the Spaniards ate buffalo steaks, they thought them "as savory [tasty] as the best beef."

Other wild animals such as deer, turkeys, and prairie chickens provided plenty of food for the travelers. Much less welcome were annoying insects and poisonous snakes, which were found at almost every campsite. Spaniards in the Aguayo *entrada* liked to walk through great fields of beautiful wildflowers but had to be careful not to stumble onto rattlesnakes. At night the campers were made miserable by mosquitoes, ticks, and chiggers.

In May the travelers ran into heavy rains that lasted for several days. The size of the expedition made crossing open meadows and the smallest of streams extremely difficult. Spaniards remarked that the land was so wet that even Indians "who carried little" had trouble walking.

During one bad thunderstorm, lightning frightened the animals and made them hard to control. One bolt came so close to two soldiers that it knocked them unconscious. Both recovered, but one of the men's hats had so many holes that it looked "riddled as if by a drill."

Because of heavy rains, Aguayo had to travel north of the Camino Real (King's Highway) in order to cross streams closer to their headwaters. He returned to the old road east of modern Bryan/College Station, where Texas A&M University is located. Even so, when the marqués reached the Navasota River, it was so swollen with floodwaters that he had to stop and build a bridge more than sixty feet in length and eight feet in width.

Crossing the Trinity River took two weeks. The large animals were strong enough to swim across, but women and small children had to be transported in a canoe. While making the crossing, the Aguayo expedition was visited by friendly Tejas Indians. The Native Americans seemed pleased that Spaniards were returning to live among them.

The Marqués de Aguayo waiting for his raft to cross the Río Grande (see p. 109) (DRAWING BY JACK JACKSON)

At about this time, Aguayo visited other Indians who had been driven from their homeland along the Brazos River by Apaches. These Native Americans had a blue and white silk flag of France, which was a sure sign that Frenchmen had passed among them. The marqués let the Indians keep the flag, but he told them that they must now pay more respect to the flag of Spain. He also promised the natives that he would set up a mission for them that was closer to their old homeland. Later, as we will note, Aguayo tried to keep that pledge at San Antonio.

A bit farther on, the Aguayo *entrada* passed through stands of pines, hickories, and oaks on the way to San Pedro Creek, where the first mission had been set up back in 1690 by Father Damián Massanet and General Alonso de León. Near the end of their march, friendly Tejas welcomed the Spaniards with gifts of flowers, watermelons, and beans. As a sign of their friendship, the Native Americans passed around a peace pipe containing a mixture of Spanish and Indian tobaccos. The Spaniards responded by giving gifts that included glass beads, knives, hoes, rings, mirrors, scissors, and blankets.

While Aguayo was camped at San Pedro Creek, Louis St. Denis came to visit from his fort at Natchitoches, on July 31, 1721. The marqués treated him with courtesy and respect, since France and Spain were no longer at war. Tired by his long ride from Louisiana, St. Denis spent the night among his old friends, the Franciscan priests he had known since 1716.

On the following day, Aguayo and the Frenchman began talks. Both of them mentioned the peace that had been signed in Europe by France and Spain. St. Denis was especially concerned about the size of Aguayo's private army, which numbered almost five hundred men. The marqués said that he would not use his soldiers against the Frenchman if he agreed to give back all the land that Spain had lost during the Chicken War. This included Los Adaes, which was only twenty miles from Natchitoches.

St. Denis said that he did not know why the Spaniards would want Los Adaes, because the land around it was no good for farming. But the Spaniards were not fooled by this argument. They had set up a mission there in 1717 and knew about the land from firsthand experience. Given the size of Aguayo's army, the Frenchman could do little but promise to pull all his people back to Natchitoches.

Aguayo then set about refounding the six missions in East Texas and western Louisiana. At each mission, his ten companies of men fired muskets and set off blasts from their cannons. This was a show of military strength to convince the Indians that Spain had come back to their lands and intended to stay there.

The last of the missions was set up at Los Adaes. To make sure that Frenchmen could not again take this religious outpost, as they had done during the Chicken War, Aguayo built a new presidio nearby. It was a solid building containing one hundred fully armed soldiers. To make doubly sure that Spain remained permanently in East Texas, the marqués refounded Presidio de los Tejas. This military outpost guarded the western part of the mission field.

In mid-November 1721, Aguayo began a difficult winter march back to San Antonio. The journey was especially hard on his horses and mules. So many died that it was necessary to send to Coahuila for replacements. While waiting for the animals to arrive, the marqués chose a new site for the Béxar presidio. He then decided to build the new structure with adobe bricks to make it stronger. Aguayo founded a third mission at San Antonio, which he had promised to Indians he met during the trek to East Texas. This new religious outpost was named San Francisco Xavier de Nájera, but its buildings were never finished. So actually San Antonio still had only two missions—San Antonio de Valero, the future Alamo, and San José, founded by Father Antonio Margil.

Aguayo then decided to set up a brand new presidio on Garcitas Creek. Perhaps you will remember that he had sent Domingo Ramón there with forty men while he was getting his animals and supplies across the Río Grande at San Juan Bautista. Another fifty men were soon on their way, and Aguayo himself went there in March 1722 with an additional forty men. The marqués directed the founding of still another well-built presidio at the exact site of La Salle's fort. His idea was to defend Matagorda Bay against the possibility of France setting up a colony there. Directly across Garcitas Creek, Aguayo helped set up a new mission for Indians in the region. The two outposts came to be called La Bahía (The Bay). When he began the return march to San Antonio, the governor left behind ninety soldiers at the presidio.

By the end of April 1722, the Marqués de Aguayo was back in San

Antonio. There he inspected the new adobe brick presidio and as-signed fifty-four soldiers to it. By then a fresh supply of horses and mules had arrived from Coahuila. And on May 5, the marqués headed back to his wife at Monclova, Coahuila.

During his stay in Texas, Governor Aguayo had been a busy man. He had refounded six missions in East Texas, ordered a new one at San Antonio, and built another near Matagorda Bay. He had also given permission for Father Margil to set up Mission San José, the most successful of the San Antonio missions. In all, the marqués had con-structed two new presidios, one at Los Adaes and a second at Matagorda Bay, and a new building for the San Antonio military gar-rison. The Spanish troop strength in Texas had increased from 60 or 70 men to 268. In doing all of this, Aguayo had spent 130,000 pesos in the service of his king.

It is well to ask at this point how long Texas benefited from the work and expenses of the Marqués de San Miguel de Aguayo. As it turned out, not long. It was the governor's bad luck that events in far-off Europe caused the government in Mexico City to change its mind about the importance of having so many presidios and soldiers in the future Lone Star State.

Aguayo was hardly back in Coahuila when relations changed be-tween France and Spain. These longtime enemies in Europe began to move closer and closer together as allies. Both countries had colonies in America, but so did Great Britain. It seemed wise for them to end their differences and join together to defend their lands against the British.

By the mid-1720s, Spain decided that it was spending too much money on its northern frontier. So the king ordered an inspection of all Spanish presidios from the Gulf of California to Texas. The in-spector was a hard-to-please general named Pedro de Rivera, who was sent to the north from Mexico in late 1724.

Rivera carried with him at all times a mountain of paper that totaled 7,000 pages! These papers included letters to and from the king, a list of each soldier at every presidio, reasons why a presidio had been set up in the first place, and the salary and rank of all mili-tary men.

As a general, Inspector Rivera carried a higher rank than anyone on the northern frontier, and not even governors could refuse to follow his orders. His instructions called on him to give a report on each presidio. Don Pedro was to set down the exact location of each garrison, the nature of the land around it, and a description of Indians in the area. He was also to explain the importance of each presidio to nearby missions or other military garrisons.

Rivera was in the field for more than three and half years and traveled about 7,500 miles—all on horseback! He began his inspection in the west and moved slowly toward Texas, where he did not arrive until the late summer of 1727. At each presidio he was to record three things: the condition of the garrison and its men, what it was like after he ordered changes made there, and what he saw as its future.

Traveling with the inspector was a sharp-eyed engineer and mapmaker named Francisco Alvarez Barreiro. Much of what we know about Texas and how it looked in 1727 comes from the pen of don Francisco. He thought the future Lone Star State to be a hot place in August, which is hardly surprising to us. Since he had to camp out at night, Barreiro complained bitterly about the mosquitoes that made his sleep miserable. In East Texas, don Francisco noted that the cry of a bird at night—probably a hoot owl—was so sad that it made those who heard it sad too. But overall he thought Texas had lands that were very good for raising crops.

For the most part, Rivera and Barreiro did not like what they saw at Texas's presidios. At Los Adaes, Rivera thought that garrison to be mostly of no use. In his opinion, it had too many soldiers, and he ordered the number cut from one hundred to sixty.

When the inspector arrived at Presidio de los Tejas, located at the western edge of the mission field, he was completely discouraged by its appearance. Rivera described it as "a collection of huts poorly constructed of sticks and straw [that] did not deserve the honorable name of Presidio de los Tejas." The nearby missions did not contain a single Indian. In recommending the closing of this garrison, don Pedro could not have been more blunt: "There is, to my mind, no reason to spend 10,000 pesos—500 for the captain and 400 pesos for each of the 24 soldiers—on such a useless place as the presidio of Texas."

Rivera actually liked the presidio that had been set up at the location of La Salle's colony. But he decided that it, like Los Adaes, had more soldiers than were needed. It was the inspector's recommendation that the total number stationed there be reduced from ninety to forty. As he left La Bahía, however, don Pedro decided that even forty men were unnecessary. He wrote: "Although I have said that forty men should be assigned to the presidio, none is really needed."

At San Antonio, the inspector found another presidio he liked. He remarked that the Béxar garrison enjoyed "the best location of any that I have seen." Once again, Rivera believed the presidio had more men than were actually needed. He recommended the number be reduced from fifty-four to forty-four.

As he left Texas for the last time, Pedro de Rivera remarked on the province as a good place for farming. He said, "Corn, vegetables, and other crops can be grown everywhere. Even without the benefit of irrigation the land demonstrates its fertility and utility to the pagan [non-Christian] Indians who cultivate it." Referring to East Texas, he commented on the large number of bears found there. He seemed especially interested in "mice resembling baby rabbits, which serve as food for the pagans."

When Rivera returned to Mexico City, he made recommendations for saving the king's money by cutting back on the number of soldiers stationed in Texas. If accepted, the inspector's suggestions would largely undo the work of the Marqués de San Miguel de Aguayo. Spain would be much weaker militarily in the future Lone Star State and the few hundred Spaniards living there would be in danger of Indian attacks.

The viceroy accepted Rivera's recommendations and had them enforced. Los Adaes went from 100 to 60 men, La Bahía from 90 to 40, and San Antonio from 54 to 44. Because Rivera thought Presidio de los Tejas "ought to be extinguished [eliminated]," it was. This meant that the missionaries working in the three most western missions of East Texas would not have any military protection. Because they were about 300 miles from San Antonio and more than 150 miles from Los Adaes, the Franciscans did not believe they could keep their missions in operation. They pointed out that Indians armed with guns supplied by the French in Louisiana made their work too risky. The priests asked the viceroy to change his orders and let Presidio de los Tejas remain where it was. But it was not to be.

These three missions in East Texas wound up being moved to San Antonio by the early months of 1731. Thus, San Antonio came to have the five missions that it has to this day. San Antonio de Valero would become known as the Alamo, and of course it is famous for events there during the Texas Revolution in 1836. The Alamo now serves as a historic shrine, where visitors are reminded of Texas's struggle for independence from Mexico. The other four missions are active Catholic churches where religious services are held each week.

Overall, the proposals of Pedro de Rivera and their enforcement by the viceroy certainly weakened Spain in Texas by the 1730s. At that same time, Apache Indians stepped up their attacks on settlers at San Antonio. And of course the presidios, with fewer soldiers, could not offer as much by way of military protection. What is certain is that Spanish settlers found Texas a much more dangerous place to live. In the interest of saving money, Spanish officials undid much of the work of the Marqués de San Miguel de Aguayo.

Indian problems for Spanish settlers in Texas would get worse instead of better over the years. Much of this was caused by Comanches who began to enter West Texas in the early 1700s. These Native Americans hated the Apaches, defeated them in battles, and drove them toward San Antonio. We will look at this serious problem in our later chapters.

For now, let us look at the last years of the Marqués de San Miguel de Aguayo. After returning to his wife at Monclova in 1722, the marqués lived at San Francisco de los Patos. At the great hacienda, he saw his work in Texas come undone. As Spain and France patched up their differences in Europe, it was no longer necessary to worry about another war between French Louisiana and Spanish Texas.

The new presidios at Los Adaes and La Bahía seemed not so important any more. Aguayo watched as Spanish officials weakened Spain's presence in Texas in the late 1720s and early 1730s. His wife died in 1733, and he on March 9, 1734. The Chicken War Redeemer had spent 130,000 pesos and weakened his health while serving the king of Spain. He and the marquesa died knowing that their work and the cost of reclaiming East Texas from the French invasion of 1719 was largely unappreciated. The best intentions and actions of some people do not always earn them the recognition that they deserve.

SOURCES

Materials used in preparing this chapter are described below. You can find more information about these sources in the Bibliography at the end of the book.

Books

Robert S. Weddle's *San Juan Bautista: Gateway to Spanish Texas* is useful for background of the Chicken War. Donald E. Chipman and Harriett Denise Joseph's *Notable Men and Women of Spanish Texas* has a more detailed sketch of the Chicken War Redeemer.

Articles

Good sources on Aguayo are Eleanor C. Buckley's "The Aguayo Expedition into Texas and Louisiana, 1719–1722," *Quarterly of the Texas State Historical Association* 15 (July 1911): 1–65, and Charles W. Hackett's "The Marquis of San Miguel de Aguayo and His Recovery of Texas from the French, 1719–1723," *Southwestern Historical Quarterly* 49 (October 1945): 193–214.

Quotes

Quotes in this chapter are from the following sources: Richard G. Santos, translator, *Aguayo Expedition into Texas, 1721*; Testimony of the Rivera Project (June 2, 1730), Archivo General de Indias (Seville), Guadalajara 44; Thomas H. Naylor and Charles W. Polzer, compilers and editors, *Pedro de Rivera and the Military Regulations for Northern New Spain, 1724–1729: A Documentary History of His Frontier Inspection and the "Reglamento de 1729"*; Jack Jackson, editor, and William C. Foster, annotator, *Imaginary Kingdom: Texas as Seen by the Rivera and Rubí Military Expeditions, 1727 and 1767*; and Donald E. Chipman, *Spanish Texas, 1519–1821*.

CHAPTER NINE

Felipe de Rábago y Terán
SINFUL CAPTAIN

In colonial Texas, presidios or forts played an important role in defending the province. Spanish soldiers and their captain were expected to work closely with Catholic missionaries to Christianize and civilize the Indians. However, in the 1740s one presidial captain came into serious conflict with the clergy because of his sinful behavior. Violence erupted. A missionary and a civilian were killed, and Captain Felipe de Rábago y Terán was accused of being involved in the murders. For many years he was deprived of his freedom. Searching his soul, the Spanish officer repented (regretted) his evil ways. When he was again put in command of a military post on the Texas frontier, the changed Rábago did his best to be an honorable man. Dying in his forties, he could hope to be judged for his good deeds—not for his sins.

The early life of Felipe de Rábago is largely unknown. He seems to have acquired a great deal of wealth from silver mines in Mexico. Success probably brought him to the attention of King Ferdinand VI of Spain, who named don Felipe as commander of a new presidio to be established in central Texas. The royal appointment, dated March 6, 1750, was carried to Mexico City by Rábago himself.

In the late 1740s, three missions had been founded on the San Gabriel River near present-day Rockdale, Texas. Their purpose was to convert Tonkawa, Orcoquiza, Bidai, Deadose, and Coco Indians. The Spanish wanted a fort to protect the San Xavier missions, as they were called, from Apache raids and to help discipline the mission Indians, called neophytes. In 1751 the viceroy of New Spain instructed Rábago to recruit at least fifty soldiers for the new presidio. Additionally, he was to find civilian settlers who would live near the missions.

At the time of his appointment, don Felipe was in his early thirties. He was handsome and conceited, and he proved to be a bad choice to command the fort.

On the way to his post, Rábago stopped at Querétaro to meet with officials of the Franciscan missionary college, who would provide additional priests for the San Xavier missions. Don Felipe asked the Franciscans to make an arrangement that they would later regret. The friars agreed that any disputes arising between missionaries and the military at San Xavier would be dealt with locally, rather than by authorities in Mexico City or Querétaro.

As he passed through village after village on his way to San Antonio, don Felipe revealed himself to be an immoral man. He had intimate relations with Indian and Hispanic women, whether married or single. The priests who were traveling with the captain were of course horrified at his behavior.

At San Antonio, Rábago recruited civilian settlers for the San Xavier enterprise. One was a tailor named Juan José Ceballos. The young man had an attractive wife, and trouble was not long in coming. When don Felipe began to behave improperly with Ceballos's wife, the husband angrily objected. When he did so, don Felipe responded by putting the tailor in chains. Then, on reaching San Xavier, Rábago had Ceballos placed in a cell.

Captain Rábago was unhappy with what he found on the San Gabriel River. Only eighteen ragtag soldiers were present. The rest had deserted or been reassigned to other presidios. The missions were also in a pitiful state. One had 109 neophytes, another had 25, and the third had none! Don Felipe wanted to move the missions to a different location, but the priests refused. The commander reluctantly chose a location nearby for the new presidio, named San Francisco Xavier de Gigedo.

Because Rábago continued to have a sexual relationship with Ceballos's wife, the priests wanted the woman returned to San Antonio. But don Felipe refused. Matters worsened during Christmas Eve celebrations at the presidio, when Ceballos broke free from his chains. The fugitive then ran to the chapel of Mission Candelaria. Rábago disgusted the missionaries by riding his horse into the chapel in pursuit of the escapee. There he seized Ceballos, returned the tailor to his cell, and beat him badly.

Father Miguel Pinilla, one of the missionaries, was outraged. He demanded a public apology from Rábago and the release of Ceballos. On December 27, the captain let Ceballos return to the mission but offered no apology. Father Pinilla and Captain Rábago were locked in a contest of wills.

Don Felipe sent a letter to Pinilla's superior in San Antonio and asked that the missionary be replaced as chaplain, but Rábago's request was denied. Not surprisingly, in mid-January 1752 the clergy at San Xavier broke their pledge to settle differences at the local level and appealed for help to their superiors at Querétaro. The Franciscans had many complaints, but above all the clergymen spoke out against "the malice [harmful intent] of this man [Rábago]."

With the captain as their role model, the soldiers at San Xavier also began to behave improperly with Indian women living at the missions. Neophyte men lost their wives and daughters to the soldiers and suffered insults "every moment of the day." Some of the Christianized Indian women were troubled by their intimate contacts with Spaniards and confessed their sins to the mission fathers. The priests, who were working to civilize and Christianize the natives, were again horrified.

Father Miguel Pinilla decided to punish the captain and his entire garrison. In February 1752 he announced that Rábago and his soldiers had committed gross sins with Indian women and were excommunicated. This meant that all soldiers at the presidio were denied membership in the Catholic Church. They could not be forgiven until they repented and changed their ways. Rather than change their behavior, however, the soldiers tore up the excommunication decree (formal order) and burned it. In the end, however, Pinilla won this conflict. The soldiers soon became afraid for their souls. One by one they begged to be forgiven, and the priests accepted their pleas.

While the missionaries were objecting to Rábago's sinful actions, he was complaining about them to the viceroy. Don Felipe charged that the priests neglected their religious duties, caused too much trouble, and encouraged the Indians to rebel.

Spanish officials in Mexico City were confused by the situation at San Xavier. They found fault with both Rábago for his behavior and Pinilla for his actions. To try to settle the matter, the viceroy ordered the head of the missionary college at Querétaro to look into affairs at San Xavier.

Before any action could be taken, tragedy struck at Mission Candelaria on the night of May 11, 1752. Juan José Ceballos and two priests, Miguel Pinilla and José Ganzabal, were eating their evening meal. Because the night was warm, the outside door was open to let the breeze in. A single candle provided light.

Suddenly there was the blast of a Spanish weapon called a blunderbuss. Its ball hit Ceballos in the chest and killed him instantly. Father Ganzabal grabbed the candle and rushed to the door to look out into the darkness. At that moment, a Coco Indian arrow struck the priest and entered his heart. As he fell dying, the candle went out. This probably saved the life of Father Pinilla. Firing another blunderbuss as they left, the murderers fled into the night.

The finger of suspicion pointed quickly at Captain Rábago. His affair with Ceballo's wife and his dispute with Father Pinilla made him a likely suspect. Don Felipe knew that he was in trouble and tried to blame the Coco Indians for the murders.

Ten days before the murders, the Cocos as a group had deserted Mission Candelaria. There had been difficulties between these Indians and the missionaries. The natives were probably also upset over quarrels between the priests and the soldiers. And they had had a disagreement with Rábago. On May 1, 1752, two Cocos had entered Presidio San Xavier armed with bows and arrows. The captain had the Indians seized and beaten. This caused all of the Cocos to flee, and don Felipe did little to track them down and return them to the missions.

Juan José Ceballos was a resident at Candelaria at this time. Earlier, he had come upon two or three Cocos who had killed a mission cow without permission and were skinning it. Scolding them, he tried to take the butchered animal from the natives. A fight started, and Ceballos struck a Coco with the handle of his knife. This caused several more Indians to attack him. To protect himself, the tailor fired his blunderbuss and wounded a Coco chief in the thigh. Because of this incident, the Cocos had reason to dislike Ceballos.

There was also bad blood between Father José Ganzabal and a soldier named Martín Gutiérrez over a young Indian woman. Luisa was a twenty-two-year-old native who had been converted to Christianity. She was married to an Indian named Andrés. Because Luisa was an attractive woman, Martín Gutiérrez wanted her. The soldier made a deal with Andrés. He would loan the Indian a horse for "three moons" in return for sexual favors from Luisa. Luisa apparently told Father Ganzabal of the agreement between Andrés and Gutiérrez. The missionary, of course, disapproved strongly of the arrangement. He likely scolded both Luisa and her husband Andrés.

What is certain is that Gutiérrez was one of five assassins at Mission Candelaria on the night of May 11. And Andrés later admitted to having fired the arrow that took the life of Father Ganzabal.

After the murders, Andrés fled to San Antonio with his wife. There he was questioned about the events of May 11, and at first he claimed his innocence. He not only made conflicting statements that drew suspicion but also knew many details about the killings. Finally, he confessed, but Andrés placed the blame on Martín Gutiérrez and three other soldiers.

Andrés said that on the afternoon of May 11 he saw four Spaniards near a creek. Two had blunderbusses, and two had bows and arrows. The men were waiting to ambush Father Miguel Pinilla at his favorite fishing hole, but the priest did not come. So they decided to wait for night and use the cover of darkness to kill both priests and Ceballos. They offered Andrés a horse if he would be their bowman. Because he disliked Father Ganzabal, the Indian agreed.

According to Andrés, the Spaniards dressed themselves like Indians, and they crept to the house where the victims were dining. Gutiérrez fired the fatal ball into Ceballos's chest, and Andrés let fly the arrow that killed Ganzabal. The five men then fled without killing Father Pinilla. Andrés and Luisa set out immediately for San Antonio, and the soldiers returned to the presidio.

Rábago later told his version of the events of May 11, 1752. He was dining with friends when he heard the sound of the blunderbusses firing. Don Felipe mounted a horse and galloped to Mission Candelaria, where he found the bodies of Ceballos and Ganzabal.

On May 14 Rábago sent word of the murders to the viceroy in Mexico City. The captain knew that he would be in trouble if any of his men had committed the murders. So he placed all blame on the Cocos and asked permission to make war on them. That request was denied.

When Andrés confessed at San Antonio, Rábago insisted that the Indian was lying about soldiers being involved in the murders. Don Felipe and others pressured Andrés to change his story, and the native finally said that he had lied. This was not enough, however, to clear Captain Rábago.

The truth of what happened in the double murder on May 11, 1752, is not clear. But Rábago bears at least some blame for those tragic events. Martín Gutiérrez had reason to be angry with Father Ganzabal. But why were the two other Spanish soldiers involved as assassins? They probably disliked Father Miguel Pinilla because of the long-standing disputes between the soldiers and the missionaries. This situation was also Rábago's fault. And Ceballos and don Felipe were the bitterest of enemies. The fact that the tailor was also the target of the murderers certainly raises questions about the captain's innocence.

It is doubtful that the Cocos played any role in the murders. These natives had little or no experience with firearms. One of the murder weapons, however, was a blunderbuss. How would Coco Indians get such a musket and learn to fire it accurately? And remember that the natives in question had been gone from Mission Candelaria for ten days. Even Rábago admitted that his soldiers could not find any trace of those Indians after they fled on May 1, 1752.

Overwhelming evidence pointed to the involvement of Felipe de Rábago y Terán in the double murder. He was removed from command at San Xavier and sent to a presidio in Coahuila, Mexico. Although he still held the title of captain, he was under house arrest for eight long years. Suspiciously, the Indian Andrés and his wife went with don Felipe and remained under his control for those eight years. The Spanish assassins disappear from the written record at this time. One died while in jail. The others somehow managed to escape.

As time passed, the events of May 11, 1752, began to fade in the memories of many people. However, the Franciscans never forgot the loss of one of their own—Father Ganzabal. In the future, they would have to deal with Captain Rábago again.

The desertion of the Coco Indians, combined with the murder of Ceballos and Ganzabal, helped doom the missions at San Xavier to failure. A long drought in 1753 made matters worse. By August 1755 the missionaries and the soldiers of the presidio moved to the San

Marcos River. They also had little success there. In late 1756 they moved again to the Guadalupe River.

During these years, the missionaries were trying to get permission to work with the Lipan Apaches on the San Saba River to the northwest of San Antonio. These Indians were dangerous enemies of the settlers, and in the 1730s they had begun making raids on San Antonio. The Spanish sent expeditions against the Apaches but failed to end the raids. To the Franciscan Father Mariano de los Dolores, the best solution was to missionize the Lipans in their own lands.

Meanwhile, the Apaches were under increasing pressure from their arch enemies, the Comanches. This forced the Lipans to make peace with the Spaniards. In August 1749, four Apache chiefs with their followers buried a hatchet and other weapons of war in a peace ceremony at San Antonio. The Lipans appeared willing to accept Christianity. In reality, these natives wanted protection from the Comanches rather than religious conversion.

About the time that the San Xavier efforts ended, Father Alonso Giraldo de Terreros started the first mission for the Apaches. Mission San Lorenzo, set up in 1754, was south of the Río Grande, far from the natives' own lands. In less than a year, the neophytes at San Lorenzo rebelled, burned the mission, and fled. The Franciscans, however, were not discouraged. They believed that the Lipans would cooperate with missionary efforts closer to Apachería, as their area was known.

The Franciscans needed permission and funding to enter Apache lands and establish a mission-presidio complex. Certainly, the government was interested in converting pagan Indians and claiming new lands. The lure of wealth, however, also influenced Spanish officials. Scouting expeditions brought reports of valuable minerals in Apachería. For all these reasons, soldiers, missionaries, and civilians were destined to move to the San Saba River in the late 1750s. Their efforts on the San Saba would be a disaster, but it would give Felipe de Rábago a chance to redeem his reputation.

After Mission San Lorenzo had been destroyed, Father Alonso Giraldo de Terreros went to Mexico City. His rich cousin, Pedro Romero de Terreros, was willing to finance missionary efforts among the Apaches in their own lands. This was on condition that Father Alonso be placed in charge of the enterprise, and the viceroy agreed to don Pedro's terms. The government would pay the military costs of the San Sabá project. And everyone at San Sabá must report directly to the viceroy in Mexico City, rather than to the governor of Texas.

Colonel Diego Ortiz Parrilla was in command of the soldiers at San Sabá. This officer was an experienced and capable veteran, but he was arrogant. Don Diego never took advice or admitted mistakes. In this case, it was his misfortune to have "come at the wrong time to the wrong place."

First, Ortiz Parrilla inspected his ragtag soldiers who had been at Presidio San Francisco Xavier de Gigedo. He was shocked by the condition of the men and moved them to San Antonio. Second, the colonel was concerned about the sincerity of the Apaches. He was not sure that they would peacefully cooperate with the Spanish, even if a mission were set up for them in Apachería.

There were problems among the clergy also. Father Mariano de los Dolores was angry. He felt unappreciated. After all, he had tried for years to get missions for the Lipans. Now Father Terreros would be in charge, just because he had a rich cousin.

Ortiz Parrilla's expedition finally left San Antonio in the spring of 1757. It had tons of supplies, dozens of soldiers and their families, six missionaries, and many Indian allies. Also taken were hundreds of horses, mules, cattle, and sheep.

The expedition got to the San Saba River on April 17, 1757. After some exploration, Ortiz Parrilla was concerned. He had not seen a single Apache. The officer thought that all of the Spaniards should return to San Antonio, but the six Franciscans would not hear of it. Soon Mission Santa Cruz de San Sabá and Presidio San Luis de las Amarillas took shape near present-day Menard, Texas.

Aware of the problems that had happened at San Xavier, the priests insisted that the presidio be located well away from the mission. They did not want the Indians exposed to bad influences on the part of the presidial soldiers. Having the two outposts about 3 1/2 miles apart lessened contact between the soldiers and the neophytes, but it also made defending the mission more difficult.

During its short life of less than a year, Mission Santa Cruz de San Sabá failed to attract even one Apache to live there. The Lipans did appear in large numbers from time to time, but they were always heading somewhere else. The Indians, however, were shrewd. They gave the Spaniards just enough hope to keep them from abandoning the enterprise. Even so, three of the priests became so discouraged that they returned to San Antonio. Plans for a second and third mission were dropped.

In the meantime, the Lipan Apaches were plotting to create conflict between their enemies, the Comanches, and the Spaniards. When the Apaches raided enemy camps to the north, they purposely left behind Spanish articles such as shoes. They wanted the Comanches to believe that the Europeans at San Sabá were at least partly to blame for the attacks. This tactic apparently worked.

The extremely cold winter of 1757–1758 brought misery to some four hundred people at the presidio. Weather was not their only problem, however. The Spaniards learned from scouts that hundreds of Comanches and their allies were drawing nearer to San Sabá.

Colonel Ortiz Parrilla felt that his major duty was to protect the 237 women and children at the presidio. He could spare only a few soldiers to guard the mission. He asked the three priests to move to the presidio for safety, but they refused. Fathers Terreros, Miguel de Molina, and José de Santiesteban chose to remain at the mission.

Early on the morning of March 16, 1758, a mission guard "heard an outburst of Indian yells resembling their war cries when going into battle." Firing their muskets, hostile natives began to surround the mission. The attackers got into the fortified area of the mission by shouting that they did not wish "to fight with the Spaniards, but only to maintain friendship with them; that they only wanted to kill Apaches, for whom they were searching."

Fathers Terreros and Molina confronted the Comanches and their allies inside the mission gate. Molina "saw nothing but Indians on every hand, armed with guns. . . . Besides the paint on their faces, red and black, they were adorned with the pelts and tails of wild beasts, wrapped around them or hanging down from their heads, as well as deer horns. . . . All were armed with muskets, swords, and lances, . . . and [he] noticed also that they had brought with them some youths armed with bows and arrows, to train . . . them in their cruel and bloody way of life."

In a dispute over his favorite horse, Father Terreros was shot to death, but Father Molina escaped. A second priest, Father Santiesteban, died within the chapel, and at some point his head was cut off. The Indians looted everything of value and killed a total of eight people. Then they set fire to the buildings and left the ruined mission.

Two days later, Ortiz Parrilla visited the ruins. The sights he saw were shocking. The Indians had scalped some victims, cut the heads off others, and gouged out some people's eyes. They had even killed the mission cats and oxen, sparing only a few sheep. Mission Santa Cruz was never rebuilt. It was unique in being the only Texas mission destroyed by outright Indian attack.

After the disaster at San Sabá, Spain felt it had to punish the natives who destroyed the mission. Colonel Ortiz Parrilla was chosen to prepare a military expedition against the Comanches and their allies. While arrangements were underway, Indians "all armed with guns" raided the horse herd at San Sabá on March 30, 1759. The attackers killed twenty soldiers and stole more than seven hundred horses and mules. All of the victims died from bullet wounds. Since the Spanish could not legally sell firearms to the Indians, the muskets were almost certainly supplied by the French. The deadly events of March 30 only increased the Spaniards' desire to let even the Indians in remote areas know that "they would not be secure from the long arm of Spanish vengeance."

Later in 1759, don Diego with more than five hundred troops went from the San Saba River to the Red River. On October 7, he and his men fought a heated battle with Indians that lasted for several hours. The results were far from satisfactory. At Spanish Fort, near present-day Nocona, Texas, Spanish troops suffered their worst defeat in Texas's history. Including dead, wounded, and missing, the colonel's losses totaled fifty-two. He also lost two cannons and other equipment.

When he returned to San Sabá, Ortiz Parrilla blamed the failed campaign on the poor quality of the troops he led. Don Diego insisted that he, however, had served with "zeal [and] valor . . . in inflicting punishment on the enemy." But words alone could not turn defeat into victory. In 1760 Ortiz Parrilla was removed from command at San Sabá. The new commandant would be the sinful scoundrel and suspected murderer, Felipe de Rábago y Terán.

By this time, don Felipe had been under house arrest and imprisonment for eight years, but he was still determined to free himself. Rábago was in the Monclova public jail when he filed an appeal for his freedom in 1759. He claimed that he had serious illnesses and needed to "repair his broken health." The captain insisted that he had been innocent of the deaths of Father José Ganzabal and Juan José Ceballos.

Once again, Rábago blamed the murders at San Xavier on the Coco Indians. His lawyer attacked the testimony of the Indian Andrés, which had placed blame on presidial soldiers. The lengthy appeal declared that the Cocos had been seeking revenge against Ceballos for wounding their chief. Don Felipe's attorney also pointed out that the accused soldiers were no longer available for punishment. One had died and the others had escaped. So the charges against Captain Rábago should be dropped.

A new viceroy, the Marqués de Cruillas, had recently arrived in Mexico City. In the summer of 1760, he ordered don Felipe, the soldiers, and Andrés cleared of all charges. The viceroy also appointed Rábago as commander at San Sabá, because the San Xavier garrison that had been moved there was don Felipe's old command.

The Franciscan clergy protested the appointment. They remembered Rábago for his "bad conduct in the time he had served as commander of San Xavier." Nevertheless, the Marqués de Cruillas ignored their protests. He was determined that don Felipe be in charge at San Sabá. In fairness to the viceroy *and* Rábago, the choice proved to be not that bad.

During the eight years that Rábago was under house arrest on suspicion of murder, the sinful captain had "a great change of heart." Perhaps his lack of freedom gave him time to search his soul and change his evil ways. At any rate, he became committed to "the conversion of the natives [to Christianity] and their reduction to mission life."

Upon gaining his freedom, Rábago had the good sense to avoid contact with his Franciscan enemies at San Antonio. As he traveled to his new post on the San Saba River, the captain blazed a new trail. Arriving in late September 1760, he found depressing conditions. The presidio had exactly one hundred soldiers. Most were disabled veterans, elderly soldiers, raw recruits, and "boys too young for military service." None had adequate clothing or equipment.

Rábago used some of his own money to get supplies, weapons, and ammunition for his command. He also acquired several hundred horses. With his men properly equipped, the new captain turned his attention to the presidio itself. The wooden walls of the stockade were replaced with stone and encircled with a moat. Don Felipe thought that the remodeled fort looked like a castle, and he gave it a new name—Real Presidio (Royal Presidio) de San Sabá.

The commander also sent expeditions into the plains separating Texas and New Mexico. These increased knowledge of the geography and of the Native Americans in the region.

Rábago showed impressive skills in dealing with the Lipan Apaches. Several chiefs visited the presidio regularly. Whenever possible, don Felipe talked to them of his desire to set up missions for the Lipans. Apparently the Spanish captain wanted to make up for his sins against the Catholic Church at San Xavier.

Despite Rábago's apparent sincerity about converting the natives, his efforts with the Lipans were his undoing. Once again, these Indians used Spaniards to achieve their own goals. The Lipan chieftains said that another mission at San Sabá was out of the question. That location was too close to their enemies' war parties, as proven by the earlier attack on San Sabá. The chiefs argued that a mission farther south in safer lands was needed.

For food, the Apaches relied in part on *rancherías*, or temporary campsites. There they scratched out small fields and crude gardens. When it was time to plant or harvest crops, the Lipans' enemies, especially the Comanches, knew exactly where to find them.

The Apaches asked Rábago to build a mission halfway between San Sabá and the Río Grande, a favorite site for their *rancherías*. The Indians hoped that the presidial soldiers would protect not only the religious outpost but Apache crops as well. Don Felipe, however, did not have authority to found missions anywhere except San Sabá. When he agreed to the request of the Lipan chiefs, the captain made a serious mistake.

In seeking a priest for the new mission, Rábago was wise not to approach the clergy at San Antonio, because the Franciscans there disliked him so much. So he asked Father Diego Jiménez at San Juan Bautista, located just south of the Río Grande, to take charge of the new mission enterprise. The priest accepted.

The new mission, San Lorenzo de Santa Cruz, required a guard of twenty men. This mission was barely started when the Lipans asked for a second one about ten miles to the south. Rábago again agreed to the Indians' request and established Nuestra Señora de la Candelaria del Cañón. This meant taking ten more soldiers and even more supplies from San Sabá. San Lorenzo and Candelaria did attract some Lipan neophytes, mostly women and children. But the drain of men and supplies to the El Cañón missions, as the two outposts came to be called, weakened San Sabá.

Worse, the Lipans continued to engage in deceitful practices. When the Apaches raided Comanche camps, they again purposely left behind Spanish articles. The Lipans also attacked Spanish settlements and left Comanche belongings. This double-dealing caused the Comanches to be angry at the Spaniards for supplying the Apaches. And the Spaniards wrongly blamed the Comanches for raids carried out in fact by the Lipans. The Apaches' devious actions, however, did not go undetected for long. It added to many complaints against these plains Indians, which later targeted them to be killed or sent to foreign lands.

Felipe de Rábago checks
for signs of Indians
(DRAWING BY JACK JACKSON)

At this moment, however, it was Rábago and his men who paid a high price for being friends with the Lipans. In five years, don Felipe spent more than twelve thousand pesos (dollars) on supplies, clothing, and livestock for the presidio. To make matters worse, the Comanches and their allies robbed about half of the supply trains. These natives also attacked Presidio de San Sabá, with some of the attacks lasting for two months. When Rábago asked Mexico City for help, his pleas were denied, because the viceroy was angry with don Felipe for founding the El Cañón missions without his permission.

In the spring of 1769, the presidio at San Sabá was under almost constant threat of attack by Comanches. The soldiers and their families dared not leave the fort to plant crops. Lack of healthful foods caused the residents to suffer terribly from a disease called scurvy. Rábago himself was covered with sores and had failing health.

The sickly captain also faced discontent from his soldiers. He became so desperate that he abandoned his post and relocated it at the site of Mission San Lorenzo. When the viceroy learned of this move, made without his permission, he ordered don Felipe back to San Sabá. The commander refused. Instead, he traveled to Coahuila, probably to buy supplies for his troops and the others stationed at the mission.

In April 1769, Felipe de Rábago learned that the viceroy had replaced him as commander at San Sabá. Don Felipe set out for Mexico City. He hoped to be repaid for the money he had spent supporting the presidio at San Sabá for nine years. The captain never completed his journey. Still in his mid-forties, Rábago died at San Luis Potosí in 1769.

The life of Felipe de Rábago is hardly the tale of a good man. His evil conduct at San Xavier corrupted his command and created tensions. That he personally ordered Ceballos and Ganzabal to be killed is unlikely. That he played a role, perhaps a serious one, in those events is possible. He probably complained about "meddling priests" and "that damned Ceballos." Maybe his soldiers carried out the unspoken wishes of their captain on the night of the murders. Guilty or not, don Felipe spent eight years under suspicion and in disgrace. He apparently realized the error of his ways, and he emerged from that experience a changed man.

When given a second chance, Rábago attempted to correct his ways. In his command at San Sabá, don Felipe revealed a good heart but bad judgment. Even his enemies, the Franciscans, could find little wrong with his personal sacrifices and devotion to the Lipan Apaches. Is it not in the nature of priests to forgive those who repent? Perhaps in the end, Felipe de Rábago deserves sympathy for trying so hard to do good works and make up for his earlier sins.

SOURCES

Materials used in preparing this chapter are described below. You can find more information about these sources in the Bibliography at the end of the book.

Books

The best treatments of the San Xavier missions are Gary B. Starnes's *The San Gabriel Missions, 1746–1756* and Carlos E. Castañeda's *Our Catholic Heritage in Texas, 1519–1936*, volume 3. For Rábago's service at San Sabá, see Robert S. Weddle's *The San Sabá Mission: Spanish Pivot in Texas*. Donald E. Chipman and Harriett Denise Joseph's *Notable Men and Women of Spanish Texas* has a more detailed biographical sketch of Rábago.

Quotes

Quotes are from the following sources: Carlos E. Castañeda, *Our Catholic Heritage in Texas, 1519–1936*, volume 3; Juan Agustín Morfi, *History of Texas, 1673–1779*, translated and edited by Carlos E. Castañeda, volume 2; Robert S. Weddle, *The San Sabá Mission: Spanish Pivot in Texas*; Depositions of Andrés de Villareal and Father Fray Miguel de Molina, in *The San Sabá Papers: A Documentary Account of the Founding and Destruction of the San Sabá Mission*, edited by Lesley B. Simpson; Statement of Diego Ortiz Parrilla, March 30, 1759, Archivo General de Indias, Seville, México 1933A; Henry E. Allen, "The Parrilla Expedition to the Red River in 1759," *Southwestern Historical Quarterly* 43 (July 1939): 61; Merits and Services of Diego Ortiz Parrilla (May 3, 1770), Archivo General de Indias, Seville, Guadalajara 515; Statements Concerning Don Felipe de Rábago y Terán, Captain of the Presidio of Santa Rosa del Sacramento in Coahuila, 1759, Center for American History, Austin, Dunn Transcripts; Proceedings of the *fiscal*, April 20, 1761, Archivo General de Indias, Seville, Guadalajara 368; and Statement of Felipe de Rábago on Review of Seventy-seven Men, October 15, 1760, Center for American History, Austin, Dunn Transcripts.

CHAPTER TEN

José de Escandón y Elguera
FATHER OF SOUTH TEXAS

When José de Escandón died in Mexico City in 1770, he was accused of serious offenses. He had faithfully served the king of Spain for many, many years as a successful soldier, explorer, colonizer, and official. So why was he on trial?

It seems that Escandón's successes made enemies, some of whom were simply jealous of his accomplishments. Those people claimed that don José was guilty of many abuses. He had also made some serious mistakes in his career, which left him open to attack. Escandón worked hard to prove his innocence, but he died before a long legal process was over.

Even after Escandón's death, his children had to defend their dead father. They wanted to clear his good name, but much more was at stake. If the court decided that don José was guilty, his family could lose the wealth, power, and titles that he had gained.

Did José de Escandón deserve to die in disgrace? Was he found guilty of any of the charges against him? What happened to his family? The answers lie in this chapter. In it, you will learn about the life of this famous Spanish colonizer and Father of South Texas, as well as what happened after his death.

José de Escandón y Elguera was born on May 19, 1700, in Soto la Marina, Santander, Spain. His father was Juan de Escandón; his mother was Francisca de la Elguera. The family was fairly wealthy, so young José had the opportunity to do what he wanted. At age fifteen, he came to America. For six years, he was part of a mounted (on horse-back) military unit in Yucatán. Because José was a cadet training to be a soldier, he did not get paid. But the young man so impressed the local governor that he reported favorable things about him to the king in Spain.

In 1721 Escandón was sent to Querétaro, where he served for a number of years—again at his own expense. He helped punish Indians who were attacking Spanish settlers. These Native Americans had been rebelling for a long time, and don José gained fame for his ability to crush their uprisings. At the same time, he also was known for his good treatment of Indian prisoners. With each success, he rose in military rank and power.

One of the areas on the frontier that alarmed Spaniards was named the Costa del Seno Mexicano (Gulf of Mexico). This included part of what is today northern Mexico and South Texas. Indians felt this was their region and raided areas settled by Spaniards. Because of the raids, colonists in New Spain tried to convince the king that the Costa should be explored and the Indians dealt with. A special *junta* (committee) was formed to decide a course of action for the Costa. But this *junta* was very slow to make any decisions. In fact, nothing happened for years!

In the meantime, José de Escandón had been busy. He had returned to Spain in the 1720s, where he married Dominga de Pedrajo in 1727. She died in 1736. A year later, don José married Josefa de Llera y Bayas of Querétaro. The couple would have seven children, including a first-born son, Manuel.

Don José became very important in a region to the east of Querétaro known as the Sierra Gorda. It contained rugged mountains that gave shelter to warlike natives. Parts of the Sierra Gorda had never been explored by Spaniards.

Escandón organized and led four expeditions to explore the Sierra Gorda. He helped to pacify (bring peace to) the region. He returned Spaniards to places that had been deserted and helped to settle new areas. He was able to pay for all of these activities with money he made as a merchant, mill owner, and rancher.

Members of the *junta* in Mexico City and the king in Spain came to value Escandón's loyalty and ability. These officials were especially impressed that don José had spent so much of his own money to help

● Settlements		○ Future Settlements	
➤ José de Escandón			
▪▪ Blas María de la Garza Falcón		◀ Francisco de Sosa	
◆ Miguel de la Garza Falcón		➤ Antonio Ladrón de Guevara	
▶ Juan Francisco Barvarena		•• Joaquín Orobio Basterra	N

The seven expeditions of José de Escandón and his lieutenants
(CENTER FOR MEDIA PRODUCTION, UNIVERSITY OF NORTH TEXAS)

his country. So they chose José de Escandón as the best person to explore a newly created province in northern Mexico and South Texas. The viceroy agreed. He named don José as the first governor of Nuevo Santander. The name of the province was chosen to honor Escandón's place of birth in Spain. Nuevo Santander was very large, and it was mostly unknown. The province also was home to Indians who were hostile to Spaniards and did not want them on their lands.

By this time, the mid-1700s, don José was one of the best-organized people in Spanish America. A good planner, he knew how to get things done quickly but effectively. He arranged for seven divisions (groups) to enter Nuevo Santander at the same time. Each would leave from a different place, explore a specific area, and meet in about a month.

Governor Escandón led the main group himself. It left Querétaro in January 1747. Later that same month, the other expeditions left from Texas, Coahuila, and Nuevo León, as well as from towns in the south of Mexico. All were to meet at the mouth of the Río Grande in late February.

As Escandón's group moved toward the coast, other Spaniards and a few Indians joined him. He made his main camp at the Río de las Palmas in northern Mexico. Then, with a smaller band, he reached the Río Grande near the sea in late February. He found that one of his captains, Blas María de la Garza Falcón, had already arrived there a few days earlier.

With two dozen men, don José did more exploring and also learned about the region from natives. Among the Indians don José met were the Comecrudos, or raw-meat eaters. They had never seen Spaniards before but were friendly.

Even though the governor was a careful planner, not all of the seven divisions were able to meet as he had hoped. For example, one group of Spaniards exploring along the north bank of the Río Grande had problems caused by snow and then lack of drinking water. With their leader, Miguel de la Garza Falcón, they returned to Mexico without making contact with Escandón.

Of the seven expeditions, twenty-five soldiers from the presidio (fort) at Los Adaes in East Texas made the longest trip. Led by Captain Joaquín Orobio Basterra, they were joined by another twenty-five soldiers from La Bahía on the coast. This division explored along the San Antonio River. Escandón hoped that this river would become the northern border of his province.

Orobio Basterra's men suffered greatly during their journey. If Indian guides had not helped them, they probably would have died from thirst. When they reached the south bank of the Río Grande, the Texas soldiers got orders from Escandón to return to their forts. Based on what they had been through, Orobio Basterra declared that South Texas had "little promise for settlement."

In early March, Escandón went back to his main camp at the Río de las Palmas. He named the place where the river entered a large inland bay La Ría del Nuevo Santander. Then, as he made the return trip to Querétaro, the governor explored frontier areas along the Sierra Gorda. Upon reaching his home base, he released his troops. Once again, the new governor had paid the entire cost of the seven expeditions. Thanks to good planning and good luck, all of don José's men came back alive.

After his journey, Escandón drew a map of his new province and set down a plan for colonizing the area. He wanted to found fourteen settlements with missions. But to do this, he had to get the approval of officials in Mexico City. Don José said that he could attract colonists by offering them one hundred to two hundred pesos in cash. Also, they would not have to pay taxes for ten years. At first, land would be shared in common, rather than divided among the settlers.

Soldiers would be placed in the new towns to protect them, but only for the first few years. After that, the civilians should be able to take care of themselves. Missionaries would minister to both Spaniards and Indians.

A *junta* in Mexico City looked at Escandón's plan and approved it. In May 1748, the viceroy officially named José de Escandón to pacify and settle Nuevo Santander. Once again the governor acted carefully but quickly. He spread the news of his project and had little trouble recruiting settlers. They were attracted by the rewards being offered. Some were ranchers with many cattle in northern Mexico, and they needed more land for their herds. Others simply wanted a fresh start.

A new life awaited settlers willing to face the dangers of the northern frontier, but they had confidence in Escandón's ability to make the Nuevo Santander project a success. When he again left Querétaro in December 1748, José de Escandón led one of the largest expedi-

*Escandón shows his map
to Spanish officials*
(DRAWING BY JACK JACKSON)

tions ever sent to settle the frontier of New Spain. As the body traveled along, the governor founded many towns and missions in his province.

The first, Santa María de Llera, was set up on Christmas Day with forty-four Spanish families, several Indians, and eleven soldiers. Mission Peña del Castillo was begun close by. Then the governor placed forty families at San Fernando de Güemes and thirty at San Antonio de Padilla.

Problems slowed Escandón's progress, however. The main camp was hit by illnesses, probably caused by bad water. Things were so terrible that the settlers called the campsite "hell." They had to move to another place, but it was not much better. The natives were also a threat. One group visited the camp and acted friendly. However, they later attacked at night and killed several horses.

Escandón did not let diseases or Indians stop him. In February 1749, he founded his capital, Villa de Nuevo Santander, with more than four hundred people present. Along with successes came some failures. Natives hostile to Spaniards moving onto their lands killed a missionary and eight soldiers who were taking some settlers to the Nueces River area in Texas. The surviving Spaniards had to wait eight months for don José to decide where they should go. Finally, he sent them to Soto la Marina. Led by Juan José Vázquez Borrego, they settled in the town named for the governor's place of birth.

Meanwhile, a site down the Río Grande from Camargo was granted to Carlos Cantú. He had brought families and soldiers from Nuevo León in northern Mexico. The *villa* (town) they started is present-day Reynosa, Tamaulipas, which is across the river from McAllen, Texas.

Escandón had to spend time visiting the new towns near his capital. He also started another town, Villa Altamira, in May 1749. However, he could not devote himself just to colonizing. Hostile Huastec Indians were a threat to Spaniards in the province. So don José launched military action against those natives. Despite this problem, in the same month the governor founded Santa Bárbara on the eastern slope of the Sierra Gorda. With this, Escandón felt a sense of pride at having settled so much of Nuevo Santander.

In June 1749, don José wrote the viceroy of his activities in the southern Sierra Gorda. Thirteen towns had been created, and hundreds of Spaniards and friendly Indians lived in or near them. There were also troops nearby for protection. Ninety thousand pesos had been spent to do all of this. It had cost more than the governor had expected, but a lot had been accomplished.

King Ferdinand VI was pleased with don José's efforts. The king granted him the titles of Count of Sierra Gorda and Viscount of the House of Escandón. Ferdinand VI wanted to honor the governor for stopping warlike Indians, exploring the Costa, and colonizing Nuevo Santander.

As mentioned earlier, Escandón had enemies. Not everyone approved of his methods of settling the province. For example, two different groups of Catholic friars (priests) wanted control of the missions in Nuevo Santander, and they did not always agree with Governor Escandón's decisions.

The count was lucky, however, because he had supporters too. An important official came to his defense. This man, the Marqués de Altamira, insisted that Escandón was a good colonizer. He claimed that don José had done "more in one year than could have been done in a hundred years" by anyone else. So no action was taken against him.

The governor spent a lot of time visiting his existing towns, while starting new settlements. Two of these outposts were placed north of the Río Grande in what is today Texas. They were Nuestra Señora de Dolores in 1750 and Villa Laredo in 1755. The first of these came about because José Vázquez Borrego needed more land for his cattle and horses. He offered to settle Dolores at no cost to the crown. Five years later, Tomás Sánchez started Laredo, also at his own cost. Dolores did not prove permanent, but Laredo is still an important border town in Texas.

Founding settlements did not mean, of course, that they would succeed. Many problems hit the colonists, and they looked to Escandón for help. During the early years, there was drought or lack of rainfall. This hurt crops and made the price of seed corn very high. Then, when the drought ended, some places flooded because of too much rain.

Even greater danger came from the natives, some of whom were hostile to the colonists. The governor knew that one of his jobs in Nuevo Santander was to control the Indians, to civilize them, and to make them Catholics. He tried to do this peacefully when possible.

When don José moved with his family to Villa de Nuevo Santander, he needed workers to build his house and tend his livestock. So he moved thirty families of Pame Indians from Río Verde in Mexico to his lands in Nuevo Santander. Each Pame family head was paid four pesos a month and received some maize (corn). The governor also put five of these families in the nearby mission to serve as good examples for less civilized Indians.

Don José was pleased that some Indian nations, such as the Comecrudos, were choosing on their own to come to Spanish missions. But he knew that they probably came to get gifts of tobacco and clothing, rather than from a sincere desire to become Christians.

When he had to do so, Escandón made war against Native Americans who were hostile to the Spaniards. For example, Indians of Mission Ygollo in Santa Bárbara rebelled in the early 1750s, so don José sent armed men against them. In cases like this, he punished the natives harshly to make an example of them.

In addition to the threat of hostile Indians, the governor had other concerns as well. The Spanish government was very demanding. On behalf of the king, the viceroy required long reports about everything going on in Nuevo Santander. The crown would not keep paying its share of the costs for the province unless the governor could prove that the money was well spent.

In February and May of 1753, the Count of the Sierra Gorda sent the viceroy "reports on the condition of the twenty new towns in the Colony of the Seno Mexicano." He bragged about his province and told of the many cattle, horses, and mules there. He also wrote of progress with the Indians.

In his reports, don José was surprisingly honest. Although he stressed his successes, he did admit to some failures. He noted that the settlement of Camargo had to be moved because of flooding. He also said that there were still many "pagan [non-Christian] Indians" in Nuevo Santander. Because of this, some of his new settlements had to be set up to help protect others from the natives. And he admitted that the missionaries did not have enough money or supplies.

Unfortunately, when don José wrote about matters in Nuevo Santander, he did not send any proof to support his claims of success. He thought that his word was good enough. This made government officials in Mexico City most unhappy with him. So the viceroy ordered Escandón to prepare another report on his province. This time he must prove what he claimed.

The governor finished the report in 1755 and came to Mexico City to present it in person. As before, he bragged about the good land, abundant crops, and great number of livestock in Nuevo Santander. He also described many hardships, ranging from natural disasters to warlike natives.

Despite this, Escandón declared that three thousand natives had been "settled in missions" and introduced to Christianity. Even so, the governor was sad to report that other Indians had been turned away because of the lack of missionaries and supplies.

In his report, don José also talked about his belief that it was better for the colonists to share land than to divide it among them. This manner of ownership kept them from being jealous of each other. It also made them live and work together.

Escandón reported that twenty sites had been settled in Nuevo Santander with a total of 1,389 families. He said that his only goal in doing this had been to serve the crown. While declaring the conquest to be basically concluded, don José also advised that more remained to be done. To protect the new towns and colonists, other areas had to be populated. Care must be taken to prevent Indian rebellions.

Because the king was far away in Spain, he could not be sure that Escandón was making honest reports about Nuevo Santander. Remember that his enemies were saying bad things about him. So the crown wanted to know more about the "progress and present state" of the province. Specially appointed, trustworthy officials must be sent to find out the truth about Escandón's claims.

Acting on instructions from Spain, the viceroy ordered an inspection tour of Nuevo Santander. Captain José Tienda de Cuervo was named judge-inspector. Agustín López de la Cámara Alta, an engineer and army officer, was to help him. The two men had a list of questions to ask the colonists in order to gather information. They were also supposed to see for themselves what was happening in Nuevo Santander.

The inspectors traveled through the province and then reported back to the viceroy. They told of the twenty settlements in Nuevo Santander and gave detailed facts about the number of colonists and livestock there. The two officials confirmed that some of the towns and missions were promising, while others faced serious problems.

Tienda de Cuervo and López de la Cámara Alta said that much more needed to be done with the Native Americans. At some missions, not even one baptism had taken place. They believed that this was because missionaries were living in the towns with the Spaniards. The friars ought to be living among the Indians instead.

The inspectors also found fault with Escandón's policy about land ownership, because the colonists were unhappy about having to share land with others. They advised that land grants should be given to individual settlers. The two inspectors also reported that the crown was spending too much money on Nuevo Santander. They likewise came up with ideas for cutting costs, such as reducing military expenses, and made other suggestions for the province.

In the ten years following the inspection tour—from 1757 to 1767—José de Escandón was busy meeting the needs of his growing province. He was involved with a flood-control project, building a road, and moving some towns. The count also arranged for Fray Vicente de Santa María to write a history of Nuevo Santander.

Don José was allowed to found three more settlements from 1765–1770, but he refused to give individual land grants to the colonists. If they got their own lands, he thought that they would move into the country and desert the towns. He insisted that it was better for the colonists to share land and live together in towns for their safety.

Years earlier, as noted, the two inspectors had advised the crown to save money by cutting the number of soldiers and the pay of officers in Nuevo Santander. By 1763 the government had finally decided to make some of those changes. This upset don José. He opposed the proposed changes, because he felt they placed the province in danger. To save money in this way "sounds good," he admitted. But there were still many warlike natives in Nuevo Santander. Spain must be careful or she could lose "in a few months that which had been achieved in so many years, . . . only to save money."

The 1760s proved hard for José de Escandón in many ways. His wife, Josefa, died in 1762. She was the mother of his seven children. Also, the governor again found himself under attack by his enemies. Colonists were upset about land grants and other matters. They let the royal officials know that they were unhappy. At the same time, leaders in the Catholic Church blamed Escandón for lack of progress in converting Indians to Christianity.

In 1766 the viceroy ordered the governor to come to Mexico City to discuss these charges and other matters. To gather more information, the viceroy planned for still another inspection, called a *pesquisa*, of Escandón's province. Beginning the following year, the head inspector was Juan Fernando Palacio, who was assisted by José de Osorio y Llamas. They were to study the "conduct of Escandón" and find out the true state of affairs in Nuevo Santander.

Palacio was also told to divide the land among the settlers. He first did this with great ceremony at Laredo in May 1767 and then at other towns as the expedition went along. Water was important to settlers in Nuevo Santander. So land grants, called *porciones*, were made along the Río Grande. These grants bordered the river on one side. Larger amounts of land were given for grazing herds of animals. The officials also provided lands for missions in the province.

When they got back to Mexico City, the two inspectors declared that many of the charges against the count were unfair. They did agree that he had done some things wrong. For example, he should have created more settlements in Nuevo Santander. They seemed to forget that the count had been forced to come to Mexico City to defend himself, which kept him away from his province and prevented him from doing more.

The results of the inspection tour, together with years of complaints by his enemies, caused bad things to happen for José de Escandón. He was charged with thirty-eight separate crimes as governor of Nuevo Santander.

One of the charges was that the count had not fulfilled the goals he had promised to the Spanish crown. Furthermore, he had spent too much of the king's money in settling Nuevo Santander. Because he desperately wanted to attract colonists, don José had failed to check them out properly, which had allowed evil people to settle in the province. Escandón was also accused of getting wealth and power for himself by cheating the soldiers, settlers, and Indians. And he had ignored requests from the colonists for land grants.

The governor was also said to have abused the Indians. Instead of bringing them to the Christian God, don José had killed or imprisoned them. He was blamed for taking land from the Indians to give to the missionaries. He had also brought Native Americans, such as the Pames, far from their homes to work on his lands. Other natives had been forced to work in *obrajes*, or sweatshops, where workers were paid low wages and forced to work long hours under poor or dangerous conditions.

The above charges against don José teach us that the king of Spain expected officials in America to be honest in their dealings with settlers and natives alike. Officials were expected to obey and enforce Spanish laws, as well as Christianize the Indians. Failure to do any or all of these things could lead to trial and punishment.

Was don José guilty of the crimes discussed above? He and his family said no. But what would the court decide? It would take a long time to determine the answer to that question.

With the support of his family, the Count of Sierra Gorda worked hard to prove his innocence. He argued that he had spent more than fifty years serving Spain. He had done what he had promised, and much more. Instead of fourteen towns, Nuevo Santander by 1757 had twenty-two settlements with almost thirteen hundred Spanish families. These colonists were like other people in New Spain—some good, some bad.

Escandón's defense stated that he had worked for the crown for twenty years without pay, "with the sole hope of earning honors." Yes, he had done business in Nuevo Santander, but this was not illegal. Rather, it was a widely accepted way for officials to make a living, because they did not receive any direct salary from the king. Don José reminded the crown that he had spent much of his own money to explore and settle Nuevo Santander. His house, which his enemies called a palace, had been built at his own expense.

The defense also explained why Escandón had not awarded land titles to the colonists for so many years. He had been busy founding settlements and doing the other tasks of his office. He also feared that dividing the lands would cause unhappiness and jealousy, because not all were of equal value. Equally important, colonists granted lands far from settled areas would be in danger from Indians. So the governor chose to provide enough land for each settler, soldier, and Indian, with ownership in common.

As for the Indians, Escandón insisted that more than one thousand of them in Nuevo Santander had been baptized into the Catholic Church. The count had always used "quiet" or peaceful means in dealing with the natives when this was possible. Escandón insisted that the natives brought from Río Verde to Nuevo Santander were not forced to relocate. They did so willingly and were paid for their labor. As for the Indians who had been forced to work in sweatshops, they were being punished for making war and killing ten soldiers.

The defense also noted that great men were often the target of others who were jealous of them. These people made up lies about successful leaders, such as Escandón. Among these liars was María Bárbara Resendi. She called herself a defender of the Jaumave Indians and claimed that the governor abused them. None of this was true, argued the defense. In fact, doña Bárbara could not be a true protector for the Indians, "because she was a woman."

José de Escandón hoped to be found innocent of all thirty-eight counts against him, but he did not live to see the results of this massive *pesquisa*. As stated at the beginning of this chapter, the count died in September 1770 while the trial was still in progress. His death was doubly sad. A man who had spent his adult life capably serving the crown died under a cloud. If he was found guilty, his children might lose everything.

It fell to Escandón's family to finish the lawsuit. His first-born son, don Manuel, had to defend his father's name. He also had to convince the king that he should inherit his father's wealth, titles, and position.

Don Manuel's supporters said that he was loyal and loved the king. As José de Escandón's son, he had also served in the military in Nuevo Santander. He was noted for good conduct, military skills, and royal service. Don Manuel had helped to subdue the Indians and was a good choice to continue his father's work.

Finally, justice was done. In January 1773, a royal decree (formal order) completely cleared José de Escandón. He was found innocent of all charges. The king also named Manuel de Escandón as Count of Sierra Gorda with the right to govern Nuevo Santander.

José de Escandón y Elguera's province included part of Texas south of the Nueces River, as well as part of the present-day Mexican state of Tamaulipas. He founded twenty-three settlements in Nuevo Santander, and the Franciscans set up fifteen missions there. Two of Escandón's sites were in the present Lone Star State. The towns he started brought hundreds of colonists and their livestock to both sides of the Río Grande.

In Rio Grande City, Texas, a monument (written memorial) was erected to Escandón in 1936. It says that he was the "greatest colonizer of Northern Mexico" and that he "founded missions, opened roads and established settlers, 1746–1755."

There are people in South Texas today who belong to a club called the Las Porciones Society. Their ancestors were among the "first families" to come into Nuevo Santander with don José. These true pioneers of the region got land grants along the Río Grande in Starr, Hidalgo, and Cameron Counties.

To be sure, Escandón was not perfect. For years he would not let the early colonists have their own lands, but at the same time he took vast private lands for himself. Even though he had some faults, the count settled the Costa del Seno Mexicano (Gulf of Mexico). This was something that other Spaniards had not been able to do in more than two hundred years. In the process, José de Escandón helped to start both ranching and farming in modern-day South Texas. He died under a cloud of suspicion, but the sun shines today on a region the Father of South Texas helped to settle.

SOURCES

Materials used in preparing this chapter are described below. You can find more information about these sources in the Bibliography at the end of the book.

Books

The best account of Escandón and his accomplishments is found in Donald E. Chipman and Harriett Denise Joseph's *Notable Men and Women of Spanish Texas*. Also useful are Robert S. Weddle's *The French Thorn: Rival Explorers in the Spanish Sea, 1682–1762* and Lawrence F. Hill's *José de Escandón and the Founding of Nuevo Santander: A Study in Spanish Colonization*.

Quotes

Quotes in this chapter are from the following sources: Robert S. Weddle's *The French Thorn: Rival Explorers in the Spanish Sea, 1682–1762*; J. B. Wilkinson, *Laredo and the Rio Grande Frontier*; Auditor's Assessment of Escandón's Report, August 21, 1753, Béxar Archives Translations, Reel 4; Decreto de Agustín de Ahumada, March 29, 1756, and Escandón al Marqués de Cruillas, November 9, 1764, in *Estado general de las fundaciones hechas por D. José de Escandón en la colonia de Nuevo Santander*; Legal Proceedings Relating to José de Escandón, 1769–1773, and Statement of Domingo Valcarcel to Viceroy Bucareli, October 10, 1774, Center for American History, Austin, Hackett Transcripts; and Hubert J. Miller, *José de Escandón: Colonizer of Nuevo Santander*.

Athanase de Mézières
TROUBLED INDIAN AGENT

Early in life, Athanase de Mézières experienced loss and rejection. Following the death of his father, young Athanase's mother sent him from France to the French colony in Louisiana. He adapted remarkably well to life in America. Living with Indians, he allowed his entire body to be tattooed. This experience later made him a useful agent in the service of the French crown. However, in the 1760s the king of France gave Louisiana to Spain. At that time, Athanase de Mézières became an Indian agent for the Spanish crown on the Texas-Louisiana frontier. His familiarity with the natives, their languages and customs, and their lands proved valuable. At the same time, many Spaniards distrusted him because he was French, and they were jealous of his power. He spent much of his wealth and the last ten years of his life serving the Spanish in America. In doing so, don Athanase was an early example of multiculturalism. Studying his life teaches us about an exceptional man. We also learn about the complex relationships between the French, the Spanish, and the Indians in early Texas history.

Athanase de Mézières was born in Paris, France, in 1719. His father, Louis Christophe, died when the boy was about fifteen years of age. His mother, the attractive Marie de Mauget, quickly remarried to a handsome, rich nobleman. Wanting to be rid of the children from her first marriage, she sent her daughter to a convent and Athanase to a boarding school. She later declared her son "an undesirable subject" and exiled him to Louisiana in 1738.

From Louisiana, Athanase ventured up the Mississippi River to Canada. Presenting himself as an abandoned child, he lived among Indians who valued tattooing. During his four years with people he called "savages," De Mézières learned several native languages. At the same time, he was determined not to forget his European education. He wrote words and numbers on bark tablets and saved them with the greatest of care. When he was twenty-two, his Native American friends made him a chief.

He soon left them, however, to join the French army. Returning to Louisiana as a junior officer around 1742, De Mézières was stationed at Natchitoches. The commander there was Louis St. Denis. He and Athanase had important similarities. Both knew Indians and spoke some of their languages. Their family ties deepened when don Athanase married St. Denis's daughter in 1746. The De Mézières couple had a daughter that same year. Sadly, Athanase's wife died in 1748.

The young Frenchman soon became actively engaged in the Indian trade. His efforts earned him promotions in the 1750s, and he became lieutenant commander at Natchitoches. He also married a second time to a young woman from New Orleans. His new wife, Pelagie Fazende, gave birth to Athanase's first son in 1756, and the couple eventually had seven more children.

During the 1750s and 1760s, De Mézières's homeland of France became involved in a war with England. This Seven Years' War proved disastrous for France and her ally, Spain. Both nations lost valuable territory in America to England. The French king wanted to repay Spain for its losses. By a secret treaty (1762), he gave the Louisiana Territory west of the Mississippi River to King Charles III of Spain. In a separate and public treaty (1763), France's lands east of the Mississippi River were taken by the English.

French colonists living in Louisiana objected to their coming under Spanish rule, and it was hard for Charles III to gain control of this new territory. Spain and France had been allies in the Seven Years' War, but on earlier occasions, as we have noted, the two nations had been enemies. Finally, in August 1769, Alejandro O'Reilly and more than two thousand troops took possession of Louisiana in the name of Charles III.

Charles feared that English colonists east of the Mississippi River might eventually threaten Spanish claims to the lands west of the river. Hostile Apaches were another problem that Spain faced on the frontier. These natives raided civilian settlements and Catholic missions, stole horses and mules, and carried out other acts of revenge.

Important Indian groups also lived on both sides of the Red River, the boundary between Louisiana and Texas. These Nations of the North (Norteños) could be important allies to help Spain against her English and Apache enemies.

In the past, Norteños had relied on trade with the French and received gifts from them. At the same time, these Indians had been hostile to Spain. After the Seven Years' War, the Nations of the North found themselves living on Spanish soil as subjects of Charles III. Somehow, Spain had to persuade these natives to become allies rather than enemies.

Spain had used two major approaches in dealing with natives on the Texas frontier. The most common was the mission-presidio system. This method used Catholic missionaries who tried to Christianize and "civilize" the Indians. At times, Spain also used military force. Neither of these approaches had worked well with the Nations of the North. Spain needed to find better ways of dealing with these Native Americans. It was suggested that Spain could learn lessons from what had worked for the French in Louisiana.

Gradually, Spain developed a new Indian policy. It aimed at gaining the friendship of key tribes and keeping them hostile to foreigners. Royal officials would use trade to pressure the Norteños into cooperation, because these Native Americans wanted European goods, especially weapons. Spain could also turn some tribes against each other. While using Indians to its advantage, the Spanish crown would honor its promise to convert Native Americans to the Catholic faith.

How could Spain best accomplish its goals on the isolated northern frontier? When Alejandro O'Reilly took control of Louisiana, he ordered Athanase de Mézières to come to New Orleans to give "correct information regarding everything relating to your district." Impressed with the Frenchman, O'Reilly named him lieutenant governor of Natchitoches. So by 1769 De Mézières was a commissioned soldier (officer), a skillful trader, and a successful planter. He also owned about three dozen slaves, including some Indians. Don Athanase took his new appointment seriously. He helped get the people of Natchitoches to accept Charles III and Spanish rule. He enforced the law, took a census, and performed many other duties. In 1770 O'Reilly wrote about "the good opinion which I have formed of his [De Mézières's] personal conduct."

Not everyone approved of the Frenchman's activities, however. Some criticized him for doing too much; others, for doing too little. And he made enemies. Despite these obstacles, he served Charles III and was loyal to him for the next ten years.

De Mézières's greatest contributions to Spain involved his work with Indians such as the Nations of the North. O'Reilly told don Athanase to select and license traders. These men would exchange European goods with the friendly tribes for furs and crops. Spanish officials would copy the French practice of giving annual presents to the natives to win their loyalty. Don Athanase was assured that he would receive guns, blankets, and other gifts for the Indians of his district.

The lieutenant governor was determined to restore the "peace, so disturbed by the ferocious and numerous gentiles [non-Christian Indians] who surround us." He also knew that unfriendly tribes must be told that the French and Spanish were no longer enemies. De Mézières advised his superiors that war was not the best way to deal with the Nations of the North. He proposed better methods to gain the "love" and "gratitude" of the Norteños. Spain should use royal officials to influence the friendly chiefs, while cutting off supplies to warlike natives.

Early in 1770, don Athanase told two chiefs, named Tinhioüen and Cocay, that Charles III had chosen them as medal chiefs. This was a great honor. In a ceremony at Natchitoches, these leaders of the Kadohadacho and Yatasi nations each received a medal and a flag. For these gifts, they signed an agreement to give up their lands to the Spanish king. The chiefs vowed to love, respect, and obey Charles III. They also agreed to help keep the peace and not give military supplies to enemy tribes.

De Mézières worked closely with the friendly chiefs like Tinhioüen, also called Bigotes (Whiskers). The Frenchman used them to arrange a meeting with the leaders of some hostile tribes. Don Athanase hoped to convince these Native Americans to go to San Antonio and meet with the governor of Texas, the Barón de Ripperdá.

To do this, don Athanase needed gifts to persuade the chiefs to cooperate. He asked Governor Ripperdá for goods, ranging from flags to muskets to mirrors. De Mézières said that he would pay for the presents out of his own pocket to serve God and his new king.

Don Athanase waited at Natchitoches for official permission to proceed with his plan. While he waited, three friendly caciques (chiefs) came to that post with many followers. They wanted to take the Frenchman to a site where heads of the enemy nations were waiting. De Mézières decided to proceed without formal orders from his governor.

He took soldiers from forts at Natchitoches and Los Adaes with him. A Catholic missionary named Father Miguel de Santa María y Silva also went on the expedition. The party crossed the lands of various Indian tribes to reach San Luis de Cadodachos. Seven chiefs of the hostile Taovayas, Tawakonis, Yscanis, and Kichais were waiting there to negotiate. Some had come great distances to talk with the Indian agent.

At San Luis in October 1770, Athanase de Mézières delivered a forceful speech. He informed the Indians that Louisiana now belonged to Spain rather than to France. And he assured the chiefs that Charles III would grant them peace if they deserved it. But, if not, the armies of the most powerful king in the world would fall upon them. The choice was theirs.

The enemy leaders defended their past actions. They complained that Spain had aided other natives who were the worst enemies of the Nations of the North. This had created bad feelings between the Norteños and the Spaniards. Those problems, however, were in the past. The chiefs insisted that they now desired peace.

De Mézières replied that Texas had been the scene of many outrages committed by the Norteños. He asked the caciques to go with him to San Antonio and beg forgiveness from Governor Ripperdá, but the Indians were suspicious and feared a trap. Because they would not cooperate, he refused to give them the gifts he had brought.

When he returned to Natchitoches, don Athanase reported these events to his superior officer, Governor Luis de Unzaga. The Frenchman admitted that his methods for peace had not yet worked. He stressed, however, that the Indians had agreed to meet with him again in the spring. The French officer also wrote of the fierce Comanches, who were "so skillful in horsemanship that they have no equal; so daring that they never ask for or grant truces." To defeat them, he said, would be "costly and difficult." So he planned to create conflicts between the Comanches and other Indian nations.

Even though Athanase de Mézières was working to the best of his ability for his new king, he had enemies among the Spaniards. Perhaps they distrusted the lieutenant governor because he was French, or maybe they were jealous of his power and position. In one case, a sergeant complained that relations with the Nations of the North had actually become worse and blamed the French agent. The soldier claimed that the Indians were angry at not receiving the gifts De Mézières had promised. Father Santa María y Silva also charged that the October expedition would result in "graver insults" from the natives. Others criticized Don Athanase for giving special treatment to his young sons, who were cadets at Natchitoches.

Why were the Frenchman's sons cadets at Natchitoches? To carry out his duties as lieutenant governor and Indian agent was expensive. De Mézières had debts and had to sell his plantation and slaves to pay his bills. After doing that, he could not support his sons at home. So Alejandro O'Reilly had agreed to allow them to be cadets at the Natchitoches fort where their father was stationed. That way, the sons would have food, clothing, and shelter. They would also be near their father.

Don Athanase admitted that he had been made "a little depressed" by those who criticized him, but he would not resign. Instead, he promised to serve honorably the king and the Spanish nation.

Fortunately for don Athanase, Governor Unzaga paid little attention to unfavorable rumors about his Indian agent. He gave the Frenchman his full support. However, the governor of Louisiana insisted that "boys under the protection of their parents and not subject to the discipline . . . of the army become effeminate [sissies] and useless for military service."

With don Athanase under personal attack, the Barón de Ripperdá continued efforts to pacify the Norteños. He sent gifts to Chief Bigotes of the Hasinais, who convinced four other caciques to make peace with the Spaniards.

With Bigotes's help, De Mézières organized a "peace party" in 1771 to invite the Norteño chiefs to come to Natchitoches. The caciques of the Yscanis, Tawakonis, Kichais, and Cahinnios accepted the invitation. Treaties were signed. The European and Indian leaders wrapped themselves in the same Spanish flag as a sign of unity. Don Athanase presented gifts to the four cooperative chiefs. Bigotes then went to San Antonio, where Governor Ripperdá also gave his approval to the treaties.

Still, complaints about De Mézières continued. Nevertheless, both Governor Unzaga and Barón de Ripperdá were impressed with the Frenchman's skills in pacifying the Native Americans. And the lieutenant governor continued to prove his capabilities.

In late October 1771, the French officer signed a treaty with the Taovayas. These natives (Wichitas) also claimed to speak for their friends, the Comanches. The Taovayas promised to stop attacking Spanish forts and accepted responsibility for the good behavior of the Comanches. As proof of their word, the Taovayas publicly buried a hatchet. Anyone who used it again would die. Don Athanase joined other officials in signing this treaty with the Taovayas. By the end of the year, he also reached an agreement with Gorgoritos, medal chief of the Bidais.

Despite these alliances, the situation on the frontier remained unstable. Royal officials did not know if they could trust the promises of their former enemies. Rumors also spread that the warlike Apaches were trying to undermine Spanish relations with other tribes. Other alarming reports stated that some of the treaty nations had been in communication with the English. This, of course, was absolutely forbidden.

Once again, the Spanish chose De Mézières to negotiate with the Indians. Accompanied by interpreters and a small troop of soldiers, he left Natchitoches in March 1772. On an expedition that lasted for months, he made contact with several key tribes. Don Athanase strengthened their commitment to Spain and investigated rumors of an English threat.

The French agent noted that the Tonkawas were nomadic Indians with no fixed homes. They had little interest in "instruction and civilization." Don Athanase concluded that these Indians would never change their ways. Only through fear of their enemies would they accept peace.

De Mézières said that the Comanches also had no fixed homes. They lived in continual motion in many small bands. Comanches would rather lose their lives than lose their liberty. Interestingly, they adopted their captives and were disgusted with other natives who feasted on human flesh. De Mézières believed that because the Comanches were divided into so many small bands, it would be easier to conquer them if necessary. He hoped that they would someday live in "fixed settlements" and become farmers.

As the French officer continued his journey from one tribe to another, friendly Indians joined him. Don Athanase and seventy natives reached San Antonio in June. At a formal ceremony, several chiefs did a feather dance as a sign of peace and wrapped Governor Ripperdá in buffalo skins.

At this time, De Mézières offered to lead a military campaign in the spring against the increasingly hostile Apaches. He proposed inviting the Nations of the North to participate. The Frenchman offered to supply them with weapons at his own expense. Ripperdá approved of the plan and sent it to the viceroy in Mexico City. Nothing could be done without that official's approval.

The reaction in Mexico City was negative. The *fiscal* was an important legal adviser to the viceroy. This official strongly opposed giving guns and ammunition even to friendly Indians. There was also the danger that hostile natives might become involved in this trade and acquire Spanish weapons. These enemies could then find themselves armed and powerful enough to make war on Spain's settlers. The *fiscal* thought that the Indians should be given tools of agriculture rather than weapons of war.

As for Viceroy Antonio María de Bucareli, he feared that a war with the Apaches would make the situation in Texas even worse. A council of war should make the final decision. In the meantime, De Mézières should return to his post in Louisiana.

Back in Natchitoches, the French officer learned that several Apache chiefs were on their way to the Bidais and Kadohadachos to make a treaty. Don Athanase ruthlessly sent orders for a medal chief named Sauto to kill these enemies of Spain. The cacique followed his brutal instructions. Sauto murdered three Apache leaders who had accepted the hospitality of his own home!

Meanwhile, Luis de Unzaga had increasing suspicions about don Athanase's effectiveness as an Indian agent. He hired a spy to report on the Frenchman's activities. The informant, José de la Peña, claimed that the lieutenant governor had lied about his "great doings." Peña also charged De Mézières with trying to prevent unfavorable reports about him from reaching Governor Ungaza.

Perhaps to escape from this hostile environment, De Mézières asked the Spanish crown for permission to visit Europe. Giving business and health as his reasons for making the trip, he received a passport in April 1773. The Frenchman spent nearly a year in Europe and acquired the rank of lieutenant colonel from the king of Spain. During a visit to France, don Athanase displayed his tattoos. He had flowers imprinted on his chest and arms, as well as snakes on his legs. The sight of a Frenchman with these designs on his body astonished his upper-class family and friends.

Athanase de Mézières
shows off his tattoos in Paris
(DRAWING BY JACK JACKSON)

When De Mézières returned to America in 1774, he was still the object of rumors and suspicion. However, don Athanase enjoyed the support of Charles III. The king was concerned about reports of trade between the "savage" nations and the English. He expressed confidence in the French officer's ability to stop the illegal trade.

The treaty chiefs clearly regarded Lieutenant Colonel De Mézières as the man with whom they should deal. Upon his return from Europe, they visited Natchitoches to assure him of their pledge to peace and harmony.

Don Athanase's ability to work effectively with the Indians was complicated by many problems over which he had no control. As an example, Louisiana and Texas belonged to different governmental units, even though both were part of the Spanish empire. Louisiana was under the direct authority of a royal official stationed in Cuba. The province of Texas was part of a vast area known as New Spain. The viceroy in Mexico City was the chief official in America with control over New Spain, and thus over Texas.

Rules for dealing with Indians differed from one province to another. When the Spanish crown acquired Louisiana, for example, it decided to continue the French practice of legal trade with Indians in that province. But trade with Native Americans in Texas was not permitted.

Matters got more complicated when the viceroy reacted to negative reports about questionable activities on the frontier. It was charged that De Mézières in Louisiana and Governor Ripperdá in Texas were making personal profits from trade with Indians, not all of which were legal. So in the mid-1770s, the viceroy ordered De Mézières not to have any contact with the governor of Texas. Similarly, Ripperdá received orders to "cut off communication" with the French in Louisiana.

Don Athanase was very upset over these instructions. The Nations of the North did not confine themselves to just one province or the other. They lived and operated on both sides of the Red River. These restrictions on royal officials made it difficult for De Mézières to carry out his duties.

Don Athanase's problems were not limited to his work as an Indian agent and royal official. In 1777 a severe epidemic hit Natchitoches. Among the dead were the Frenchman's wife, one son, and perhaps another child. The lieutenant governor, who never remarried after this, was left a single parent with several children. The epidemic, possibly smallpox, killed many Native Americans as well.

Ironically, at this time of great personal loss things began to go better for De Mézières in his career as a Spanish Indian agent. In 1776–1777 major changes occurred in Spain's American empire. Bernardo de Gálvez became governor of Louisiana. He encouraged liberal trade policies that allowed don Athanase a freer hand in Indian matters.

More important, the northern provinces of New Spain became part of a new governmental unit known as the Interior Provinces. This included Texas. Teodoro de Croix was appointed commandant general of the Interior Provinces, which were now almost independent of the viceroy in Mexico City. Croix also removed many restrictions that had caused problems for officials like De Mézières. All of this made it easier for the Frenchman to do his job.

In Texas, Governor Ripperdá reported to the new commandant general about his problems with Native Americans. The Comanches and Apaches posed serious threats. Croix knew that many tribes of Indians lived in the Interior Provinces. Some were friendly, but others were not.

The new commandant general asked for advice on Indian matters. He called for a council of war to be held at Monclova in northern Mexico. Officers with "highest rank, longest experience, and greatest knowledge" of Indian affairs attended this meeting in December 1777. Croix asked them if Spain should ally itself with the Lipan Apaches to make war on the Comanches and Nations of the North. But he also asked whether it would be wiser to do the opposite—join with the Comanches and Nations of the North to make war on the Apaches. He was open to either possibility!

The men at the Monclova council advised that Spain make war on the Lipan Apaches, because these Native Americans were not to be trusted. Besides, the Northern Nations and the Comanches were believed to be more numerous and more powerful, and they were already enemies of the Apaches.

Members of the Monclova council had no personal knowledge of the Nations of the North. So they suggested that a second war council be held at San Antonio and a third at Chihuahua. Afterward, a final decision based on information from the three meetings could be made.

The second war council began in San Antonio in early 1778. Delegates agreed that peace treaties with the "lying" Lipans were useless. They also said that De Mézières's treaties had improved relations with the Norteños. These agreements, however, did not include the Comanches. The San Antonio group suggested that Croix have don Athanase come to San Antonio without delay. The Frenchman would know the best way to get an alliance of other Indian tribes against the Apaches.

Lieutenant Colonel De Mézières arrived in San Antonio by February 1778. He studied the secret records of the second war council and prepared a report for the commandant general. According to the Frenchman, trade conducted from Louisiana was important to ensure the friendship of the Indians. If trade did not win over the Comanches, however, he thought Spain should use arms.

Don Athanase stressed the need for secrecy in organizing a military campaign against the Apaches. He wrote a carefully detailed plan. It proposed to use more than a thousand warriors recruited from the treaty nations. Three hundred Spanish soldiers would also participate. A combined military force from the Interior Provinces and Louisiana should be used to show the unity and cooperation of all Spanish subjects.

De Mézières then traveled among tribes along the Trinity, Brazos, and Red Rivers. He wrote detailed accounts of his meetings with the natives, which he sent to the commandant general. Among the groups De Mézières visited were the Taovayas, a settled people of Wichita Indians who lived on both sides of the Red River. Don Athanase gave them gifts in Croix's name. They, in return, gave up two bronze cannons that had been abandoned years earlier by a Spanish expedition.

Don Athanase was unhappy to learn that the Taovayas had ten Spanish captives from New Mexico, which they had bought from the Comanches. The prisoners, of course, begged for freedom. Despite their pleas, the French officer did not try to pay ransom for their release. He believed that this would only encourage the Indians to take more Spanish captives. He could not lose sight of his major goal—to get the Taovayas to ally with Spain against the Apaches.

De Mézières learned that the Comanches had been raiding and killing Spaniards in Texas. He therefore refused to negotiate directly with them at that time. He sent word that if the Comanche leaders sincerely desired peace, he would meet with them at another time.

Croix was pleased with don Athanase's reports of his travels among the Indians. The commandant general also appreciated the Frenchman's energetic efforts and good judgment. But he waited until the third war council met before making his reply.

While secret plans for making war against the Apache were underway, other important events were occurring. Domingo Cabello y Robles was appointed governor of Texas to replace Barón de Ripperdá. It would take time, however, for Cabello to travel to Texas from his post in Nicaragua.

The third war council at Chihuahua suggested that don Athanase should return immediately to San Antonio. The Frenchman should replace Ripperdá until Cabello arrived. Croix agreed that don Athanase should serve as interim (temporary) governor of Texas. His "knowledge, practical experience, zeal, and conduct might contribute much to the success" of the commandant general's overall Indian policy.

De Mézières received orders to proceed immediately to San Antonio, but he chose not to do so. He claimed that the rivers he would have to cross were at flood stage. In truth, he probably hesitated to leave his children and his friends. He actually attempted to go to New Orleans to plead his cause before Governor Bernardo de Gálvez. Unfortunately, Don Athanase suffered an accident and had to return to Natchitoches. However, he wrote the governor and asked to remain under his command rather than go to Texas. If he did have to go there, he asked permission to take his sons with him.

In the meantime, Cabello arrived in San Antonio in the fall of 1778 to assume the office of governor. This meant that De Mézières would not have to hurry to Texas. In the following year, don Athanase asked Bernardo de Gálvez to approve still another visit to the Norteños. Among his reasons was a desire to contact the Comanches who were interfering with trade in Louisiana and Texas. The lieutenant colonel asked for goods from New Orleans to give as presents to the Indians.

Governor Bernardo de Gálvez granted don Athanase's requests. He provided muskets, hatchets, glass beads, tobacco, and other gifts. The governor also sent equipment and supplies for the Spanish troops that were to accompany the Frenchman.

Weather conditions and swollen rivers delayed the proposed expedition to the Indians. When it did depart, the lieutenant colonel learned that colonists in East Texas needed help. The new town of Nacogdoches was poorly defended. Settlers there were afraid of the

Comanches and other natives. Heading to Nacogdoches, don Athanase had a serious accident near the Attoyac River. His horse pitched him down the side of a steep hill. He had "such a shock . . . that fever, delirium, and other symptoms resulted." His condition became so grave that servants carried him back to Natchitoches on a stretcher. Experiencing two serious accidents in a matter of months took a toll on don Athanase's health.

After two months in bed, De Mézières improved enough to complete the journey to Nacogdoches. Arriving there, he scolded the settlers for being cowardly, and he showed little sympathy for their situation. Continuing on his way to San Antonio, the French agent distributed many gifts to Kichai, Tonkawa, and Tawakoni Indians.

The new governor of Texas was unhappy about the arrival of De Mézières and his party. Domingo de Cabello complained about the cost of providing food and housing for don Athanase and the Native Americans who accompanied him. At church services, don Domingo placed a chair next to his for don Athanase. The governor also provided medicines, because De Mézières suffered from a serious case of diarrhea and a sexually transmitted disease.

Despite ill health, the French officer tried to carry on his duties. He sent a forceful letter to Teodoro de Croix. Perhaps De Mézières's words were so strong because he realized that he had only a few more days to live.

Don Athanase wrote about the province of Texas. He asked why so little progress had been made there. Then he answered his own question: It was laziness on the part of the settlers. He warned that the English posed a serious threat, one that Texas was ill-prepared to meet. The sick man warned the commandant general not to be blind to the discouraging situation in Texas, because it placed Spain's interests at risk. His own desire, De Mézières insisted, was for the whole of Texas to be prosperous and happy.

On October 12, 1779, don Athanase received word that he been appointed to replace Cabello as governor of Texas. The French officer had little desire for the position. Writing to Croix, he begged to be excused. He claimed to be unfit and inexperienced for that office. He was also in poor health and had no money. Don Athanase insisted that his experience could best be used in Louisiana. Besides, he wanted to return to his family in Natchitoches. If Croix insisted, De Mézières would "sacrifice his own views and his personal comfort" in order to do what the commandant general ordered. In that event, his family should be brought safely to San Antonio. He asked Croix to provide protection for his sons, the youngest of whom was only twelve.

De Mézières never assumed the office of governor of Texas. His health declined rapidly. The Frenchman was "overcome with . . . a strong melancholy [sadness], knowing that he was dying." He wrote out his will, but he had little to leave to his family.

Don Athanase also penned a final letter to Teodoro de Croix. It was in his native language of French, because he was so ill that he could no longer think or write in Spanish. The Frenchman stated that he had only debts to leave his daughters. The debts were the result of his journeys on behalf of the Spanish crown. Don Athanase asked the commandant general to arrange for his two daughters to receive a military pension.

Athanase de Mézières received the Catholic sacraments and died at one o'clock in the afternoon on November 2, 1779. He was buried the next day at the parish church of San Antonio for a cost of five dollars.

Croix was saddened by the death of this remarkable Frenchman who he felt had such "excellent" qualities. He took steps to secure a pension for the Frenchman's daughters, and he arranged for the cadet sons to be placed in a frontier presidio.

Athanase de Mézières was an exceptional individual. Despite the death of his father and rejection by his mother, this Frenchman had a productive life in America. Because he was French-born, his loyalty to his new king and country were often questioned. But he never let these or other obstacles defeat him.

Tattooed don Athanase served the Spanish crown for a decade. He willingly faced the challenges of being a military officer and Indian agent on the Texas-Louisiana frontier. He recognized the importance of trade and gifts in winning the allegiance of Native Americans. De Mézières was also a practical man. He knew the Spanish could use peaceful approaches with some tribes. He thought other tribes must be dealt with by using military strength. And he was ruthless when he considered it necessary.

Twice a widower, De Mézières did his best as a single parent to care for his children. However, his duties as an official on the Spanish frontier often took him away from his family and put him in debt. Before he died, he tried to provide for his children's future.

By studying the life of this Frenchman who dealt with Native Americans for the Spanish crown, we learn about Texas and Louisiana in the colonial period. There are also valuable lessons about one man's ability to make the best of any situation that faced him.

SOURCES

Materials used in preparing this chapter are described below. You can find more information about these sources in the Bibliography at the end of the book.

Books

The most important collection of documents and letters relating to De Mézières is found in *Athanase de Mézières and the Louisiana-Texas Frontier, 1768–1780*, edited and translated by Herbert E. Bolton. A more complete biographical treatment of the Troubled Indian Agent may be found in Donald E. Chipman and Harriett Denise Joseph's *Notable Men and Women of Spanish Texas*, which draws heavily on the contents of Bolton's two-volume work.

Quotes

Quotes in this chapter are from the following sources: Betje B. Klier, "Théodore Pavie" (unpublished manuscript in the possession of the authors); Herbert E. Bolton, editor and translator, *Athanase de Mézières and the Louisiana-Texas Frontier, 1768–1780*; Lawrence Kinnaird, editor, *Spain in the Mississippi Valley, 1765–1794: Translations of Materials from the Spanish Archives in the Bancroft Library*; Juan Agustín Morfi, *History of Texas, 1673–1779*, translated and edited by Carlos E. Castañeda; and Cabello to Croix, November 12, 1779, Béxar Archives Translations, Reel 11.

CHAPTER TWELVE

Domingo Cabello
COMANCHE PEACEMAKER

Because Texas was located on a distant frontier that included Indians who did not wish to share the land with Spaniards, its governors were always military men. They carried the rank of lieutenant colonel or full colonel in the Spanish army. This high rank meant that colonial governors had started their military careers outside of Texas. For the most part, they were born in Spain and entered the army as teenage cadets.

Being governor of Texas was a difficult job that carried many responsibilities. San Antonio in the late 1700s was also not a very attractive place to live, especially for army officers who had lived in Spain or more settled parts of the Spanish empire in America. This chapter looks at Domingo Cabello, who was governor for eight years in the 1770s and 1780s. Those years were important ones for Texas.

During that time, Cabello spent much of his time handling problems that Spain had with Native Americans in Texas. His main worries were the Karankawas and Comanches. Often he could not deal with these Indians as he might have wished, because Spain was at war with Great Britain during the American Revolution (1776–1783). His king ordered him to overlook problems with Native Americans, because Texas needed to support the more important war in Europe and America. This meant providing Texas beef for Spanish troops who were fighting the English along the lower Mississippi River. It also meant trying to keep peace with Native Americans by ignoring their attacks on Spaniards.

As you read about Domingo Cabello, keep in mind that he did not like being governor of Texas or living at San Antonio. But did this mean that he would not do a good job for his king and country?

When the Spanish crown appointed Domingo Cabello as governor of Texas, he was fifty-three years of age. He began life in the Spanish city of León around the year 1725 and entered the army as a teenager in 1741. Over the next thirty-seven years, don Domingo earned the ranks of first lieutenant, major, lieutenant colonel, and colonel. Most of his fighting as a soldier came on the island of Cuba, where he suffered a leg wound. Later, the British captured Cabello and made him a prisoner of war for about a year.

Before coming to Texas as its governor in 1778, don Domingo had served as governor of Nicaragua for a period of twelve years. There he dealt with problems the Spanish had with Indians in Central America. Caribs and Mosquitos particularly angered Cabello. These Indians raided the villages of peaceful Native Americans, burned their houses, and sold them as slaves to English woodcutters on the coast of Honduras. As a result of his experiences, don Domingo came to distrust all Indians, even those who lived peacefully in missions. Like most military men, Cabello saw force as the only way to bring Native Americans under Christian and Spanish control.

Cabello liked being governor of Nicaragua and did not want to leave there to take up his duties at San Antonio. He was a good soldier, however, and followed the orders of his king. When he arrived in Texas, the new governor described himself as "robust" (strong and healthy).

Domingo Cabello began his eight-year term of office in October 1778. His first serious problem had to do with Karankawa Indians. Less than a year before, the governor of Louisiana had sent a Spanish ship along the Gulf Coast toward Texas. The ship's captain, Luis Antonio Andry, carried instructions to explore the coast and make a map of it as far west as Matagorda Bay.

On board *El Señor de la Yedra* were a dozen crew members and Andry's son, who was only twelve years of age. This must have seemed like high adventure to the young cadet! One of the adults on board had lived in Texas and served there as a soldier. Another was a young Maya Indian named Tomás.

The ship had little trouble reaching Matagorda Bay, and the mapping had gone smoothly. Unfortunately, the men had eaten most of the provisions on the *Yedra*. A hunting party of five led by the former Texas soldier went ashore in hopes of killing fresh game. These men were hardly out of sight before they were set upon by Karankawas and killed.

As time passed, Captain Andry became worried about the missing sailors and there was even less food on board. Hoping the men would respond, he fired off a small cannon and raised a flag. Instead, two Karankawa Indians named Joseph María and Mateo appeared on shore. Both Indians spoke some Spanish, because they had lived for a time at a nearby mission. They asked to be brought aboard the vessel, and Andry sent a small boat to pick them up.

The Indians asked Andry to send three men back to shore with them and promised to return with fresh meat. The captain agreed. When the Spaniards disappeared from view, the Karankawas set upon them and murdered them, too. This left Andry with a crew of only five, including his young son.

In a short while, Joseph María and Mateo again appeared on shore and asked to be brought aboard the vessel. This time they brought freshly killed deer meat, and they informed Andry that his three men had stayed ashore to feast on a recent game kill. As the starved captain and his skeleton crew sat down to eat, they did not notice other Karankawa warriors as they slipped aboard the vessel. On signal, the Indians seized the sailors' guns and murdered them with their own weapons, sparing only the young Maya Indian. Joseph María claimed him as a slave.

Later, a friendly priest was able to gain the freedom of the Maya. Tomás traveled to San Antonio, where he described the murder of the ship's crew to Governor Cabello. The young Indian also added grisly details about the death of Captain Andry and his son, as well as the destruction of the Spanish vessel. The Karankawas killed the captain with daggers, followed by his cadet son as he clung to his father's body. They then stripped the ship of its guns, threw the dead Spaniards in the bay, and burned the vessel.

Armed with Spanish guns, the Karankawas began a bloody rampage along the lower Río Grande. To increase their numbers, they encouraged the Indians at Mission Rosario to take flight and join them.

One of the mission residents was the elderly mother of Joseph María and Mateo. When the poor woman could not keep up with the other Indians from Rosario, Joseph María stabbed his mother with a spear and left her to die along a trail!

When Governor Cabello learned of these awful events, he asked permission to make all-out war on the Karankawas. Those Indians had become so bold that they left the coast and even raided near the very outskirts of San Antonio. But don Domingo was told that he could not wage war on the Karankawas. For one thing, he did not have the military strength to do so, and for another, the war with the English was more important. Joseph María and Mateo could not be punished.

Cabello had learned just how weak Texas was when he was in his early days as governor. On January 20, 1779, a party of four hundred friendly but fully armed Indians came to San Antonio. Don Domingo had only two soldiers at the Béxar presidio, and both were sick. All of the others were on assignments: ten were out scouting; twenty were accompanying the former governor out of Texas; another twenty guarded a new settlement of Spaniards near San Antonio; and twenty-four guarded more than a thousand horses at a distant pasture.

To deal with the Indians, Cabello relied on his long military experience. He boldly told the Indians that they were welcome at Béxar but could not bring their weapons into the town. His bluff worked. The Indians filed into San Antonio's town square "without a bow or arrow, a gun or rifle, a tomahawk, or scalping knife." Don Domingo then gave them food, candy, and cigarettes, and they left with no one hurt.

The whole experience, however, left the new governor shaken. He wrote that the idea of a "friendly Indian" was a joke, and that even Indians at San Antonio's five missions could not be trusted. He said that Indians would only behave themselves if they were given gifts or feared punishment for their misdeeds. Once again, Cabello had great difficulty accepting the idea that Spaniards could trust Native Americans. He urged that Texas be given enough soldiers and guns to make the Indians accept Spanish rule and the Christian religion. His views of Indians were the same as those of most other military men of that time.

As Spain's involvement in war with the English increased,

Domingo Cabello found it impossible to build up the military strength of Texas. Instead, problems with Indians actually got worse. Native Americans recognized that their attacks on Spanish ranchers and other civilians went unpunished, and they became even bolder.

Worse, from Cabello's point of view, the governor of New Mexico formed an alliance with Ute Indians and Jicarilla Apaches. In 1779, don Domingo's first year on the job as governor of Texas, the Comanches suffered a huge defeat in New Mexico. As it turned out, this was bad news for Cabello and Texas. These powerful Plains Indians then turned their attacks on the Spanish in Texas, because it was a weaker province than New Mexico.

In August 1780, one year later, Cabello reported that Texas was overrun with Comanches. The Indians had stolen so many horses and mules from the Béxar presidio that he could not carry out military campaigns against them. His superiors in Mexico recognized that their settlements in Texas were in serious trouble but could offer no help. They informed don Domingo that he must overlook attacks by Indians and not try to punish them. Instead, the Comanches and other Indians were to be shown the benefits of peace by giving them gifts. For a military man like Cabello who believed punishment to be the best solution to all problems with Indians, this was hard to accept. Don Domingo kept as many soldiers armed and ready to fight Indians as he could put in the field.

Throughout 1781, Comanche raids on Spanish settlements in Texas increased almost day by day, and week by week. On one occasion, Cabello learned that Comanches had been spotted on the Medina River near San Antonio. He rounded up his soldiers and sent them to attack the Indian camp, believed to contain about eighty people. A furious fight lasting for several hours followed. At the end of it, eighteen Comanche warriors and their chief lay dead. The chief must have been a important one, because he wore a headdress made of horns and a shirt with Spanish scalps attached to it. In the Comanche camp, Spanish soldiers found clothing and jewelry belonging to settlers in the Béxar area—clear evidence that these Comanches were raiders.

Comanches were known to get even for raids on their camps, and Spaniards at San Antonio feared attacks against them. Signs of Comanches were apparent, such as smoke signals in the distance and tracks of their ponies, but there were no raids on Béxar itself. It fact, almost a year went by with no actual sightings of Comanches. It seems that these Indians suffered terribly from huge outbreaks of smallpox that killed hundreds of men, women and children in 1782. They could no longer brag, as they had to Athanase de Mézières, that their numbers were greater than the stars.

Smallpox was especially deadly to Native Americans because they had no immunity (natural defenses) against the disease. On the other hand, smallpox was not nearly as deadly to Europeans. It was a disease with a long history in Europe, and people such as Spaniards had much less need to worry about dying from it. Over the centuries, parents and grandparents had survived smallpox and passed on some immunity to the next generation. It was also at this time that some of the first experiments in vaccinating humans were taking place in Europe.

For whatever reason, the Comanches remained quiet throughout 1782. Peaceful relations with them ended in the spring of the following year. Governor Cabello learned that a large Comanche camp had been sighted on the Guadalupe River. Once again, don Domingo rounded up soldiers and marched to the Guadalupe. In this case, Comanche scouts spotted the Spanish, and so the Indians fled their *ranchería* (encampment), leaving behind the frames of forty tepees. Fearing revenge, Cabello ordered an alert for San Antonio. Just as before, there were signs of Comanches but no attacks by these plainsmen.

Another fifteen months passed. Then in the summer of 1784, violence again broke out between Spaniards and Indians. While chasing Wichita Indian raiders, a company of presidio soldiers came upon forty mounted and armed Comanches on the Guadalupe River. When the smoke of an eight-hour battle cleared, ten Comanche warriors lay dead, and an equal number had been captured. As before, Governor Cabello warned settlers at San Antonio to be especially careful. But just as before, there were no attacks by Comanches.

While all of these incidents were taking place, Domingo Cabello had tried to make peace with the Comanches by sending agents among them. Although this was not what he preferred to do as a military man, he had been ordered by his superiors in Mexico to try this approach. In the long run it worked, although it took five years to pull it off.

As early as 1780, Cabello sent agents who were skilled in Indian languages into Comanche lands. These efforts, however, had little success until the late summer of 1784. From that time onward, events moved quickly toward peace with the Comanches. Don Domingo's agents understood Comanche languages and customs much better than at first. Spain was also no longer at war with England, thanks to the Treaty of Paris in 1783, which ended the war for independence of the United States.

The first of Cabello's agents to score success among the Comanches was Juan Bautista Bousquet, a trader from Louisiana. Bousquet visited Wichita Indians and carried the message that Spaniards wanted peace with them. His words were believed by Wichita and Taovaya chiefs, and four of them traveled with Bousquet to San Antonio, where they met with Cabello. Don Domingo gave small gifts to all the Indian leaders, and a medal to the most important of the Taovaya chiefs, a man named Guersec.

Traveling with Bousquet were three non-Indians who had successfully traded among the Norteños. The most important of the trio was French-born Pedro Vial. Vial spoke only a little broken Spanish and knew little about the Comanches, but he would soon be a vital key for Cabello as Texas's Comanche Peacemaker.

Don Domingo gave Vial many gifts for Comanche chiefs and sent him back to the north. With the governor's new agent went a companion named Francisco Xavier Chávez and the medal chief, Guersec. Guersec guided Vial and Chávez to a huge Comanche *ranchería*. This camp had a large meeting tent of tanned buffalo hides and more than two hundred warriors. But these numbers of Comanches were small when compared to what the Spaniards would face within a week.

The Comanches told Vial and Chávez to remain at their camp until they could bring two of their high chiefs to meet them. During that time, the two white men crammed their heads full of information about the Comanches. They learned more of the Comanche language and culture and how to give gifts that matched the importance of an Indian leader.

At the end of a week, two high Comanche chiefs came to the big buffalo-hide tent. Vial called them "Capitán de Camisa de Hierro" (Captain Iron Shirt) and "Capitán de Cabeza Rapada" (Captain Shaved Head). The Indian leaders were so named because one wore a chain mail upper garment, which he claimed to have taken from a dead Apache chief. The second had no hair on one side of his head and very long hair on the other side.

Vial approached the high Comanche chiefs and about a dozen

"little captains" who traveled with them. The French-born agent drew on what he had recently learned about Comanche customs. He gave each of the chiefs gifts of tobacco, knives, vermilion (red dye), and other items that were in keeping with their rank. All were impressed that a white person could know so much about them. Vial's cram course on Comanche culture had armed him with knowledge that was extremely useful.

The Comanches then led Vial and Chávez to a nearby gathering of their people, where the agents stood at the center of hundreds of Native Americans who formed rings around them as far as their eyes could see. Vial began talking, and all listened. Although he spoke in the Taovaya language, which he knew much better than Comanche, the Indians understood him perfectly. Comanches and Taovayas had long been allies and learned how to speak each other's languages.

Vial reminded his audience that he and Chávez were not strangers to them. Years ago, the Comanches had captured Chávez but later sold him to the Taovayas. When his Indian owner died, Chávez became a free man. At that time he had traveled to San Antonio to be with his own people. Vial, on the other hand, had visited Comanche *rancherías* for many years as a trader.

Vial reminded the Comanches that he and Chávez were good and honest people who had always treated them fairly. While living among Indians, the two traders had first learned of Capitán Grande, or Big Captain (Cabello), who lived at San Antonio. It was said that the Big Captain was a fair man. When the two white men were in San Antonio, they met with Cabello and learned that he had collected a lot of presents to give to the chiefs of friendly Indians. However, there were no gifts for Comanches. Instead, the Capitán Grande had brought together many soldiers, guns, and powder in order to make war without end on the Comanches.

Vial was a gifted actor and good speaker. He said that when he and Chávez learned that the Comanches were not to receive any gifts, tears came to their eyes. They remembered how kind the Comanches had been to them. Clearly, if Cabello only knew Comanches better, he would come to see them as fine Indians who deserved presents, not war. Vial also reminded the Comanches that on many occasions he had seen them so poor that they did not "have a knife to cut meat, a pot with which to cook in, nor a grain of powder with which to kill deer or buffalo."

Vial said that he and Chávez had begged the Capitán Grande to include Comanches and Taovayas in his gift giving. At first, Cabello had angrily said no. He reminded the traders of the many times that Comanche warriors had killed unarmed Spaniards who were merely trying to find food on the plains. Indians who would do such an awful thing were "without a good heart." Certainly, they did not deserve gifts.

Vial and Chávez did not give up easily. They had argued and argued for their Indian friends, and slowly Governor Cabello began to change his mind. The traders urged him to think of Comanches as "good people, very generous, and very friendly to their friends." At last, the Big Captain asked, "Is this certain?" Both men quickly replied that their words about Comanches were "extremely true."

Cabello had then told Vial and Chávez to carry this message to the Comanches and their Indian allies: "If they want to be my friends, and friends of the Spaniards, I will promise not to kill them, and to stop sending my soldiers, those who make war on them." If they would come to San Antonio to meet with him, he "would forget the many deaths which they had caused among his people, as they must forget those which my people did to them." But Cabello also said something that really appealed to the Comanches. He would have nothing to do with the Lipan Apaches. He did not wish to make friends with these Indians; rather, he wished "to make continual war against them." This was good news to Comanches, because they hated Lipans more than Spaniards. They had fought Apaches for more than eighty years.

Cabello's final message to the Comanches was this: If they wished peace, they must send two or three of their chiefs back to San Antonio with Vial and Chávez. After Vial reported all of this, the two white men returned to their tent. The Comanche chiefs must have time to discuss the offer and decide what to do.

Throughout the rest of the day and into the night, the Comanches talked and talked. They were so loud and so excited that they kept the two Spaniards awake all night. The Indians looked for certain omens (signs) that would tell them if the white men spoke the truth about Cabello. There had been no wind, no cloud had cast a shadow across the sun, and the smoke from their pipes had not twisted. All were favorable omens.

On the following morning, the high chiefs gave their answer to the Spaniards: "[We will] forget the deaths of our fathers, sons, and brothers caused by the Spaniards . . . and from now on the war with our brothers the Spaniards is finished, we will not kill, nor make any raids or rob. And there will be three little captains from our nation [the Comanches] named to go with you to hear what the Capit[á]n Grande says about . . . peace."

In October 1785 the three little captains arrived in San Antonio to talk with the Big Captain. The Comanche chiefs got down from their horses, approached Cabello, and hugged him one at a time. To a hard-nosed military man like Cabello, being embraced by Indians whom he had hated and made war on was an absolutely astonishing experience. He said so in a letter to his superiors in Mexico.

On this occasion, Spaniards and Comanches signed a remarkable treaty. With only a few exceptions, this agreement lasted throughout the final years of Spanish Texas. Both sides would no longer make war on each other. The Comanches agreed not to let foreigners, such as the English or Americans, into their *rancherías*. Each year, Spaniards would give goods to Comanches in exchange for their animal hides. Friends and enemies of one side were to be friends and enemies of the other. Neither side could ally with the Lipan Apaches. Instead, these Indians would be the enemies of both parties. Finally, Spaniards would give gifts each year to Comanche chiefs, as long as they kept the peace.

The October 1785 treaty with the Comanches was an amazing agreement. Comanches received such items as medals, flags, daggers, knives, razors, scissors, iron kettles, mirrors, combs, glass beads, bells, tobacco, hats, shoes, long coats, and stockings. People in late Spanish Texas remarked that it was strange to see Comanche chiefs dressed in frock coats and hats.

As the years passed, Comanches and Spaniards generally kept the peace. Annual gifts to the Indians came to include guns, bullets, and powder. Of the things desired by Indians, Spanish guns were considered the most important of all. As one Spaniard remarked, to an Indian there was no jewel more valuable than a musket.

The treaty with the Comanches came late in the governorship of Domingo Cabello. He considered it to be the most remarkable thing he had accomplished in Texas. But that success did not make up for don Domingo's dislike of San Antonio. From day one, he complained that Texas was far different from life in Nicaragua and Cuba, and he was probably right.

Domingo Cabello is
hugged by a Comanche chief
(DRAWING BY JACK JACKSON)

While serving at the Béxar presidio, Cabello tried his best to get a
better position elsewhere, and he never stopped complaining. In 1779,
his first year on the job at San Antonio, he wrote to his superior in
Mexico about life at San Antonio. He described his house as a "pig-
sty," meaning it was better suited for hogs than human beings. He
whined that a cook who had served him for years in Nicaragua refused to come to Texas, because it was such an awful place. Since he
had no cook, all he had to eat was tortillas and dried beef.

Athanase de Mézières, who is discussed in Chapter 11, once visited Governor Cabello in San Antonio. Governor Cabello complained
because he could not find a decent place for his guest to stay. Worse,

don Athanase traveled with several Indians in his company, and don Domingo said he had to kill and butcher one cow each day just to feed the Indians. This was bad enough, but the governor's house did not even have large pots to boil the meat. Cabello had to rent the cookware.

Cabello's letters from Béxar are filled with complaints and protests. For example, the town had dozens and dozens of dogs that ran loose in the streets. At night these animals barked and howled, which caused the governor to lose sleep. To cut down on the noise, he ordered his soldiers to shoot strays and passed laws requiring dog owners to keep their pets under control.

Many people assume that *bandadas* (gangs) of young people are something new in cities and towns of America. In Texas in the late 1700s, Cabello wrote about teenage boys who went about "giving cries and disturbing the tranquility [peacefulness] at all hours of the day and night." To stop their mischief and noise, don Domingo ordered the parents of these boys to keep their children off the streets or pay fines.

On other occasions, Cabello described adults who were just as bad in their behavior as their children, if not worse. Men and women went to noisy dances called fandangos. Don Domingo thought fandangos and songs with bad words created a climate in San Antonio that gave rise to misbehavior and sins. More serious, men got drunk and used foul language toward each other. For example, calling someone a *perro mocoso* (snot-nosed dog) was certain to cause trouble and possibly bloodletting. When people were injured or killed in fights, these cases wound up before Cabello, who also served as a judge in San Antonio.

Cabello himself often drew criticism for his actions and comments. He refused to go to church on Sunday, thereby setting a bad example for the people of San Antonio. Cabello especially upset the religious leaders of Béxar by claiming that God did not control things on earth. When asked what he meant, don Domingo said that *if* God determined what happened and what did not, why did he allow a good man like himself to suffer accidents? In this case, he referred to his falling off a horse and breaking an arm. In all, Cabello hated life at San Antonio, and many in the town did not feel any better about him.

Of all Cabello's troubles at San Antonio, none was more serious than his battles with ranchers over cattle and horses. As mentioned earlier, don Domingo had no choice but to supply Texas beef to Louisiana, where Spanish soldiers were at war with the English over control of the lower Mississippi River valley. Texas had lots of cattle that belonged to ranchers and even to some of the missions. There were also half-wild cattle and horses that ran loose in the country, and these animals had never been branded.

When Cabello began his term as governor of Texas, Teodoro de Croix, his superior in Mexico, ordered ranchers to brand all their animals within four months. Livestock not branded after 120 days would become the property of the king. It was don Domingo's job to enforce those orders, and in doing so he stirred up a hornet's nest of hatred among Texas ranchers.

Usually, people in Spanish Texas and Spanish Louisiana could not carry on direct trade with each other. The king did not permit this, because he wanted all trade in America controlled through Spain. This economic system was called mercantilism, and it was common in all Spanish colonies in America. However, when Spain entered the war against England in 1779, it was necessary to bend the rules: Bernardo de Gálvez, the governor of Louisiana, would be allowed to buy cattle in Texas.

Gálvez first sent an agent from Louisiana to buy fifteen hundred to two thousand head of Texas cattle. Domingo Cabello also received orders to supply the animals and help drive them through the piney woods of East Texas into Louisiana.

The most famous cattle drives in Texas history were those that came after the Civil War in the United States. In the late 1800s, longhorns were driven north into Kansas and Missouri. But the first real cattle drives started in the 1720s. Then, in the 1770s and 1780s, cowboys trailed beeves from Texas to Louisiana. It was these cattle drives that got don Domingo in so much trouble.

Texas ranchers claimed that Governor Cabello was guilty of dishonesty. In order to meet the needs of Bernardo de Gálvez, don Domingo ordered his soldiers to round up thousands of cattle. These animals, according to private ranchers, often bore their brands. Nevertheless, Cabello claimed that the cattle belonged to the king. They were sold in Louisiana and the money was set aside for shipment to Mexico.

The ranchers claimed that Cabello kept bad accounts of the *number* of cattle being driven into Louisiana. Ranchers insisted that don Domingo reported *fewer* animals than actually left Texas. The difference between cattle recorded and cattle sold was never reported by Cabello. His enemies declared that this money went into the pocket of their corrupt governor, Domingo Cabello.

Texas ranchers insisted that they lost 10,901 cattle that carried their brands. The value of those animals was 27,254 pesos. Other dishonest actions by their governor, such as undercounting the number of unbranded cattle, brought the total to 32,254 pesos. Since Cabello only reported sales amounting to 13,096 pesos, he owed Texas ranchers and the king more than 19,000 pesos. Cabello denied any wrongdoing, however, and insisted that he was innocent.

Matters with Texas ranchers worsened over the eight years that Domingo Cabello served as governor. When don Domingo learned that dogs belonging to Texas stockmen were wandering into town at night, he ordered his soldiers to shoot them. Most ranchers loved their dogs, which helped them work cattle on the range, and they hated Cabello. They began calling don Domingo a *mataperros* (killer of dogs). In their eyes, this was about as low as a man could sink.

When Cabello finally left Texas to take up a new post in Cuba, where his military career had begun, he did not leave behind his troubles with ranchers. They brought lawsuit after lawsuit against him for years to come. Always, Texas ranchers insisted that don Domingo owed them thousands of pesos for stolen cattle and the cost of the lawsuits themselves.

The Spanish crown looked into charges against Cabello, and it studied the case for eleven long years. In 1797 the king's *fiscal* (lawyer) decided that the charges against the former Texas governor could not be proved. The *fiscal* declared don Domingo cleared of all guilt. Finally, while still living in Cuba, Cabello left behind his Texas troubles for good.

We do not know the circumstances of Domingo Cabello's death. Perhaps he returned to Spain to die there, as many Spanish officials who served in America did. We do know that those Spanish officials who studied his record as governor of Texas thought well of him. He was praised by Teodoro de Croix, his superior in Mexico, and Athanase de Mézières, as well as by high officials in Spain.

Cabello himself always regarded his role as Comanche Peacemaker as most important. It is interesting that a man who had such a dim view of Indians, who believed even Indians living in missions could not be trusted, came to value the words and promises of Comanches. Peace with these Indians saved lives, and gift giving in the long run was far cheaper than the cost of fighting Indian wars. We think Domingo Cabello deserves credit for his good sense. His life shows that a man who hated Indians, hated Texas, and hated life at San Antonio could rise above his dislikes and still do a good job during his eight years as governor of Texas.

SOURCES

Materials used in preparing this chapter are described below. You can find more information about these sources in the Bibliography at the end of the book.

Books

Valuable information on the loss of Spanish lives and the *Yedra* at Matagorda Bay is contained in Robert S. Weddle's *Changing Tides: Twilight and Dawn in the Spanish Sea, 1763–1803*. For a scholarly book on the Comanches, see Thomas W. Kavanagh's *Comanche Political History: An Ethnohistorical Perspective, 1706–1875*. A more complete biographical sketch of Cabello may be found in Donald E. Chipman and Harriett Denise Joseph's *Notable Men and Women of Spanish Texas*.

Quotes

Quotes in this chapter are from the following sources: Carlos E. Castañeda, *Our Catholic Heritage in Texas, 1519–1936*; Elizabeth A. H. John, editor, and Adán Benavides, translator, "Inside the Comanchería: The Diary of Pedro Vial and Francisco Xavier Chaves," *Southwestern Historical Quarterly* 98 (July 1994): 40; Thomas W. Kavanagh, *Comanche Political History: An Ethnohistorical Perspective, 1706–1875*; and Odie B. Faulk, "Texas during the Administration of Governor Domingo Cabello y Robles, 1778–1786" (master's thesis, Texas Technological College, 1960).

CHAPTER THIRTEEN

Marqués de Rubí/ Antonio Gil Ibarvo

HARSH INSPECTOR AND FATHER OF EAST TEXAS

The Marqués de Rubí was a Spanish official sent to Texas in the late 1760s. His goal was to inspect the province known then as Tejas and to recommend ways for the king of Spain to save money. At this time, the presidio of Los Adaes, located in present-day Louisiana, was the capital of Texas. Nearby were three missions that were first set up by the Domingo Ramón–St. Denis expedition of 1717–1718.

As perhaps you remember from Chapter 8, the three missions were closed as a result of the Chicken War between France and Spain in 1719. The Marqués de Aguayo then refounded the missions and established the Los Adaes presidio in the early 1720s. Since that time, relations had improved greatly between Spain and France. In fact, the two countries became close allies against the English in America. In 1762 Louisiana passed from the French to the Spanish, so there certainly was no longer a threat from that territory. To the king of Spain, there seemed little reason to keep these expensive outposts, which were hundreds of miles from San Antonio. But what about Spaniards living on farms and ranches in the piney woods of East Texas and western Louisiana? Could they stay in their homes?

It may seem strange that a king in far-off Spain could tell Spaniards where they could live in America and where they could not. This, however, is exactly what happened. As a result of the Rubí inspection, everyone living near the presidio and three missions had orders to leave and move to San Antonio.

This chapter explains how recommendations by Rubí and the king's orders upset the lives of many people, and how Antonio Gil

Ibarvo gave these same people new hope. Rubí caused Spaniards to be "combed" out of East Texas. Ibarvo, by finding a way to win back their farms and ranches, became known as the Father of East Texas.

Just listing the seven names of this harsh Spanish inspector gives you an idea of his importance. He was Cayetano María Pignatelli Rubí Corbera y San Climent, as well as Marqués de Rubí. Born in Barcelona, Spain, around 1725, Rubí was the son of powerful Spanish nobles. His father was a three-star general in the king's army; his mother was the second Marquesa de Rubí.

As a boy, young Cayetano liked math and science, and he had a quick mind. Perhaps because of his noble background and good education, Rubí often appeared cold to those who knew him. When he became an adult, people remarked unfavorably on his personality and commented that he was a man more to be feared than loved. It seems that the marqués was undiplomatic (blunt) but a totally honest man. What is certain is that he could not overlook dishonesty in others. People in Texas came to hate Rubí, but then he was not there to please them. His purpose was to serve the king first and foremost. Traveling with don Cayetano was a mapmaker and engineer named Nicolás de Lafora, who was just as blunt and sharp-tongued as Rubí.

Rubí was about forty-two years of age when he arrived at the Los Adaes presidio in 1767. His king had ordered don Cayetano to inspect all presidios on New Spain's northern frontier. These military posts were scattered from the Gulf of California in the west to Los Adaes in the east. Especially important was how to protect Spanish Louisiana. Also important was what to do about Texas, now that Louisiana would act as a buffer and protect it from invasion.

An older problem was what to do about Indians who attacked Spanish settlements. These attacks took place all along the northern frontier. The raids by Native Americans killed civilians and drove off their livestock. In the minds of Spanish officials, the Lipan Apaches were the worst of all the raiders.

Rubí had started his tour in the western region of the frontier in 1766. From there he worked his way east so that Texas was one of the last provinces he visited. He was well aware that Texas had not been visited by a royal official since the Pedro de Rivera inspection in the late 1720s. Perhaps it was not surprising to him that there were problems that needed correction.

The Marqués de Rubí
arrives at Los Adaes
(DRAWING BY JACK JACKSON)

Over the previous forty years, military commanders at Texas's presidios had been guilty of serious abuses. Instead of paying their soldiers in cash, they paid them only in food and clothing. In doing so, the poor presidio soldier was charged much more than the true value of the items. He was always in debt to his commander, because his wages amounted to less than the cost of goods supplied to him. Furthermore, no soldier could leave his post without his captain's permission. Life for the common soldier was one of poor food, bad clothing, and hard labor that generally lasted until his death.

Rubí had entered Texas in the west, so that one of the first presidios to be inspected was Felipe de Rábago's old garrison at San Sabá. The inspector did not like what he found there. He thought the buildings were badly constructed. The fort was "as barbarous as the enemy [Indians] who attack it." He would later report that San Sabá served no more useful purpose than "a ship anchored in mid-Atlantic would afford in preventing foreign trade with America."

But Rubí did like the presidio at San Antonio. He also liked the appearance of the five missions there with their large number of Indian neophytes (religious beginners). As it turned out, this was just about his last favorable impression of things he saw in Texas.

When Rubí reached the mission at present-day Nacogdoches, he could hardly believe his eyes. The priest there had nothing to do. Don Cayetano remarked that for forty-six years missionaries at this religious outpost had "little more to do than baptize a few of the dying [Indians]." Nicolás Lafora was equally unimpressed. He claimed there was not one Indian living at the mission, nor had there ever been one.

Father Antonio Margil's old mission near present-day San Augustine, Texas, did not appear any better to either Rubí or Lafora than the one they had just visited. Worse, in Rubí's words, the two priests there "hid themselves upon our arrival" and refused to talk to him. Lafora thought things to be actually worse there, because the king had to pay the salary of two priests rather than just one.

The mission near the Los Adaes presidio was the third one that Rubí visited in East Texas. The two Franciscan priests at this location had accomplished "as little as those two previously cited [mentioned], for there is not one single Indian in the mission."

Rubí also described the people living near Los Adaes, which was then the capital of Texas. There were only twenty-five families located on "little ranches . . . cleared of trees and brush for that purpose." Crops grown without irrigation were so poor that the settlers did not have enough to eat. Worse, the water wells were so bad that they hardly provided enough volume for drinking.

Rubí next inspected a presidio and mission located on the lower Trinity River. While traveling there, he and Lafora ran into heavy rains that turned the lowlands into swamps "in which horses sank up to their chests." The presidio had the worst location in all of Texas. Heat and humidity along the Gulf Coast made it impossible to store food for more than a few hours without it spoiling. The nearby mission likewise contained not a single Indian neophyte.

At La Bahía, Rubí finally found another presidio that he liked. He approved of its location and the condition of the buildings. At nearby Mission Espíritu Santo, the inspector found the first Indians living among priests since he left San Antonio several weeks before. Most of the neophytes were Karankawas and other tribes from along the Gulf Coast.

From La Bahía, Rubí and Lafora set out for Laredo, which had been founded about a dozen years earlier by one of José de Escandón's officers. This poor settlement contained only "twelve huts made of branches and leaves." It left the inspector and his engineer wondering how people could live under such miserable conditions in what was called a *villa*, or small town.

When he left Texas, Rubí traveled to San Juan Bautista, south of the Río Grande. There he inspected the gateway presidio and found it to be in good order. In the following weeks, the Marqués de Rubí made the long journey back to Mexico City. During his inspection, don Cayetano had spent twenty-three months on the northern frontier, and he had covered some 7,600 miles!

In the capital of New Spain, Rubí set to work. His report on the northern frontier would be sent to the king, who was always eager to save money. Don Cayetano thought the twenty-three presidios he had inspected to be largely worthless. In Texas, for example, he would keep only the ones at San Antonio and La Bahía.

Rubí also asked why missions that cost the king a lot money should be kept open when they contained not a single Indian. Outposts such as those in East Texas and on the lower Trinity River should be closed as soon as possible. He also recommended that the capital of Texas be moved to San Antonio, along with all the settlers living in East Texas and western Louisiana.

During his inspection, don Cayetano had closely studied the Indians of Texas. He believed that, of all Native Americans, the Lipan Apaches were the greatest problem for Spain. They did not keep their promises to Spaniards, they were known to be thieves, and they belonged to a warlike tribe. Indeed, Rubí told his king that these Indians must be made to change their ways or suffer harsh punishments for not doing so.

Since Rubí did not really think that the Lipans would ever behave as the Spaniards wished, he advised that Spain form alliances or sign treaties with their enemies—the Comanches and Nations of the North. If this happened, the Apaches would be caught in a huge trap. Their Indian enemies would be in the north, while Spanish soldiers would be in the south. At some point the Lipans would have to surrender. Since the Spanish could never trust them, these Native Americans should not be placed in missions on the frontier. Instead, the Spaniards should move them from their native lands and send them far into the interior of New Spain.

After finishing his report, the Marqués de Rubí sailed to Spain from Veracruz in July 1768. In Europe he was in a position to explain and defend his suggestions for changes on the northern frontier, including Texas. Four years would pass before King Charles III decided what to do. His decision came in September 1772, and it had really important results for the future Lone Star State.

The king decided that the presidios at San Sabá and Los Adaes, as well as the one on the lower Trinity River, must be closed and the soldiers removed "at once." The missions near these forts and "others that are maintained without any Indians in the shadow of the . . . presidios" were also to be eliminated immediately. "The few settlers who live around them" were to be moved to San Antonio. There every effort should be made to find land for them to farm and houses to live in, although no property could be taken from the five missions or settlers already at Béxar.

The viceroy of New Spain and the governor of Texas had to carry out the king's orders. At San Antonio, Governor Barón de Ripperdá had the unhappy job of traveling to East Texas with the bad news. He had to inform the priests and settlers that they must give up their missions, farms, and ranches. Ripperdá did not want to do this, but he had no choice.

During his years as governor of Texas, Barón de Ripperdá had come to like the people living in the piney woods near modern Nacogdoches and Los Adaes. He knew that they had carved their farms and ranches out of the wilderness. He also knew that they were families who had lived in that frontier area of Texas for fifty years. He had also come to know and like Antonio Gil Ibarvo, the most famous and best-known man in East Texas and western Louisiana.

Born at Los Adaes in 1729 to Mathieu Antonio and Juana Hernández Ibarvo, young Antonio grew up among the French, Spanish, and Indian population of the region. He became a rancher-trader as an adult, and his business practices sometimes landed him in trouble. Other difficulties for don Antonio came from his wife, María Padilla, who was not always faithful to her husband. You will read her story later on, in Chapter 16.

In an earlier chapter, we mentioned that trade between Spanish Texas and French Louisiana was not permitted by the king of Spain. At the same time, individual settlers could not carry on direct trade with the Indians. The purpose of restrictions on trade with the French was to protect the king's economic interests in America, a policy known as mercantilism. Equally important, by prohibiting trade with the Indians, Spain hoped to force Native Americans to give up their way of life and enter the missions, where they would receive gifts and instruction in the Catholic faith. The Spanish hoped that someday these neophytes would become tax-paying citizens, just like Spaniards.

Both goals had failed badly in East Texas. Settlers, when hungry, traded furs and buffalo hides to the French for food. As for the missions, Rubí and Lafora pointed out that they had not attracted even one Indian in all their years on the frontier.

Gil Ibarvo was the very best (or worst) at bending or actually breaking Spanish laws. At his ranch, called El Lobanillo (The Wart), he carried on trade with Indians, and he also traded with the French until Louisiana became a Spanish colony in the 1760s. Once Spain took hands-on control of Louisiana in 1769, Gil Ibarvo became a frequent visitor in New Orleans. While there, he was arrested. In his possession were horses and mules stolen from various missions and presidios, including San Sabá, La Bahía, and Béxar. Clearly, don Antonio had acquired these animals from Indian raiders.

For this offense, Gil Ibarvo was imprisoned for seven months. He was finally released, thanks to the efforts of his friend Governor Barón de Ripperdá of Texas. In fact, Ripperdá and Gil Ibarvo were on such good terms that the governor used the East Texan to illegally acquire hard-to-come-by items not found on New Spain's northern frontier.

So it was difficult for Governor Ripperdá to have to carry bad news to Gil Ibarvo and others in East Texas. It was nevertheless his sad responsibility to tell the settlers that they must give up their homes and move to San Antonio where they would be strangers. Just imagine an order today from the president of the United States telling Texas ranchers that they must give up their land and move to Oklahoma! Well, of course, that cannot happen under our present system of government. In Spanish Texas, it could and did happen in 1773. The king's orders had to be obeyed.

The settlers in East Texas were given only five days to prepare for the long march to San Antonio. Since the order came in June, they had no opportunity to gather their spring crops, and there was little time to round up scattered livestock. For some, the thought of leaving their homes for an uncertain future at San Antonio was just too awful to accept. Perhaps thirty-five settlers at Los Adaes fled into the woods, where they lived with their Indian friends. It seems an equal number did the same thing near Nacogdoches. But about four hundred East Texans did what the king ordered. They packed their most valuable possessions, left their houses and fields, and joined the march to Béxar.

Because they had such a short time to get ready for the long march, the East Texans did not have much food to take along. They also had not had time to round up their best horses. Lack of rain and summer heat made them miserable at first, and then hard rains and swollen rivers made their trek even more difficult. Ten children died on the march, and most of the adults had to travel on foot until they reached the Brazos River.

At the Brazos, the footsore East Texans did better. Governor Ripperdá had sent them fresh horses to aid their travel on to Béxar, where they arrived on September 26. In all, more than thirty lost their lives on the ninety-day journey, and thirty more would soon die of illnesses caused by the march.

Although the king had ordered that these East Texas refugees be given new lands, the best farms and ranches had already been claimed for miles around San Antonio. No East Texas families wanted to live isolated by themselves, where they might be easy targets for Apache and Comanche arrows. Within eight days, seventy-eight men signed a petition (request) asking Governor Ripperdá to let them return to their homes in the piney woods. The baron was truly sympathetic but could do nothing—his hands were tied by orders of the king and the viceroy in Mexico City.

Antonio Gil Ibarvo's name appears first on the list of seventy-eight signatures, and it seems likely that he wrote the petition himself. Don Antonio then asked the governor if he and another East Texan could carry their petition all the way to the capital in Mexico, some nine hundred miles away. Ripperdá agreed.

Joining Gil Ibarvo was Gil Flores and an important chieftain named Texita, a Tejas Indian who wanted the Spanish back in East Texas. The three men left Béxar in December for a two-month trek in the dead of winter. They reached Mexico City in February and arranged a meeting with the viceroy, Antonio María de Bucareli.

Viceroy Bucareli listened as the three men begged for permission to return to their homes. He then asked a *junta* (special committee) to give its advice. Its members saw the advantage of keeping in close contact with the Tejas, and the viceroy agreed. However, there was the matter of illegal trade between the settlers and Indians, as well as foreign agents operating at Natchitoches. Since Gil Ibarvo was perhaps most guilty of smuggling and engaging in illegal trade, this was a big concern.

The final decision was less than the three had hoped for but still something of a victory. Yes, the East Texans could return, but they could settle no closer than one hundred leagues (about 260 miles) from Natchitoches. This they could do immediately. In the meantime, the viceroy would write to Charles III with the hope that the king would agree to this compromise (middle course of action). As it turned out, the king and his advisers did not object.

The two Spaniards thanked the viceroy for giving them some money to live on in the capital, for they had none. They then hurried back to San Antonio with exciting news—the East Texans could at least go halfway home. Always looking for an edge, Gil Ibarvo asked Ripperdá if he could return to his ranch, El Lobonillo. But the Wart Ranch was too close to Natchitoches, and the governor of Texas could not change the viceroy's orders.

The East Texans could, however, set up a town on the Trinity River at a place known as Paso Tomás. The new settlement would be named Nuestra Señora del Pilar de Bucareli. Part of the name, of course, honored Viceroy Bucareli who had made it all possible.

The new *villa* (town) was never very successful. It lasted for only five years. During that time, the settlers always hoped to return to their original homes to the east. Then, in 1779, they had a good excuse to move. In February of that year, much of the *villa* was washed away in a flood that also drowned most of the cattle. The finishing blow came when Comanches attacked the town and drove off the last of the cattle.

Everyone then moved east to the location of modern-day Nacogdoches, which they reached toward the end of April 1779. Not much was left at the old mission, where no one had lived for six years. The few broken-down buildings were quickly patched and then jammed with people anxious to have a roof over their heads. Unfortunately, the East Texans could not get a crop in the ground or scratch out gardens until May. So the first year there was one of hunger and discomfort.

Antonio Gil Ibarvo took charge of establishing good relations with the Indians, who helped the settlers get through the winter. In the following year, don Antonio remembered well the hunger of that first experience at Nacogdoches. To store food and supplies, don Antonio began construction of a large stone house that served as a granary. This building, now called the Old Stone Fort, is still in Nacogdoches and is one of the few buildings in Texas that date from the Spanish period.

Gil Ibarvo became lieutenant governor of Nacogdoches and chief judge of criminal cases in October 1779. In the following year, he was appointed as a judge in charge of handling smuggled goods. When one considers his past record as a trader in East Texas, this was like choosing a fox to guard a henhouse! In the years to come, he would be accused of illegally trading with Americans east of the Mississippi River.

Don Antonio served as lieutenant governor for a dozen years. In looking at his governorship, one gets an interesting view of what life was like in a raw East Texas town. By looking at the laws that he drafted, you can know the kinds of illegal activities that concerned this Nacogdoches official.

Gil Ibarvo noted that "crimes of every description" were occurring, and "disorders of all kinds" were spreading "amongst persons of both sexes." To deal with such lawless behavior, the lieutenant governor issued fifty-four laws. They prohibited swearing in public, saying unkind things about the king, setting fires, and committing murders. The punishment for murder was being hanged and quartered (carved into four pieces). Other offenses covered by law included practicing witchcraft, dueling, mistreating women, breaking and entering houses, stealing livestock, breaking out of jail, resisting arrest, drinking and gambling, conducting illegal lotteries, protecting criminals, failing to clean soot from one's chimney once every fifteen days (to prevent houses from catching on fire), and selling liquor to Indians.

Despite laws that seemed to cover every possible offense, Gil Ibarvo had trouble keeping order in Nacogdoches. His records show that he had to deal with a master criminal and escape artist named Juan José Peña. Like many lawbreakers, Peña had various aliases (fake names), including the Little Braggart and Sky-Blue Breeches.

Peña first appeared in Nacogdoches in 1789 when he robbed a trader and stole six horses from different owners. Caught by hunters, he was brought before don Antonio, who placed him in handcuffs and leg irons. The Little Braggart broke loose, stole a gun and another horse, and then killed a milk cow. While still on the loose, Peña mistreated an Indian woman. Other Indians came to her aid, captured the criminal, and turned him over to Gil Ibarvo for punishment.

This time, the judge placed Peña in stocks (a wooden frame with holes for securing ankles and sometime wrists), added ball and chains, and then placed him inside the town jail! In Gil Ibarvo's words, "By some miraculous way he escaped again." Once again, the arch criminal committed crime after crime—including stealing three horses. But he was soon captured and turned over to don Antonio, who threw him in jail. Several days later, in Gil Ibarvo's words, "By the same miracles that freed him before, he once more evaded the law."

Antonio Gil Ibarvo
punishes Juan José Peña
(DRAWING BY JACK JACKSON)

Bent on revenge, for he had made public threats against the lieutenant governor, Peña broke into Gil Ibarvo's house at night. Luckily, don Antonio was awake and drove the Little Braggart from his sleeping quarters. However, he could not catch the housebreaker, who fled into the country. With the help of citizens from Nacogdoches, Gil Ibarvo again caught this arch criminal. On this occasion, he said, he "took particular care that the thief was securely detained." Yet Peña escaped again, and stole three horses before he was again arrested!

More than a little angry, Gil Ibarvo "took the greatest precaution of placing the evildoer in double handcuffs and double ankle-chains." Peña escaped again, taking the handcuffs and ankle-chains with him! This time, the thief remained at large for about four months, during which he stole more horses, broke into more houses, and walked off with personal possessions.

At last, Peña was captured again. In Gil Ibarvo's words, "This time . . . I took all the means of precaution in my power to guard against his escape, and I my own self took charge of the jail and guarded him." Don Antonio finally rid Nacogdoches of this evil man by sending him under heavy armed guard to San Antonio. There he apparently met his end. At least he was no longer a problem for Gil Ibarvo and the people of Nacogdoches.

As the years passed, Gil Ibarvo grew tired of his duties in Nacogdoches. In March 1791 he described himself to the governor of Texas as "now worn out by my advanced age, which exceeds sixty years." Although he still wished to serve his king in Spain, he could not do so because of ill health. He asked for retirement pay, but that request was not granted.

Suspected of being an illegal trader, Gil Ibarvo was placed under arrest in early 1792 and taken to San Antonio. After four years of trial, he was declared innocent of all charges. However, he was told that he could never return to Nacogdoches. His presence there was thought to be against the best interests of its citizens.

Meanwhile, his first wife had died. While still in San Antonio, don Antonio married a second time to María Guadalupe Herrera. He and doña María were permitted to visit Nacogdoches in 1799 and pick up their belongings. Even then, a royal agent looked at every piece of furniture and every brand on the cattle, horses, and mules. In his view, Gil Ibarvo was still not to be trusted.

The last ten years of life for Antonio Gil Ibarvo were filled with bad health and problems of old age. Worse, children from his two marriages quarreled over the few possessions still left in the Gil Ibarvo household. Near his death, Spanish officials finally permitted don Antonio to return to the Nacogdoches area, where he died in 1809. His family descendants still live in East Texas and elsewhere in the United States. The modern family name has many different spellings—including Ybarbo, Ybarvo, and Ibarbo.

Antonio Gil Ibarvo certainly deserves to be known as an important person in Texas history. He was a skillful but not always legal trader. He bent the law by taking advantage of market opportunities in French and Spanish Louisiana. He was also a successful rancher at El Lobonillo for many years. And he was the main founder of modern Nacogdoches.

It is clear that he and the Marqués de Rubí were very different men. One had no sense of humor. He is what we call a bottom-line official, meaning the only thing that mattered to him was to follow laws and save money for the king. Gil Ibarvo, on the other hand, learned to make do on a distant frontier. He was an excellent example of a pioneer leader and organizer.

Perhaps Gil Ibarvo's finest moment was a decision to make an nine-hundred-mile trip to Mexico City, where he met with Viceroy Bucareli, the highest official in New Spain. At that time, don Antonio had no money and not much experience in such matters. How could a rancher from East Texas without the best record for honesty hope to change the decision of the king of Spain? Yet, he did just that. True, he did it for himself, but at the same time he helped his fellow East Texans, who were stuck at San Antonio without hope and without their homes and ranches.

More than anyone else, Gil Ibarvo found a way to reoccupy East Texas after the king decided to accept the recommendations of the Marqués de Rubí—the Harsh Inspector on the Texas scene. On a remote frontier, he also established a fine record of helping fellow settlers when their lives had been upset in the interest of saving money for a king in far-off Spain. Don Antonio's legacies (things to remember him by) include a fine city in East Texas where Stephen F. Austin State University is located.

Father José de la Garza, a longtime missionary at Nacogdoches, offered a stirring tribute (compliment) to their lieutenant governor in 1787. In his view, the settlers in East Texas thought of Antonio Gil Ibarvo as "the father, protector, and comforter of their recovered homeland." Yes, he was not perfect in his personal conduct and honesty. Leaders, whether Anglo-American or Spanish, have the same faults that we all share. In the long run, the people of East Texas remember the Father of East Texas for his accomplishments, not for the flaws in his character.

SOURCES

Materials used in preparing this chapter are described below. You can find more information about these sources in the Bibliography at the end of the book.

Books

Imaginary Kingdom: Texas as Seen by the Rivera and Rubí Military Inspections, 1727 and 1767, edited by Jack Jackson and annotated by William C. Foster, is the best source for the Rubí inspection. Donald E. Chipman's *Spanish Texas, 1519–1821* has a useful overview of Rubí and Gil Ibarvo's role in Texas history, while Donald E. Chipman and Harriett Denise Joseph's *Notable Men and Women of Spanish Texas* contains biographical sketches of the two men.

Quotes

Quotes in this chapter are from the following sources: Jack Jackson, editor, and William C. Foster, annotator, *Imaginary Kingdom: Texas as Seen by the Rivera and Rubí Military Inspections, 1727 and 1767*; Carlos E. Castañeda, *Our Catholic Heritage in Texas, 1519–1936*, volume 4; Sidney B. Brinckerhoff and Odie B. Faulk, *Lancers for the King: A Study of the Frontier Military System of Northern New Spain, with a Translation of the Royal Regulations of 1772*; A Criminal Code for Nacogdoches, 1783, Robert Bruce Blake Collection, Center for American History, Austin, volume 45; "Gil Ibarbo," Blake Collection, volume 45; Letter from Gil Ibarvo to Manuel Muñoz, March 22, 1791, Blake Collection, volume 52; and Father José de la Garza's Affidavit on the Character and Service of Gil Ibarvo, November 14, 1787, Béxar Archives Translations, Reel 17.

CHAPTER FOURTEEN

Bernardo Gutiérrez de Lara/ Joaquín de Arredondo

REBEL CAPTAIN AND VENGEFUL ROYALIST

For more than three hundreds years, Spain claimed a huge empire in America. At one time, it stretched from California to Texas to Florida in the north, and to Argentina and Chile in the south. However, by the mid-1820s that empire was almost completely gone. All that remained of it were Cuba and Puerto Rico, and even they were gone in less than one hundred years.

As the early centuries of the Spanish Empire in America passed, some colonists did not do as well as others, and these poorer folk became increasingly unhappy with Spain. A chain of events in Europe during the early 1800s, combined with long-term discontent in America, sowed seeds of revolution in New Spain (Mexico). That rebellion overflowed into Spanish Texas with deadly results, as you will see in looking at the lives of Bernardo Gutiérrez de Lara and Joaquín de Arredondo. Their story is a mixture of courage, blood, loyalty, and brutality.

As mentioned, some Spanish colonists in America had not fared as well as others. Success depended partly on where colonists were born. Spain's leaders believed that Spaniards born in Spain (*peninsulares*) were more reliable and more dependable than Spaniards born in Spain's American colonies (*criollos*). So, after a while, *peninsulares* sent across the Atlantic Ocean held the highest positions in the government, in the church, and in the army. This seemed unfair to New World–born *criollos* who came to love their place of birth.

Even though they did not enjoy the same rights as European-born

Spaniards, *criollos* could educate their children, own land, run businesses, and make money in America. But there were still others in Spanish society for whom life was much harder. Many of these people belonged to *castas* (mixed-race groups). Those people whose parents (or grandparents or great-grandparents) were Spaniard and Indian were called *mestizos*. Other people with Spanish and black parents were called *mulatos*. Still other people had Indian and black parents and were called *zambos*. And just as there were pure-blooded Spaniards in New Spain, there were pure-blooded Indians, as well as pure-blooded African Americans. All of Spanish America had black slavery, the same as the English colonies that became the United States.

Despite the fact that millions of people in New Spain were poor with little hope for a better life, they hardly thought about trying to become independent from Spain. In the past, Spain had shown that it was capable of dealing with rebels in a brutal manner. Punishment for traitors included cutting off their heads and carving their bodies into four parts.

As it turned out, it was events in faraway Europe, rather than in America, that actually triggered rebellion in New Spain. In 1808 the famous Napoleon Bonaparte of France forced the king of Spain, Charles IV, to give up his throne. At the same time, Napoleon captured Ferdinand VII, who was next in line to become king, and made him a prisoner in France.

Napoleon then made his brother, Joseph Bonaparte, ruler of Spain. This was not acceptable to Spaniards. Although Charles IV was not a good king, the people of Spain would never agree to a French ruler who was forced on them by Napoleon's armies.

Most Spaniards loved Ferdinand, the son of Charles IV. They called him El Deseado (the Desired One), and they had high hopes that he would be become a much better ruler than his father. So on May 2, 1808, patriotic Spaniards in Madrid began what they called the Spanish War for Independence. This meant that they wanted independence from France and the right to choose their own king.

News of Charles IV's retirement, of the capture of Ferdinand VII, and of the Spanish War for Independence reached New Spain in the summer of 1808. This led to a power struggle between *peninsulares* and *criollos*. The *peninsulares* said that they should continue to run Mexico, but in the name of Ferdinand VII. On the other hand, *criollos* saw this as a chance to increase their power. They insisted that New

Spain should be governed by *criollo* committees (called *juntas*)—also in the name of El Deseado. Note that both groups claimed loyalty to Ferdinand but disagreed over who should run New Spain.

Within two years, this disagreement resulted in the first move toward Mexican independence, which was led by a *criollo*, Father Miguel Hidalgo. On September 16, 1810, Father Hidalgo issued his famous Grito de Dolores (Cry of Dolores). This call for rebellion was answered by hundreds of people from the lower classes, especially Indians and *mestizos*.

Father Miguel Hidalgo's revolt of September 1810 moved northward out of Mexico and reached Texas on January 21, 1811. On that date, Juan Bautista de las Casas led a strike against royalists (supporters of the king) in San Antonio. Las Casas and his followers seized Manuel Salcedo, the governor of Texas, and his military staff on the following morning. Elsewhere, rebels took control of Nacogdoches and other places in Texas.

Unfortunately for the rebels, Las Casas made mistakes. He failed to build support among the people in San Antonio. This and other errors allowed royalists to quickly overthrow him. In fact, the Las Casas government lasted for only thirty-nine days. Royalists wanted to make an example of this rebel leader. After a brief trial in Coahuila, Las Casas was found guilty of treason and sentenced to death. He was shot in the back as a traitor, and then his head was cut off. It was salted, boxed, and shipped to San Antonio, where it was placed on a pole in the military plaza. This was intended to serve as a warning to anyone else thinking of rebellion.

When captured, a similar fate awaited Father Miguel Hidalgo and his top three *criollo* officers. They were tried in Chihuahua City, convicted of treason, and likewise shot. After death, Spaniards cut the heads off the four bodies and shipped them south to the area where Hidalgo's Grito de Dolores had started the revolt. The heads were placed on public display, where they hung in iron cages for ten years.

The trials and deaths of Hidalgo and Las Casas did not stop rebellion in Mexico or Texas. Another priest in Mexico, Father José María Morelos, took Hidalgo's place as leader of the rebels in southern Mexico. In the north of Mexico, leadership fell to Bernardo Gutiérrez. Don Bernardo had family ties in Nuevo Santander dating back to when it was settled by José de Escandón.

Born at Revilla on August 20, 1774, Bernardo was the son of Santiago Gutiérrez de Lara and María Rosa de Uribe. Shortly before the century ended, he married a widowed cousin, María Josefa de Uribe, and they had five sons and a daughter. A blacksmith/business-man by trade, don Bernardo quickly answered Father Hidalgo's Grito de Dolores.

Bernardo Gutiérrez's first act as a rebel was to get his brother, Father Antonio Gutiérrez, to join the cause. The two men sent their agents throughout much of northern Mexico to convince others to throw off Spanish control. The success of their efforts was soon obvi-ous, because hundreds of frightened royalists fled into Coahuila, where they felt safe.

Enjoying success in Nuevo Santander, the Gutiérrez brothers next turned their attention to Coahuila and Nuevo León. Once again they produced good results. Both provinces soon joined the rebellion. This meant that revolutionaries controlled much of northern New Spain from San Luis Potosí to Monterrey.

Father Antonio Gutiérrez then agreed to promote rebellion in towns as far north as the Río Grande. And again those efforts enjoyed so much success that in February 1811 the former governor of Nuevo Santander said that "revolution and terror raged in the settlements along the Río Grande." By that time revolution had already swept into Texas, where it produced the short-lived victory of Juan Bautista de las Casas.

As noted, Las Casas was in control at San Antonio for only a little more than a month before royalists overthrew him. After holding the trial of Father Hidalgo and his *criollo* officers in Chihuahua City, Manuel Salcedo returned to San Antonio and resumed his governor-ship. By then, the faint hopes of rebels in the north of Mexico lay almost entirely in the hands of Bernardo Gutiérrez.

As royalists regained control of Texas and much of northern Mexico, don Bernardo believed that his best chance for success against them was to seek aid from the United States. With a fellow rebel named José Menchaca, Bernardo Gutiérrez left his family in Revilla and made the dangerous trip across Texas, which was controlled by Spaniards loyal to the king. Just before reaching United States soil at Natchitoches, the two men were attacked by either thieves or royal-ists. In making their escape, Menchaca and Gutiérrez lost "everything," including the papers that identified them as agents for the Mexican rebels.

After spending a month in Louisiana, don Bernardo traveled overland to Washington. Reaching the capital on December 11, 1811, the rebel was favorably received by U.S. officials, including President James Madison. But in the end, Gutiérrez did not get the support he had hoped for. This "first unofficial representative from the Mexican people to the United States" received only the unofficial encouragement of Secretary of State James Monroe. The Mexican rebel needed much more than just good wishes.

U.S. officials had to be careful in their dealings with Gutiérrez, because they did not want to make Spain angry. They did give don Bernardo a letter of introduction to Governor William C. C. Claiborne in New Orleans. The rebel captain sailed from Philadelphia and reached New Orleans on March 23, where Claiborne introduced the former blacksmith to William Shaler. A special agent for the United States, Shaler was to watch over Gutiérrez and go with him to Natchitoches.

At Natchitoches, don Bernardo lost no time in preparing for an invasion of Texas. As it turned out, volunteers were easy to come by. One of the men eager to join him was Augustus William Magee, a West Point graduate and former artillery officer in the United States army.

William Shaler's support caused other Americans to join the Mexican revolutionary movement. Gutiérrez also got the help of Samuel Davenport, an experienced Indian trader in Spanish Texas and successful merchant of Nacogdoches. That Americans were part of the quickly organized Bernardo Gutiérrez–Augustus Magee expedition reveals the goals of the United States in Texas. U.S. officials wanted Texas if they could get it without risking war with Spain.

Calling themselves the "Republican Army of the North," Gutiérrez and Magee crossed the Sabine River on August 8, 1812. Anglo-Americans had joined the movement "for reasons of land, loot, and adventure." Don Bernardo, on the other hand, wanted to bring Texas into the camp of the Mexican revolutionaries, still fighting in the south under Father José María Morelos.

The Republican Army of perhaps 130 men soon swelled to around 300. As Gutiérrez and Magee headed inland in mid-September 1812, they learned that the presidio at La Bahía was poorly manned and marched directly to that outpost. The fort's few defenders fled. This allowed the rebels to take a stone fort and capture two or three cannons.

Three days later, a royalist army arrived at La Bahía. It was led by Colonel Simón de Herrera and Governor Manuel de Salcedo, the youngest governor in Texas history. They opened a four-month siege to try to force the rebels to surrender. During this difficult period, Gutiérrez wavered in his desire to make Texas a part of an independent Mexican nation. Apparently he feared that the rebellion was doomed without outside help. Writing to William Shaler, don Bernardo offered Texas to the United States in return for military aid and protection. However, nothing came of the proposal. And Gutiérrez's fears proved unfounded. In all armed clashes with the royalists, the Republican Army won.

Leadership of the Republican Army of the North changed in February 1813 when Augustus Magee died. Gutiérrez then took command of the rebel army, and new volunteers continued to join the revolutionaries. Some were Spaniards, deserting from Governor Salcedo's army. Republican Army agents also managed to recruit Lipan and Tonkawa Indians as allies.

On February 19, 1813, Salcedo and Herrera gave up the hopeless siege and retreated to San Antonio. Two days later, the Republican Army marched on Béxar. To defend the capital of Texas, Colonel Herrera made a stand at Salado Creek, about eight miles southeast of San Antonio. In the resulting battle, a combined force of Anglo-Americans, Mexicans, and Indians soundly defeated the royalists. Although the fighting lasted no more than twenty minutes, 330 royalists were killed and 60 captured. The Republican Army lost only 6 men, with 26 wounded.

The defeated royalists left baggage, cannons, and supplies on the battlefield. These items fell into the hands of Gutiérrez and his officers. Don Bernardo then approached San Antonio and set up his headquarters at Mission Concepción. As Gutiérrez prepared to lay siege to the capital, several hundred men in San Antonio switched sides and joined the rebellion. This left Manuel de Salcedo and Simón de Herrera with little choice other than to surrender. The royalist officials asked for some promises from the rebel leaders. These included protection for the lives and property of innocent people, as well as protection of church property.

The reply from the Republican Army warned that only uncondi-
tional surrender (surrender with no terms set or promises made) would
prevent an attack on San Antonio. On April 2, 1813, the governor and
town council of Béxar surrendered. To celebrate their victory, a rebel
honor guard raised the green flag of the first Republic of Texas over
the military plaza at San Antonio.

Royalist soldiers were given a choice. They could enlist in the
Republican Army or become prisoners. This offer, however, did not
include Governor Salcedo, Colonel Herrera, or their officers. These
men had no reason to hope for mercy. A mob demanding bloody revenge already moved through the streets of San Antonio. On the following day, April 3, 1813, a hasty trial brought the sentence of death
for Salcedo, Herrera, and fifteen other officers. That verdict was as
certain as night follows day.

Bernardo Gutiérrez may have tried to spare the Spanish officers
by granting them pardons. More certain were the efforts of United
States military officers who tried to save the prisoners. They wanted
the royalist officers imprisoned far from Texas, perhaps on United
States soil in New Orleans. Some of Gutiérrez's aides seemed to agree.

The seventeen prisoners left Béxar under guard on the night of
April 3. They were supposedly being taken to New Orleans, where
they would be safe. The captives, with their hands tied behind their
backs, were in the company of sixty Mexican soldiers. Captain Antonio Delgado was in command. At the site of the recent battle at Salado
Creek, the defenseless Spaniards were unhorsed, humiliated, and attacked with knives. Governor Salcedo and his men died of stab wounds
and slit throats! Their bodies were left where they fell and even denied decent burial until sometime later.

With the capture of San Antonio, Gutiérrez was in a position to
determine the destiny of Texas. At this point, he began to act in a
very independent manner. This upset his United States allies. Don
Bernard made it clear that he would no longer consider any plans to
annex (join) Texas to the United States. Instead, he intended to make
Texas a part of Mexico. Not surprisingly, this hurt Gutiérrez's relations with William Shaler and Governor William C. C. Claiborne,
who had hoped Texas would join the United States.

In San Antonio on April 6, 1813, Gutiérrez announced a declaration of independence for Texas. His break with king and country began with the statement that "the bonds that kept us bound" to Spain

had been broken forever. "We are free and independent and have the right to establish our own government." It was a sin, he said, that in a province blessed with rich natural resources and fertile soil human beings should have to go about half-naked and half-starved.

Ignoring the role of Augustus Magee and others, Gutiérrez gave no credit to Anglo-Americans for their role in the victory of the Republican Army. Don Bernardo took all the glory for himself as liberator. He also named himself president-protector to head the government, but a special *junta* helped him draft a constitution.

Bernardo Gutiérrez reading from his declaration of Texas's independence (DRAWING BY JACK JACKSON)

Gutiérrez clearly intended for Texas to be free of all ties with the United States. Texas's first constitution stated that it was to be part of a new Mexican nation. The writers of the constitution did give some reward to Americans who had joined the Gutiérrez-Magee expedition. Those who had served for at least six months were entitled to one square league of land (4,428 acres). A draft of the constitution of 1813, completed on April 17, was sent to Shaler and Claiborne, who were naturally most unhappy with it.

Five days later, Gutiérrez made an emotional appeal to faithful *criollos*. He reminded them that they had suffered under a European king. He begged his countrymen to realize that their cause, independence, was just. The mistreatment they had suffered under Spain was against all rights of free men. He also begged the people of San Antonio to "cast off" the burden of slavery and raise their voices against the evil *peninsulares*.

Although Gutiérrez and the *junta* were breaking away from Spain, Texas's first constitution provided a government that was little different from what had existed before. The president-protector and his council made all decisions regarding government, war, and foreign relations, just as the Spanish king and his advisers had controlled those matters for centuries.

Gutiérrez knew that he had to have support in Mexico. He wrote to Ignacio Elizondo, a Spanish officer who had once supported Father Miguel Hidalgo but later changed his mind and again became a royalist. Elizondo replied that even if Gutiérrez were to hide in "hell itself," he would seek him out, burn his body, and cast his ashes "to the four winds."

Much worse lay ahead for Bernardo Gutiérrez than being threatened by a former royalist turned rebel turned royalist. The brutal murders of Governor Salcedo and his military officers had cut Spanish pride to the bone. Determined to have revenge on the Texas rebels was a no-nonsense military officer who would change the course of Texas history.

Joaquín de Arredondo was born in 1778 in Barcelona, Spain. His father was an important Spanish official who would later serve as governor of Cuba and as a viceroy in South America. Young Joaquín entered the military as a cadet in the mid-to-late 1780s. He must have been a good soldier, because he had reached the rank of colonel by

1810. In the following year, he became military commander at Tampico. His wife was Mexican-born Guadalupe del Moral.

Arredondo first showed his loyalty to Spain by crushing supporters of Father Hidalgo in the Tampico area, and he wanted to do even more. However, the viceroy of Mexico ordered him to stay out of northern Mexico. But things were about to change.

A tough general named Féliz María Calleja took office in Mexico City as the new viceroy in early 1813. Viceroy Calleja decided to name Joaquín de Arredondo as commandant general of the eastern interior provinces, which included Texas.

Arredondo, filled with self-confidence, wanted to take immediate action against the rebels in the north, but he needed Calleja's permission. He warned the viceroy that José Ramón Díaz de Bustamante, the man then serving as governor of Nuevo León and Nuevo Santander, was a "do-nothing" official. He even said that to don José Ramón himself.

In March 1813, Arredondo informed Bustamante that he was going to enter Nuevo Santander and save it from the rebels, whether Bustamante liked it or not. The governor, who had served the Spanish crown for more than thirty years, reacted angrily. He informed don Joaquín that "I am . . . the only one responsible for Nuevo Santander." Bustamante reminded the new commandant general that New Spain was being hit by rebels in the north *and* the south. Arredondo should stay where he was and defend San Luis Potosí, rather than messing in Bustamante's territory.

The governor, however, was soon to change his mind. He learned that San Antonio had fallen to the Republican Army of the North, as well as details of the horrible murders at Salado Creek. In a panic, he sent a letter begging Arredondo to "fly to his rescue."

Arredondo moved quickly. He sent mounted troops to Revilla to arrest the family of Bernardo Gutiérrez, but the rebel leader had anticipated this and wisely moved his relatives to San Antonio. Nevertheless, the Gutiérrez family suffered the loss of its house, library, and more than 4,200 pesos—all taken by the soldiers of the "cruel" Joaquín de Arredondo.

The commandant general then asked Calleja to lend him all the experienced soldiers the viceroy could spare. This plea brought results. As don Joaquín neared Laredo, he learned that a thousand Spanish troops had been sent to join his command. Arredondo also learned that hundreds of American volunteers in Texas had left San Antonio for Natchitoches. These men had deserted from the Republican Army of the North because they were sickened by the killings at Salado Creek and unhappy with Gutiérrez's leadership.

Viceroy Calleja warned his new commandant general to avoid military action without the absolute certainty of victory. Don Joaquín assured his superior that he would exercise caution. Even so, at first things went badly for the royalists.

At Laredo, Arredondo learned that Ignacio Elizondo had enlisted some seven hundred men from Nuevo Vizcaya and Coahuila for the royalist cause. Don Ignacio needed to show that he could be trusted, and he asked for a chance to set up a forward base in Texas. Arredondo agreed but provided strict orders. Elizondo could go only to the Río Frío, not one step beyond. Don Ignacio, however, ignored these orders. He did not stop his march until he reached the outskirts of San Antonio.

When Arredondo learned that his officer had failed to follow orders, he flew into a black rage. If Elizondo were to capture Béxar, it would rob the commandant general of a victory that was to have been his. On the other hand, if don Ignacio failed, it would undo months of careful planning.

Arredondo's fears that he might be denied a personal victory proved groundless. Things were bad among the rebels in San Antonio, but they put aside their differences when faced by a large royalist army.

Gutiérrez and Major Henry Perry threw together an effective fighting force, which quietly surrounded Elizondo's troops on the night of June 19, 1813. The following morning, the rebels attacked don Ignacio's men as they knelt for Catholic Mass. In the fierce battle of Alazán, which lasted for about two hours, the forces of Elizondo were defeated and scattered. Don Ignacio, who had two horses shot from under him, was lucky to escape with his life.

The victory at Alazán was the high point of Bernardo Gutiérrez's leadership in Texas. From this point onward, he fades quickly from our story. Shaler and Claiborne were upset with Gutiérrez because he did not want Texas to be part of the United States. Thanks largely to their plotting, Gutiérrez was soon forced out as president-protector in San Antonio. He was followed in power by José Alvarez de Toledo, who had not served in the Republican Army but had been an officer in the Spanish navy. Toledo had come to Natchitoches, where he joined forces with William Shaler. The two men combined efforts to spread gossip about Gutiérrez and undercut his leadership.

Because of this anti-Gutiérrez campaign, most of the Republican Army at San Antonio began to desert in large numbers. This caused the *junta* there to replace don Bernardo with Toledo. On August 1, 1813, the ex-naval officer entered Béxar in a general's uniform. He claimed authority from a popular government in Spain and from the U.S. Congress. Three days later, Toledo got the *junta's* approval as commander in chief of the Republican Army of the North.

Meanwhile, Arredondo had recovered from Elizondo's costly mistake. The commandant general left Laredo on July 26 and moved slowly toward a showdown battle with the Republican Army. By August 17, Arredondo had arrived at a location south of the Medina River.

While Arredondo was marching toward a fight with rebels in Texas, Toledo likewise had been preparing at San Antonio. On August 13 don José received word of the approaching royalist army. Some 1,400 Republican Army soldiers then left Béxar for a battle with royalists that would be the bloodiest in Texas history.

August 18, 1813, the day of the great battle at the Medina River, was like too many days in Texas summers. Dawn brought the promise of continuing, terrible heat. By early afternoon, with temperatures soaring, the Republican Army forces under Toledo and royalists under Arredondo clashed some twenty-five miles south of San Antonio. Arredondo opened the battle with a blast of artillery, followed by musket fire and a cavalry charge. The Republican Army fought bravely for almost four hours, and then the soldiers broke and ran—making themselves easy targets for royalist swords and lances. Perhaps 1,300 Republican Army soldiers, thirteen out of every fourteen, died in this battle or were shot as prisoners of war by Joaquín de Arredondo. San Antonio would soon suffer also at the hands of the Vengeful Royalist, also known as the Butcher of Béxar.

Later, in evaluating his great victory over the Republican Army, Arredondo gave little credit to the rebels' Indian allies. He reported that the Indians were the first to run. Quick to follow the flight of the Native Americans was the cowardly Toledo, who escaped. Don Joaquín was only a little more favorable in his comments about the Anglo-

Americans. He thought them capable in battle. However, the commandant general gave credit for their fighting qualities to lessons learned from Spanish traitors, who had been trained in the king's army.

The 112 Republican Army soldiers who survived the battle and surrendered at the Medina River were all shot. On August 20, having captured 215 more rebels along the way and ordered the execution of "those deserving death," Joaquín de Arredondo entered Béxar.

The killing continued. An additional forty men in San Antonio, believed to have helped the Republican Army cause, paid with their lives. The mothers, wives, and children of these men were packed into makeshift compounds (buildings), where eight of them died from lack of air. The survivors were left to cry out as shots rang out day after day, taking the lives of loved ones. Even today, the street that runs through this area of the Alamo City is named the Calle Doloroso (Street of Sorrows).

Joaquín de Arredondo deciding who will
live and who will die at San Antonio
(DRAWING BY JACK JACKSON)

Younger and more attractive Bexareñas (women of Béxar) suffered both rude insults and physical assaults. These señoritas were also forced to work long hours in royalist barracks, where they ground corn to make tortillas. Mistreatment of these unlucky females ended after fifty-four days. At that time, they were cast into the streets of Béxar without homes and with nothing.

While Arredondo took lives at Béxar, Ignacio Elizondo advanced toward Nacogdoches. Along the way, he executed a total of seventy-one rebels, as well as capturing one hundred prisoners. These included women, along with their clothing and jewelry. However, don Ignacio never reached the East Texas town.

While camped on the Brazos River, a crazed lieutenant killed Elizondo's cousin with his sword. Elizondo tried to disarm the officer, who slashed don Ignacio's hand and fatally stabbed him in the stomach. Carried on a stretcher, Ignacio Elizondo died ten days later, probably of infection. He was buried on the banks of the San Marcos River.

In all, Commandant General Joaquín de Arredondo remained in Texas for only a few weeks. This was just long enough to direct the execution of Spain's enemies and to complete his report to the viceroy on the battle of the Medina. As historian Félix D. Almaráz Jr. has written, the commandant general's revenge "on Spanish Texas was swift and hard." Taking people's property, locking them up, and killing them were the means used to restore royalist control.

Over the next four years, five temporary governors followed the unlucky Manuel de Salcedo. In 1817 Antonio Martínez began a term that would be the last for Spanish governors of Texas. By 1821, Agustín de Iturbide, the third leader for Mexican independence, defeated Spanish forces in Mexico. On July 19 of that year, the Spanish flag—the flag of Castile and León—came down for the last time at San Antonio.

Governor Martínez, a good official and a decent human being, saw the curtain fall on the province where the king's soldiers had "drained the resources of the country and laid their hands on everything that could sustain life." In don Antonio's own words, Texas had moved "at an amazing rate toward ruin and destruction." It seems certain that Texas in 1821 had a non-Indian population of less than 3,000—fewer than the 3,103 reported in the first Spanish census of Texas, taken in 1777.

What about the lives of Gutiérrez and Arredondo after their Texas careers ended? When he was removed from power on August 6, 1813, Bernardo Gutiérrez left Béxar for Natchitoches. From there he went to New Orleans, where he tried without success to organize another independence effort for Texas. During his stay in Louisiana, don Bernardo claimed to have fought in the famous battle of New Orleans (1815) under the command of Andrew Jackson. Later, Gutiérrez returned to Natchitoches, where he joined a number of military expeditions. These included James Long's unsuccessful attempts to conquer Texas in 1819 and 1821.

After achieving the independence of Mexico, Agustín de Iturbide recognized Gutiérrez as a loyal Mexican. The former blacksmith returned to Revilla as a hero in 1824. In the next two years, he served as governor of Tamaulipas, as commandant general of the state, and as commandant general of the eastern interior provinces—the very position held earlier by his enemy, Joaquín de Arredondo.

After resigning as head of the eastern region in 1826, don Bernardo spent the rest of his life in Tamaulipas. He suffered from "the bitterness of poverty, political persecution, and broken health." Gutiérrez was recalled to duty only two years before his death. At that time, he helped to defend his home state from efforts to separate it from Mexico as part of the Republic of the Río Grande. Captured, he was briefly put in prison by rebels and his home was looted. Weakened by these experiences, Bernardo Gutiérrez died at Villa Santiago on May 13, 1841, at the home of his daughter, María Eugenia.

One historian has come to some interesting conclusions about Gutiérrez. He was hot-tempered. He allowed, and maybe ordered, cruelty in the treatment of prisoners of war. A man of limited education and experience, he took himself too seriously.

On a positive note, it is well to remember that Gutiérrez had qualities as a leader that won him the approval of many Mexican and Anglo-American leaders. Even though he could not speak English and had no official papers, don Bernardo presented himself well to the highest officials in the United States. With only one exception, when his forces were under siege at La Bahía, he remained a firm supporter of making Texas part of an independent Mexico.

After Joaquín de Arredondo left Texas, his headquarters as Spanish commander of the eastern interior provinces was in Monterrey. Interestingly, while still serving as commandant general, Arredondo had to decide whether to grant Moses Austin's request to bring three hundred Anglo-American families into Texas. Governor Antonio Martínez had referred this matter to his superior, and don Joaquín gave his approval to the petition on January 21, 1821. Arredondo insisted that the new colonists had to agree to an important condition. They must either be Catholics or promise "to become so, before they enter the Spanish territory."

Within months, Agustín de Iturbide's successful plan for Mexican independence swept Arredondo from power, but not without a last-minute suggestion from him. On July 3, 1821, don Joaquín offered to support the new nation on the condition that he remain in power as commandant general. This proposal was strongly rejected by the citizens of Saltillo. In the following month, Arredondo fled to San Luis Potosí. He stayed in safety there for several months by hiding in a Catholic monastery. Then, in December 1821, the former commandant general slipped out of Mexico through a small port, and traveled to Cuba on the ship *Rosita*. Infamous in Texas history as a "butcher" because of his brutal murder of Republican Army soldiers and supporters, Joaquín de Arredondo died in Havana in 1837.

Bernardo Gutiérrez de Lara and Joaquín de Arredondo were notable men with opposite purposes in Texas's late colonial era. The first was a Mexican patriot who refused to be a willing agent of Anglo-American expansion. His loyalty to Mexico helped lead to his removal as president-protector of Texas's First Republic of 1813.

The second of these notable figures, Arredondo, was practical but vengeful. Determined to hold Texas in the Spanish Empire at all costs, the Vengeful Royalist killed rebel soldiers at the battle of the Medina River and Republican Army supporters at Béxar. Later in his career as a Spanish official, don Joaquín agreed to allow Anglo-Americans to settle in Texas. His decision had unexpected results.

While Texas was part of Mexico (1821–1836), Anglo-Americans became a majority of the settlers. On March 2, 1836, Anglo-Americans and their Tejano comrades issued a declaration of independence from Mexico. Then, almost a decade later, on December 29, 1845, Texas became part of the United States.

If Bernardo Gutiérrez and Joaquín de Arredondo had been alive in

1845, they both undoubtedly would have opposed Texas joining the United States. This might well have been the only time that these two men would have agreed on anything!

SOURCES

Materials used in preparing this chapter are described below. You can find more information about these sources in the Bibliography at the end of the book.

Books

Good information on Gutiérrez and Arredondo may be found in Félix D. Almaráz Jr.'s *Tragic Cavalier: Governor Manuel Salcedo of Texas, 1803–1813*. Details on the Battle of the Medina are best presented in Ted Schwarz's *Forgotten Battlefield of the First Texas Revolution: The Battle of the Medina, August 18, 1813*, edited and annotated by Robert H. Thonhoff. Biographical sketches of the two men may be found in Donald E. Chipman and Harriett Denise Joseph's *Notable Men and Women of Spanish Texas*.

Quotes

Quotes in this chapter are from the following sources: Odie B. Faulk, *The Last Years of Spanish Texas, 1778–1821*; Nettie Lee Benson, editor and translator, "A Governor's Report on Texas in 1809," *Southwestern Historical Quarterly* 71 (April 1968): 610; Julia K. Garrett, *Green Flag over Texas: A Story of the Last Years of Spain in Texas*; Kathryn Garrett, "The First Constitution of Texas, April 17, 1813," *Southwestern Historical Quarterly* 40 (April 1937): 293; Richard W. Gronet, "The United States and the Invasion of Texas," *The Americas* 25 (January 1969): 293; Carlos E. Castañeda, *Our Catholic Heritage in Texas, 1519–1936*, volume 6; Díaz de Bustamante to Joaquín de Arredondo (March 30, 1813), Center for American History (Austin), Operations of War, Hackett Transcripts; Félix D. Almaráz, Jr., *Tragic Cavalier: Governor Manuel Salcedo of Texas, 1803–1813*; David J. Weber, *The Mexican Frontier, 1821–1846: The American Southwest under Mexico*; and Elizabeth Howard West, "Diary of José Bernardo Gutiérrez de Lara, 1811–1812," part 1, *American Historical Review* 34 (October 1928): 61.

CHAPTER FIFTEEN

Women in Colonial Texas
PIONEER SETTLERS

Many people consider María de Agreda, the famous Lady in Blue, to be the first important European woman in Texas history. But even if her spirit came to America, she herself never set foot in the future Lone Star State. Hundreds of women did come to the Texas frontier from the late 1500s to 1821. Who were these pioneers? Why did they come to a distant and dangerous frontier? Was it by accident or on purpose? And what happened to them once they were on Texas soil? Studying the lives of these female settlers who helped shape Texas history in the Spanish colonial period can both teach and inspire us.

The first European women in Texas suffered great hardships, and many of them died young. Some were Spanish; others were French. Their nations across the Atlantic Ocean were both trying to claim areas in America that included Texas.

In 1554 four ships with about three hundred people on board left the port of Veracruz in Mexico. They were headed for Spain with no plans to visit Texas. On their way to Havana, Cuba, the ships were soon caught in a bad storm. Foul weather blew the vessels off course and back toward land. Three of the four ships, the *Santa María de Yciar*, *San Esteban*, and *Espíritu Santo*, were wrecked on the Texas coast near the southern end of Padre Island.

As many as two hundred people may have survived the shipwrecks. About thirty of them managed to get a small boat from one of the ships and sail down the coast toward Mexico, where they hoped to get aid. Their efforts took too long, however, and Spanish officials were too slow in responding to the crisis.

This meant that the other castaways, including women and small children, were left to their fate. Hoping to reach Mexico, they began walking south along the beach toward the port of Santiesteban del Puerto (modern Tampico). Indians along this part of the Texas coast were really hostile toward Europeans. They were members of the same hunting and gathering groups who had killed many of Cabeza de Vaca's companions, some thirty years earlier. These Native Americans began following the shipwrecked Spaniards, killing everyone who fell behind the others. The Indians dared not attack the larger party of Spaniards, because the men were armed with deadly crossbows.

When the Spaniards reached the mouth of the Río Grande, they found it necessary to build crude rafts from driftwood. The Great River was simply too deep and wide to wade. In crossing it, a large bundle was thrown overboard to lighten the load on a raft. Unfortunately, it held all of the crossbows, the only long-range weapons.

Losing the crossbows meant that the Europeans were now all at the mercy of the Indians. The natives mounted attack after attack, and all but two of the shipwrecked Spaniards were killed as they traveled south of the Río Grande.

One of the survivors was named Marcos de Mena. He had been left for dead among others killed by the Indians. Fortunately, he recovered from his wounds and walked to Pánuco, a province to the north of Veracruz. Thanks to Mena, we know about the awful fate of these first Spanish women in Texas, even though we do not know their names.

The next European women in the future Lone Star State were French. Although they came to Texas more than 130 years after the disaster described above, these French women did not fare much better than the Spanish females who found themselves shipwrecked on Padre Island.

In 1685 René Robert Cavelier, Sieur de La Salle, arrived at Matagorda Bay to set up a French colony on the Gulf Coast. This outpost became known as La Salle's colony. The French explorer and colonizer brought perhaps two hundred men, women, and children with him. But their numbers quickly got smaller and smaller. Some deserted the colony right away. Others died from disease, snakebite, drowning, or Karankawa arrows. La Salle himself was shot to death by his own men in March 1687. Then Karankawa Indians destroyed the French settlement in a brutal attack at Christmastime in 1688.

Who were the French women at the doomed fort and what happened to them? We have several ways to find answers to these questions. One of the colonists was named Henri Joutel. He kept a journal (diary) and wrote about what was happening to the French colony. Also, the few people who survived at La Salle's colony later told about what had happened to the others.

Another source of information did not come about until the 1990s, when one of La Salle's ships was found in Matagorda Bay. *La Belle* had been shipwrecked soon after the French arrived on the Texas coast. Although it had sunk more than three hundred years before, *La Belle*'s cargo was in very good condition. Thousands of the items on board have been recovered and studied by scholars at Texas A&M University.

The artifacts (objects) taken from the wrecked *La Belle* shed light on the French colony. They include wooden combs, shoes, rings, and mirrors that were possibly intended for use by the women colonists. Recovered items also include beautifully preserved cannons, as well as thousands of small glass beads and other trinkets intended as gifts for the Indians.

One of the women at this French colony was Isabelle Planteau Talon, who was from Paris. Earlier, perhaps in 1671 while she was living in Quebec, Canada, Isabelle Planteau had married Lucien Talon from Normandy, a province in France. The couple had three sons and two daughters. They and their children had moved back to France by the time La Salle organized his Gulf voyage of 1684.

The Talons joined La Salle's expedition, and at that time Madame Talon was again pregnant. During the voyage, she gave birth to a fourth son, Robert. In all, there were six Talon children. They ranged in age from a few months to twelve years by the time the family arrived in the Texas wilderness.

Things did not go well for the Talons. Henri Joutel wrote that the father became "lost in the woods" on one of La Salle's overland expeditions. We do not know what happened to Lucien, the father. His poor widow suffered yet another loss when her elder daughter, Marie-Elizabeth, also died.

To make matters worse, Isabelle Talon became involved in a quarrel with another family at the fort. This involved the question of who was the first child born at La Salle's colony. It was an important matter, because the French crown gave special gifts and rewards to the first child born in a new overseas colony. Even though Robert was born on the voyage to Texas, Madame Talon thought her son qualified as the first child. Gabriel Minime, Sieur Barbier, disagreed.

Joutel wrote in his diary that Sieur Barbier, "used to slip aside from the company with a young maid he had a kindness for." The woman became pregnant as a result of these secret meetings, and Barbier then agreed to marry her. Barbier insisted that his child be recognized as the first to be born at the colonial outpost. As it turned out, the dispute did not matter, because it had a sad ending. Barbier's wife had a miscarriage, and her first baby died.

When La Salle left his colony to look for the Mississippi River, he ordered Isabelle Talon to give up ten-year-old Pierre. The child must go with the expedition to the land of the Hasinai Indians. Young Pierre would be left there to learn the language of the Indians. Both mother and son were tearful when they parted. They probably suspected that they would never see each other again.

Pierre's eleventh birthday fell on March 21, 1687, the day after La Salle was shot by his own men. The young French boy was left with Hasinai Indians in East Texas, not because La Salle had ordered it, but because the adults deserted him. He spent three years with these natives before being freed by Alonso de León in 1690.

While Pierre was with the Hasinais, things went badly for the French colony. Sieur Barbier had been left in command of the colonists, which included his wife and seven "maids" (young unmarried women). Without La Salle's leadership, the settlers were a sad "band of . . . misfits, women and children who clung to a meager existence." But the worst was yet to come. From other Indians, Karankawas had learned of La Salle's death, and they decided to attack the weakened colony.

The end came in late December 1688. Karankawas quickly killed two Franciscan priests and Commander Barbier. Karankawa women tried to protect the life of Madame Barbier, who had a three-month-old baby at her breast. Warriors killed her, grabbed the crying baby by its heels, and bashed its head against the trunk of a tree. So ended the

*A French settler and her
daughter at La Salle's fort*
(DRAWING BY JACK JACKSON)

life of the first European child born on Texas soil. Luckily, Karankawa women were able to protect the Talon children and would not let warriors kill them. They also saved Eustache Bréman, an orphan child who had been living with the Talons.

The four remaining Talon children had already suffered great losses. Their father and older sister had died, and they were separated from Pierre. Now they saw their mother clubbed to death by a Karankawa warrior.

When Alonso de León arrived at the site of the destroyed French fort in April 1689, he found three bodies. One was a woman with an arrow in her back. A soldier with don Alonso became so emotional at the sad sight that he wrote a poem to the dead woman. It spoke of a "beautiful French maiden fair" who was "now so cold, so dead."

By early 1689, only one European female remained in all of Texas. Because of her youth, Marie-Madeleine Talon had not been killed by the Karankawas. The only girl among the four Talon children saved by the Karankawas, she was kept as their prisoner for eighteen months, until Alonso de León came to her rescue.

Can you imagine what it must have been like for her and the other children during those months? They had no idea how long it might be before help would come or if they would ever be set free. All they had known was life among other Europeans. Now they lived among strange people who spoke a language they did not understand.

When the Spaniards rescued Marie-Madeleine, she was sixteen, covered with tattoos in the manner of Texas Indians, and still a virgin. The Karankawa men were apparently attracted to the "quite pretty" French maiden. Luckily for her, young Eustache Bréman's quick wit kept them from molesting her. He warned the warriors that the "girl's god would make them all die" if they dared to harm her.

After being freed by Alonso de León, Marie-Madeleine and her brothers, who had also been tattooed by Texas natives, were taken to Mexico City. There they lived in the viceroy's palace with the Conde de Galve and his family. The viceroy treated them kindly, regarded them as household servants, and considered them as adopted Spanish citizens.

When the viceroy and his wife, doña Elvira, returned to Europe in 1697, they took the twenty-two-year-old French woman with them. Marie-Madeleine Talon married Pierre Simon of Paris and had a son in 1699. Her horrible experiences in America were finally behind her.

After Marie-Madeleine left for a new life in Mexico City, there were no European women in Texas. And when Mission San Francisco de los Tejas was abandoned in 1693, no Spaniards—male or female— lived in Texas for more than twenty years.

During that twenty years, Franciscan missionary activity in northern New Spain led to the founding of Mission San Juan Bautista, on January 1, 1700. Located south of the Río Grande at modern-day Guerrero, Coahuila, the mission became the gateway to Texas, because one Spanish expedition after another passed through it. At the nearby presidio, also called San Juan Bautista, one family became very powerful. They were the Ramóns.

When Louis St. Denis arrived at San Juan Bautista in July 1714, he was seeking Father Francisco Hidalgo, whom we discussed in Chapters 4 and 5. St. Denis also found Commandant Diego Ramón's stepgranddaughter, Manuela Sánchez, living at the presidio. As mentioned earlier, the Frenchman and the Spanish maiden were quickly attracted to each other, and they soon became engaged. St. Denis also had practical reasons for wanting to marry her. The young señorita had family ties to powerful people in New Spain. These relatives could help the Frenchman be accepted in the Spanish empire and succeed in business.

After their marriage in late 1715 or early 1716, Luis (as the Spanish called him) and Manuela were soon separated. The Frenchman left his bride in late April 1716 to serve as an officer in the Diego Ramón expedition to East Texas. Manuela had just celebrated her nineteenth birthday, and she was pregnant by then. Her complete name after marriage was a long one—Manuela Sánchez Navarro y Gomes Mascorro de St. Denis!

The Ramón–St. Denis expedition of 1716 was the first step in Spain's colonial occupation of Texas. That presence lasted for more than one hundred years. Unlike the earlier Spanish expeditions of the 1680s and 1690s, Ramón and St. Denis brought female colonists to the future Lone Star State.

The first recorded Spanish women in Texas were María Longoria, Antonia de la Cerda, Antonia Vidales, Ana María Ximénez de Valdez, María Antonia de Ximénez, Juana de San Miguel, and Josefa Sánchez. Aside from these women, who were all married, Ana Guerra was single and entered Texas as its first señorita.

After the Spaniards came back to East Texas in 1716, Louis St.

Denis became unpopular with officials in New Spain. They feared that the Frenchman wanted to engage in illegal trade between French Louisiana and Spanish New Spain. There were also strained relations between France and Spain at this time.

St. Denis, while trying to defend himself before Spanish officials, was put in a Mexico City prison for more than a year. When the Frenchman finally gained his freedom, he was told that he could never return to Texas.

Fearing he might be placed in prison again, Louis fled toward Louisiana. Later, Spanish officials allowed Manuela to join her husband at Natchitoches. In the meantime, she had given birth to their second child. The couple's happy reunion came sometime between 1719 and 1721.

Louis and Manuela had seven children—two sons and five daughters. When her husband died in June 1744, Manuela was left a widow at age forty-seven. At that time, she had to support three or four young children. She continued to live at Natchitoches, Louisiana, until her death on April 16, 1758.

Manuela Sánchez never actually lived in Texas. But she—like María de Agreda—is an important woman in Texas history. Her marriage to Louis St. Denis helped to influence events in northern New Spain and French Louisiana in the 1700s.

As for the eight women who came to Texas with the Diego Ramón expedition in 1716, they are Texas's first Hispanic (Spanish) female colonists. As noted, seven of these pioneers came as the wives of soldiers, and Ana Guerra soon married one in Texas.

Still, because Texas had only a small number of Spanish settlers, officials in Mexico City worried that the French would try to gain control of Texas. To prevent this, Spain decided to build more presidios and place more missions in the province. But the viceroy and his advisers knew that soldiers and priests alone were not enough to keep Texas out of the hands of Spain's enemies. More Spanish settlers were needed. To encourage their moving to the frontier, promises of land and financial support might be necessary.

A wise official, Juan Manuel de Oliván Rebolledo, also pointed out that soldiers at the presidios should have the necessary skills for farming. Hopefully, they would stay in Texas after their military service was over. The soldiers should also be married. Don Juan Manuel believed that having wives would cause them "to take root more firmly" in Texas. They would "fill their presidios with the children that their wives bear them."

As it turned out, important events were happening in Texas that would help bring in more settlers. In 1718 Martín de Alarcón headed a major expedition. Its purpose was to set up Mission San Antonio de Valero and Presidio San Antonio de Béxar. These were to serve as a way station between the Río Grande and the eastern missions. Priests at San Antonio were also to begin converting Native Americans of that region to Christianity. It is well to remember that Alarcón's expedition contained civilian families. From the very beginning, Villa de Béxar had farmers, muleteers, artisans, and aides to the missionaries.

In all, the Alarcón expedition had a total of seventy-two persons, including thirty-four soldiers. Seven of these soldiers were married and brought along their families. Probably not all of the seven families remained at Villa de Béxar, because Alarcón went on to the six missions in East Texas. But any families in East Texas would have come back to San Antonio after the Chicken War of 1719, which we discussed in Chapter 8.

By 1726 there were forty-four families at the Béxar presidio. Only four households did not include soldiers. This group grew over the next five years to about twenty to twenty-five households. The growth in civilian settlers was partly due to better relations with the Indians, which made San Antonio much safer for frontier families.

Some of the soldiers' daughters also became old enough to get married. For example, in the early 1720s two children of Cristóbal Carabajal and Juana Guerra married soldiers. Overall, eight daughters of the first Bexareños (original settlers at San Antonio) wed and remained in Texas. By 1730, about forty married couples lived in San Antonio. Other important changes were about to occur.

In 1731 fifty-five settlers arrived at San Antonio from the Canary Islands, near Africa. This was the result of a plan proposed years earlier. An official in Spain thought it would be a good idea to find people in the Canary Islands who would move to Texas. But it was hard to find families willing to come to a rough and distant frontier province. The project also proved expensive, and there were lots of official rules and red tape (routine matters) that slowed things down.

Above all, the Spanish crown was trying to save money in America.

Pedro de Rivera's expedition, which we discussed in Chapter 8, had presented some ideas for cutting back expenses in Texas. This meant closing three of the six missions in East Texas and moving the people to San Antonio. As it turned out, the Canary Islanders arrived at Béxar at the same time as the East Texans.

The older settlers at San Antonio were not happy about the arrival of the newcomers from East Texas and the Canary Islands. The new colonists needed land and water for their crops. On the other hand, the original Bexareños liked things the way they were. They did not like changes, and they did not welcome outsiders.

So it proved difficult for the more recent arrivals to fit in at Béxar. To make matters worse, Apaches in the 1730s began new attacks on the town. But without doubt, the biggest problem was finding ways to accommodate the Canary Islanders at San Antonio.

The fifty-five Isleños (Canary Islanders) were members of fifteen different families. Because not everyone had survived the long trip from the Canary Islands to San Antonio, widows headed two of the families. These women were María Rodríguez Robayna and Mariana Delgado Meleano.

Doña María was said to have a "good figure . . . long face, fair complexion, black hair and eyebrows." Although she was only twenty-seven years old, the young woman had six children. They ranged in age from one month to thirteen years. The other family head, Mariana Delgado, traveled with two children, ages two and sixteen. These widows remind us that Isleño women were not just wives and mothers. They also headed two of the fifteen pioneer families that are important in the early history of Béxar.

By the 1730s, San Antonio was a raw frontier town with many different kinds of people. For them to form one successful community was not easy. The manner in which this happened has been studied by historian Jesús de la Teja. As you will note, women played an important part in that process.

Pioneer women contributed a lot at Béxar and elsewhere in Texas. Most came as wives and daughters, and little is known about them except for their names that appear in church or census records. Because none of them could write, these Bexareñas apparently left no letters or diaries.

It is possible, however, to learn something about these women by

A Canary Island woman and her child on their way to San Antonio
(DRAWING BY JACK JACKSON)

studying legal records, such as wills and lawsuits. In the next chapter, you will meet some of these "faceless" women who lived on the Texas frontier. You will also learn about the laws that affected them and the rights they enjoyed under these same laws.

Before turning to women and Spanish law, we need to look at the other pioneer women in Texas history. Not all were in San Antonio, although that was the most important area of settlement.

In Chapter 13, you read about Antonio Gil Ibarvo, the founder of Nacogdoches and Father of East Texas. That town grew rapidly after the Spaniards returned to East Texas in the late 1770s. By the end of the century, its population had reached 660.

Census records from 1799 to 1809 provide bits of information about colonial women on the East Texas frontier. Of special interest are the twenty-four women who headed families there in 1799. They ranged in age from thirty-four to eighty-five. These widows were from very different backgrounds. They included Hispanics, *castas* (women of mixed races), Indians, French, and one "American."

The two youngest widows were María Benites and Vicenta Medina. Benites was a Hispanic woman born at Los Adaes. She had two small children, ages four and five. Medina was a *mulata* (Spanish and black ancestry) from Béxar. She had a twelve-year-old son and a thirteen-year-old daughter. The oldest widow, Rita Vergara, was in her eighties. The only person living with her was an eighteen-year-old grandson.

Nacogdoches was certainly more diverse (varied) than San Antonio, where most people were Hispanic. For example, two French women, who could not read or write, lived in Nacogdoches in 1809. They were Marie-Madeleine Prudhomme and Marie Rambin.

Madame Prudhomme and her husband had married only days before moving to East Texas from Louisiana around 1800. The couple had four children, with the husband working as a farmer. Madame Prudhomme did sewing to help earn money for the family.

Marie Rambin, her husband, and five children left Natchitoches, Louisiana, to live in Nacogdoches. In East Texas, Madame Rambin gave birth to four more children, but one died. When her farmer husband also died, the widow found it hard to support her family. She had to use the boys "in the field," and the girls were kept busy "making candles and weaving."

The hard times faced by Madame Prudhomme and Madame Rambin were very different from the successes of three Latina ranchers in the late colonial period. In 1779 the top ten cattle owners at Béxar included María Ana Curbelo, who ranked second. Doña María Ana had become the owner of Las Mulas ranch on Cíbolo Creek when her husband died in 1778.

Also included in the list was Leonor Delgado, who was tied for fifth place in the number of cattle owned. Doña Leonor had been the object of gossip in the 1750s, because she had a child without being married. She later wed Juan José Flores de Abrego. As his widow, she owned 150 head of cattle by the late 1700s.

The position of María Ana Curbelo and Leonor Delgado is minor, however, when compared to that of María del Carmen Calvillo. Born at Béxar on July 9, 1756, María del Carmen was the eldest of six children. Her parents were Ygnacio Calvillo and Antonia de Arocha.

In the 1790s doña María's father owned the famous Rancho de las Cabras (Goat Ranch) in present-day Wilson County. By then María del Carmen had married Juan Gavino de la Trinidad. The couple had two sons and adopted three other children.

In the previous chapter, you read about the rebels in Texas in the early 1800s and Joaquín de Arredondo's brutal treatment of them. Doña María's husband, don Juan, approved of the rebellion. So he had to flee the ranch to escape Arredondo's executions. The Gavinos apparently separated at that time. In any event, don Juan never again lived at the Goat Ranch.

Doña María's father was murdered at the ranch in April 1814. At that time, she became owner and manager of Rancho de las Cabras. She apparently did a very good job, because the ranch grew tremendously in the 1830s when Texas was part of Mexico.

This notable woman died on January 15, 1856. She had lived almost one hundred years! María del Carmen Calvillo made sure that the Rancho de las Cabras would remain in the family by passing it on to two of her adopted children.

The stories of these Latina ranchers show that women, when given the chance, competed very favorably with men on the frontier. Often that chance came because of the death of a husband or father. In that case, women were left to take care of the family, its land, and other possessions.

Hundreds of Hispanic and mixed-race women, as well as a few French women, were among the first pioneers in Spanish Texas. They came as wives, widows, and daughters. Or they were born on the northern frontier of New Spain.

Regardless of how they came to be in Texas, women faced many of the same hardships as men. They bore their children and lived on a frontier threatened by Native Americans hostile to Europeans and by

European wars that often spilled over into America. These women definitely played an important role in Texas history.

Without these pioneer settlers, Spain could not have had a permanent civilian presence in Texas during the Spanish colonial period. Without them, the Spanish legacy (influence) would not be so strong in the Lone Star State today.

Young María Calvillo helps brand cattle at her famous Goat Ranch (DRAWING BY JACK JACKSON)

SOURCES

Materials used in preparing this chapter are described below. You can find more information about these sources in the Bibliography at the end of the book.

Books

The best book dealing with the shipwrecks of 1554 is *The Nautical Archeology of Padre Island: The Spanish Shipwrecks of 1554*, by J. Barto Arnold III and Robert S. Weddle. The best accounts of women at La Salle's colony may be found in *The French Thorn: Rival Explorers in the Spanish Sea, 1682–1762*, by Robert S. Weddle, and in *Three Primary Documents: La Salle, the Mississippi, and the Gulf*, translated and edited by Robert S. Weddle, Mary Christine Morkovsky, and Patricia Galloway. For women at San Antonio, see *San Antonio de Béxar: A Community on New Spain's Northern Frontier*, by Jesús F. de la Teja.

Quotes

Quotes are from the following sources: Henri Joutel, *Joutel's Journal of La Salle's Last Voyage*; Robert S. Weddle, *The French Thorn: Rival Explorers in the Spanish Sea, 1682–1762*; Robert S. Weddle, *Wilderness Manhunt: The Spanish Search for La Salle*; Robert S. Weddle, Mary Christine Morkovsky, and Patricia Galloway, translators and editors, *Three Primary Documents: La Salle, the Mississippi, and the Gulf*; J. Villasana Haggard, translator, "Spain's Indian Policy in Texas," *Southwestern Historical Quarterly* 44 (October 1940): 241; Testimonio de las diligencias hechas por el señor factor Don Manuel Angel de Villegas Puente para el despacho y aviso de las familias que . . . pasan a poblar a la provincia de los Texas, 1730–1734, Center for American History, Austin; photostats from original documents in the possession of Louis Lenz, Lake Charles, Louisiana; and Sworn Statement of Marie Rambin, July 27, 1809, Robert Bruce Blake Research Collection, Center for American History, Austin, Supplement, volume 6.

Additional Information

For the complete text of the poem about the dead woman at the French fort, see Robert S. Weddle, *Wilderness Manhunt: The Spanish Search for La Salle*, 187–188.

CHAPTER SIXTEEN

Women and the Law
RIGHTS AND RESPONSIBILITIES

What do a young Indian woman kept as a slave and the wife of a famous East Texas settler have in common? Both became involved in legal cases that had to be decided by royal officials. Like other women in Texas, they had to obey Castilian (Spanish) laws. These laws gave women in Spain and Spanish America many rights, but they also required them to live within the rules of society.

What specific rights did women have in Texas? Did officials take women and their legal rights seriously? What happened to women who broke the law? These questions and others will be explored in this chapter. Here you will meet a variety of women. Some were good people, who benefited from the legal system. Others committed crimes and were punished for their actions.

In the late 1400s, the kingdom of Castile, a part of present-day Spain, was ruled by Queen Isabella. In 1492 she agreed to help pay for Christopher Columbus's famous voyage. She and her husband, King Ferdinand of Aragon, also supported three other voyages to America by Columbus. But Castile claimed the lands that Christopher Columbus discovered on his four voyages.

Long before Columbus discovered the New World, women played important roles in early Spanish history. This was especially true during the long wars (711–1492) between Christians and Muslims. They were settlers, wives, mothers, and "vital members of new . . . communities" on the frontiers of Spain, just as they later were in new towns on the American continents. Because they risked their lives on dangerous frontiers, Spanish women were granted special rights under Castilian law. They did not have equal status with men, but they had greater legal protection than most other members of their sex in the world at this time in history.

When Spaniards began coming to America to set up colonies, they brought their Castilian laws with them. In Texas, Spanish governors served as chief judges. Although governors of Texas were always military men, rather than trained lawyers, this was not as big a problem as it might seem. Castilian laws were very detailed and covered almost every possibility. So governors simply had to find the appropriate law and apply it to individual cases.

All women, even those who were poor and uneducated, were protected by Spanish law. It is interesting to note that women on the American frontier seemed to know a lot about their legal rights. This information was passed down, generation after generation, from grandmother to mother to daughter. One thing seems certain—women in Spanish Texas had a good idea of what they could expect from the legal system. They also knew what their society expected from them.

Most women were expected to marry and bear children. But because men fought battles with Indians, women faced the reality of widowhood. If that happened, the widow was supposed to honor her husband's memory for a year. Then she should remarry. Until she did, she had to take care of the children, property, and other family matters. Even women who did not lose husbands had to handle the family's affairs while the men were away from home.

Women also played a major role in forming family ties in the Spanish Empire. Remember that Louis St. Denis probably married Manuela Sánchez at least in part because she was a member of the powerful Ramón family, although the couple apparently were attracted to each other as well. Nevertheless, Louis St. Denis clearly understood that having the right relatives could improve a Frenchman's chances for success on the Texas-Louisiana frontier.

For men, making a proper marriage also meant that they might collect a dowry. This was money or property that a bride brought into the marriage as a gift to the groom. Remember that the Marqués de Aguayo acquired his titles and wealth through marriage. The resources of the marquesa allowed her husband to head the expedition that reoccupied East Texas in the early 1720s, established a mission-presidio complex on the Gulf Coast, and strengthened the San Antonio area.

In San Antonio, marriages were especially important in tying the community together. As discussed in Chapter 15, Béxar in the 1730s was divided by quarrels among the original colonists, the settlers who moved there from East Texas, and the people from the Canary Islands.

At first the Isleños (Canary Islanders) controlled much of Béxar—the agricultural lands, water rights, and town council positions. But their numbers were so small that they had to seek husbands and wives among the American-born settlers. An example is the offspring of Canary Islanders José Leal and Ana de los Santos. The couple's six daughters and three sons all married non-Isleños.

Within three generations, many of the people at San Antonio could claim ties to the Canary Islander families. Indeed, there was no one left at Béxar who was pure-blooded Isleño. Marriage to Isleños also helped other colonists gain higher positions and more power within the community.

Besides marriage as a means for social betterment, what did marital status mean for colonial women? Under Castilian law, women could definitely own property in their own name. Sometimes the bride brought property into a marriage as a dowry for her husband. But she kept any other property that she already owned. This was not the case in the English colonies that became the United States, nor was it the case in most European nations.

When Spanish men and women married, the husband began managing their possessions. Castilian law, however, tried to protect the wife from having her belongings mishandled or wasted by her husband. For example, the husband could not sell any property his wife had before they married without her permission.

Castilian law also contained the concept of community property. Under this arrangement, as in Texas today, the husband and wife had equal ownership of all the wealth and property that they acquired *after* they were married. They were also both responsible for any debts they made while married. This meant that a wife had to pay her share of anything that she and her husband owed.

María Melián is an excellent example of a woman who owned property. She and her husband, Lucas Delgado, were Canary Islanders. They were both poor. Neither had any property when they married. But they got rewards from the crown for agreeing to move to San Antonio. By the time Lucas Delgado died, the couple had several head of cattle among their possessions.

Later María Melián wed Juan Leal Goraz. She gave him one cow as her dowry. She did not give him "any of the five [cattle] which the king gave me when I came as a settler" to Béxar. This shows that a woman could bring a dowry into a marriage but also keep her own personal property.

Castilian laws also tried to prevent a husband from selling property that belonged to both without his wife's permission. For an example of this, there is the case of María Alexandria de los Reyes. María's husband, Pedro de Regalado de Treviño, signed a contract to sell a lot and house they owned. Doña María had to swear in writing that she would not oppose the sale "by reason of my marriage, dowry," or other rights. She also had to swear that her husband had not threatened her or forced her to agree to the contract. It is clear that don Pedro could not sell the property without his wife's approval.

Affairs of the family of José de Urrutia also reveal a great deal about wives, daughters, and property. When Mission San Francisco de los Tejas was abandoned in 1693, don José chose to live among the Tejas Indians, rather than return to New Spain. He later rejoined Spanish society, and became commander of the fort at Béxar in 1733—a post he held until his death in 1740.

During his long life, don José married twice within the Catholic Church. His first wife, Antonia Ramón, brought no dowry or property into the marriage. The couple had one daughter. After don José's first wife died, he wed Rosa Flores y Valdés. She too had no dowry or property at the time. This marriage produced a number of children, including four daughters.

The will of José de Urrutia mentions eleven legitimate children. (Legitimate means that the parents were legally married at the time that the children were born). These eleven were to "share and share alike" in most of don José's estate.

One of José de Urrutia's sons, Joaquín, was a soldier at the presidio of Béxar. He wanted to sell his share of a house and lot in Saltillo that was part of don José's estate. In order to make the sale, Joaquín had to get the approval of his wife, Josefa. Once again, a woman had to be consulted and give her permission before property could be sold.

Juana de Urrutia was a daughter from don José's second marriage. Later in life, she was a widow who lived at Béxar. In 1745 she sold her share of a house and lot in Saltillo to her brother Pedro for eighteen pesos. In the following year, doña Juana sold some property that had belonged to her and her dead husband. This included a lot in San Antonio with a house and sixteen peach trees.

By studying the settlement of José de Urrutia's estate, we can learn a lot about women's legal rights. Legitimate daughters could inherit property equally with legitimate sons. A son who inherited property from his father had to have his wife's consent to sell it, but a widow could sell inherited property whenever she wanted. Compared to English and Anglo-American law, these were astounding powers for women to have.

Another case at Béxar involved Josefa Flores y Valdés. She was an early resident who had married twice, but she outlived both of her husbands. There were people at San Antonio who owed debts to doña Josefa's dead husbands, and she wanted to collect what was due her. So Señora Flores de Valdés gave her power of attorney (legal right to represent her interests) to Francisco de Liñán of Coahuila. He was supposed to collect any money, livestock, water rights, or other valuables owed to her husbands when they died.

Doña Josefa also gave don Francisco the right to file lawsuits and swear oaths for her. To do this she had to state in writing that she gave up her rights under the laws "in favor of women." She also had to promise to go along with whatever Francisco de Liñán decided.

Papers concerning doña Josefa and her business affairs show that women were also involved in buying and selling "human" property, as well as real estate. On October 29, 1743, Señora Valdés sold Luis, a black slave, to Governor Justo Boneo y Morales. She had gotten the slave from her first husband, Miguel Núñez Morillo.

In making the sale, dona Josefa had to pledge that the slave would belong to Governor Boneo y Morales "for all time." Should anything go wrong, such as the slave having a hidden injury that would prevent him from working, she had to return the sale price of two hundred pesos. On that same day, October 29, 1743, doña Josefa bought a thirty-three-year-old slave from don Justo for 279 pesos. Thus, a woman could be both a seller and buyer of black slaves.

Under Castilian law, women had impressive rights, such as those discussed above. We also noted earlier in this chapter that women seemed to be well informed of their rights. They fully expected the legal system to protect them.

In actual practice, did Castilian law really work for women of all classes? Would the legal system provide justice even for poor women who could neither read nor write? What would happen when a woman from the lower class was involved in a dispute with someone of higher social position? Or what if the woman seeking justice was not even Hispanic?

To answer these questions, we need to look again at the affairs of doña Josefa Flores y Valdés. She was involved in an earlier incident with Antonia Lusgardia Hernández. Antonia was a free *mulata*, a woman of mixed African and Spanish ancestry. Her case shows that a woman's rights were protected under Spanish law, no matter how poor she was.

Antonia Lusgardia Hernández presented a petition (written appeal) to Governor Manuel de Sandoval in 1735. Nine years earlier, Antonia and her daughter had moved into the home of Josefa and her first husband, Miguel Núñez Morillo. While living there, the *mulata* gave birth to a son. Doña Josefa became very fond of the boy and became his *madrina* (godmother).

Antonia claimed that she received no pay while she worked in the Núñez Morillo household. She also suffered "from lack of clothing and mistreatment." To escape from this awful situation, the young woman left and took her two children with her. However, the *mulata* claimed that don Miguel secretly entered her new home, stole her son, and took him back to doña Josefa.

Naturally, Antonia was very upset. In her complaint to Governor Sandoval, she stated that her son, Ignacio, was "the only man I have and the one I hope will eventually support me." Antonia called herself a "poor, helpless women whose only protection is . . . a good judicial system."

Governor Sandoval ordered don Miguel to appear and read the petition to him. Not surprisingly, don Miguel disagreed with Antonia's version of events. He stated that the *mulata* had asked doña Josefa to be young Ignacio's godmother. According to don Miguel, Antonia "gave her the said boy" and gave up any rights to him.

Don Miguel also insisted that the boy had left his mother of his own free will. "Without being carried or encouraged by anybody," the child had walked to the Núñez Morillo home. Don Miguel argued that the boy wanted to be with doña Josefa more than he wished to be with his own mother.

It appears that the boy was returned to his birth mother, Antonia, by order of Governor Sandoval. This royal official upheld the rights of a lower-class woman of color to her child over those of a Spanish woman with a higher social position. In this case, the legal system worked for an illiterate (unable to read or write) female of mixed ancestry.

An even more impressive example of Spanish law protecting women involves a young Indian slave. María Gertrudis was a Native American of the region near Camargo. As a baby, she was sold to José de la Peña of Saltillo for fifty pesos. Don José gave her his family name, De la Peña. María Gertrudis de la Peña was passed on to two more masters before she arrived at San Antonio. At that time, she petitioned Governor Domingo Cabello for her freedom.

María's story is indeed a sad one. She did not know her exact age or even remember her parents. At the time that she presented the petition, the young Indian woman was living in the house of Angel Navarro. In that household, she was called Esclava (Slave). She claimed to have suffered "many ill-treatments" from the family and especially from don Angel himself.

Before coming to Béxar, María Gertrudis de la Peña had lived as a daughter of José de la Peña at Saltillo. But things had changed when she turned sixteen. As her body matured, José became attracted to her, and she became pregnant by her adoptive father. Wanting to avoid a scandal, he sold María to a soldier at Presidio del Río Grande.

This soldier also claimed the Native American as his daughter, not as his slave. For two years María lived with him, until he became angry with her. The soldier then took all of her clothes and sold her to Angel Navarro. Because Navarro had paid for her, he expected work in return. The new master promised to free María Gertrudis after three years. María had originally agreed to those terms but changed her mind after being subjected to "the temper and style of the household." However, when she announced that she wanted to leave, don Angel would not let her go.

This young Indian woman begged Governor Cabello for "mercy, justice, and goodwill." She also expressed the hope that at Béxar "there would not be an absence of justice as there had been at the Presidio of Río Grande."

Again the legal system worked to provide justice. In his decision, Cabello noted that Spanish law "greatly favors the freedom of Indians." María Gertrudis was "free by nature" but still had been sold as human property. The governor declared that this was illegal, and he granted María Gertrudis her freedom. No longer would she have to serve in the Angel Navarro household. Cabello then advised the former slave to return to Camargo and join her relatives, if she could find them. If, on the other hand, she chose to stay at San Antonio, she must live with "orderliness" and cause no trouble.

Cabello's warning to María Gertrudis de la Peña illustrates another important aspect of Castilian law. Women expected and indeed received protection under the law. They were also expected to behave properly. Failing to do so, they could be punished like everyone else.

Of particular interest in this regard is a case involving adultery. Adultery, which is forbidden in the Ten Commandments, involves a married person having sexual relations with someone other than the spouse (husband or wife). This was a crime punishable under Spanish law.

At San Antonio a sad triangle of love and hate came to light in 1744. It involved a woman named Rosa Guerra and her husband, Matías Treviño, as well as her supposed lover, a man named Antonio Tello. On August 21 a badly wounded Treviño staggered into Mission San Antonio de Valero. He was bleeding from a single bullet wound, and he had also been severely beaten about the head and shoulders with a gun barrel. The dying man stated that he was attacked by Antonio Tello, who screamed, "Now you'll see, cuckold"—a term used for the husband of an unfaithful wife.

Don Matías claimed that two days before, on August 19, a heated conflict had broken out in his household. It started when he scolded his wife because he suspected she was having an affair. Doña Rosa denied this and replied in anger, "I'll have you killed." Don Matías ended his deathbed statement by saying that it was "well known and rumored" that Antonio Tello had had sexual relations with his wife, doña Rosa.

A soldier at the Béxar presidio supported don Matías's version of events. He told officials at Béxar that Antonio Tello had built a log house for doña Rosa while her husband was out of town. Don Antonio apparently let her live there free of charge, but he was always there too.

Based on the evidence, Béxar officials arrested Rosa Guerra on the day of her husband's murder. They placed her in handcuffs and locked her in a room. Under questioning, doña Rosa stated that her husband and Antonio Tello had never quarreled. She also insisted that she had paid for the house that don Antonio built for her. She likewise denied that they had a secret affair. She did admit, nonetheless, that in the recent past a local official had told her *three times* to "throw him [Tello] out of her house."

As for the accused lover, Tello took refuge in Mission San Antonio de Valero. From there, he sent word to officials that he was not guilty of Treviño's murder. Three days later, Béxar officials got permission from the priest to remove Tello from the mission. However, by the time that they surrounded the church, Tello had already escaped, and they could not find him.

Unfortunately, the documents relating to this case do not tell us what finally happened. Nevertheless, the fact that Rosa Guerra was arrested and confined shows that women had to behave responsibly or face serious consequences.

Another case involving suspected adultery occurred almost thirty years later. It also resulted in murder, but teaches us a different point of law about the conduct of women during the Spanish period.

In April 1772 Juan de Sosa admitted that he had murdered Diego Menchaca. As it turned out, the dead man had lived for a while in the Sosa household. Both men were soldiers at the Béxar presidio. But problems began between them when the husband became jealous of his wife, Gertrudis Barrón, for he suspected that she had her eye on Menchaca.

Matters got worse one day while Juan de Sosa was beating his wife out of jealousy. Menchaca tried to protect the woman, and in doing so managed to slightly wound Sosa. The angry husband then ordered don Diego out of his home and told him never to return.

Don Juan, however, still suspected that his wife and Menchaca were meeting secretly. One night the husband discovered that Menchaca, a sentry (guard), was not at his assigned post in the presidio. Suspicious of what might be going on, Sosa went looking for his wife. At first he could not find her or the missing sentry.

Then Sosa saw his wife's dog, which always followed her. Realizing that his wife had to be nearby, the frantic Sosa continued his search. At about nine o'clock in the evening, Juan de Sosa found the couple alone in another house. When he entered the place, don Diego tried to throw him out. The angry husband then struck the other soldier three times with his sword, killing him.

After the deadly attack, Sosa admitted that he had committed the crime, but he stated that he had only intended to use the broad side of his blade. He certainly had not planned to kill his wife's lover. Menchaca's death was an unfortunate accident.

In the meantime, doña Gertrudis "sought protection in the sacred place" of Mission Concepción. Luis Antonio Menchaca, captain and judge at Béxar, asked permission to have her removed from the mission, "not to be immediately punished or charged with any [crime], but only to protect her."

Captain Menchaca wanted to make sure that those responsible for the murder were punished. With the permission of the local priest, Gertrudis Barrón was removed from the mission and placed under arrest. Captain Menchaca decided that the case was serious enough

Juan de Sosa kills
Diego Menchaca
(DRAWING BY JACK JACKSON)

to have her imprisoned. So he placed her in leg irons and locked her in a secure house until the matter was settled.

A lieutenant at Presidio Béxar defended Juan de Sosa's actions. He declared that the man should be freed, because the crime was committed to "save his honor." The officer added that "any man has the right to defend his honor, [and] his wife."

This case went on appeal all the way to a high court in Mexico City. An advocate general (defense lawyer) acting on Sosa's behalf said there were times when it was acceptable to commit murder. If a man and woman were found in an isolated place at night, that in itself was sufficient proof of adultery. The advocate general reminded the judge that Juan de Sosa had ordered Diego Menchaca and Gertrudis Barrón not to have any contact. Indeed, Sosa himself was the injured party. He had every right to do what he did.

At the end of the case, the point was clearly made that under Spanish law a husband who found his wife committing adultery had the right to kill her lover! He could do this even if there was only strong suspicion of that act. In Sosa's case, there was no real proof that his wife had been unfaithful. The situation, however, did explain his being so "mad at that moment, blinded by anger, and deeply hurt" that he acted without thinking. Therefore, orders came from Mexico City that Juan de Sosa should be released. As of May 1773, his sentence was changed to time already served. Interestingly, upon his release, Sosa was ordered to pay for twenty-five Masses to be said in the Catholic Church for the soul of Diego Menchaca. He did this, but probably was not happy about it.

The way that this case turned out illustrates "the unwritten law" of a betrayed husband's rights. By those rules, a husband who found his wife committing adultery had the right to kill the other man. He could not, however, kill the wife. Instead, she must be handed over to a judge for punishment. This so-called "unwritten law" of a husband's rights carried over into twentieth-century Texas.

The act of adultery by a man's wife was considered a serious offense and an insult to his honor, as we have seen. If a husband wanted to avoid using violence to separate a wife and her lover, he could appeal to the legal system for help. Antonio Gil Ibarvo, the famous colonizer and Father of East Texas, used this approach in the 1760s.

Gil Ibarvo's wife, María Padilla, was publicly carrying on an illegal affair with a soldier named Andrés Chirinos. When other measures did not work, Governor Angel de Martos arrested Chirinos. The man was accused of public drunkenness and immoral relations with Gil Ibarvo's wife. At first, the soldier was released but sent far away to the presidio at La Bahía, and Chirinos was sternly warned never to return to Los Adaes.

Apparently the lure of María Padilla proved too great. When the soldier reappeared at Los Adaes, he was quickly arrested and again ordered to leave the capital. But within a short time, Andrés Chirinos returned yet again to Los Adaes.

Gil Ibarvo was fed up. He again petitioned Governor Martos for relief. Don Antonio asked to be spared the shame of having everyone know that he and his wife "were living in a constant state of . . . anxiety and discord on account of Andrés Chirinos."

Efforts to separate the adulterer and Gil Ibarvo's wife within Texas had obviously not worked, according to don Antonio. So he asked the governor to send Chirinos to a "distant location" or to grant him "license to move" with his family "from this presidio." Gil Ibarvo believed that only one or the other of these solutions would improve his marital problems and bring peace to the family.

The governor decided that removing Chirinos was a better choice than letting the Gil Ibarvo family move away from East Texas. That was an important decision, especially when one considers the role that Antonio Gil Ibarvo would play in East Texas in later years.

Governor Martos's decision was to sentence Andrés Chirinos to serve the crown without pay for four years at El Morro, a fort in Havana, Cuba. Sending the soldier so far away would hopefully allow don Antonio to have some peace in his marriage. And Gil Ibarvo would not have to resort to murder.

The story of María Padilla, her husband, and her lover reminds us that not all women lived in San Antonio. After the founding of modern Nacogdoches in 1779, the East Texas town grew rapidly. By 1783 it had attracted some undesirable elements. Antonio Gil Ibarvo was concerned, saying, "Disorders of all kinds are spreading . . . amongst persons of both sexes."

As lieutenant governor, he issued a set of laws for the colony. These rules and regulations may well have been influenced by problems with his wife, María Padilla. Gil Ibarvo's criminal code had specific sections that applied to immoral women and their lovers. Don Antonio spelled out what would happen to any women having

*María Padilla attracts the attention
of Andrés Chirinos at Nacogdoches*
(DRAWING BY JACK JACKSON)

sexual relations with a man other than her husband. The penalties became more severe if the woman kept repeating the crime. Harsh punishment at Nacogdoches awaited those guilty of adultery.

Obviously, don Antonio hoped that threats of severe penalties would keep women from acting immorally. He also wanted to protect women from being the victims of crime. Under Gil Ibarvo's legal code, anyone who violated "a maiden" faced the death penalty. "Rape in a secluded and deserted place" could cost a man his life. So could committing violence against "a woman living honestly." Likewise, allowing one's wife to be a prostitute, a woman paid for having sex with others, carried stiff punishment. In East Texas, as in San Antonio and elsewhere, the rule of law was imposed on both women and men.

Women who were involved in the legal system in Spanish Texas were a varied group. Some early pioneers, like Canary Islander María Melián, owned cattle that they had received from the crown for coming to San Antonio. Others, such as the widow and daughters of José de Urrutia, inherited property. Josefa Flores de Valdés bought and sold human property (slaves), while María Gertrudis de la Peña was freed from slavery. These women enjoyed important rights under Spanish law.

Still others ran into trouble because of their suspected immoral behavior, as in the murder case involving Rosa Guerra. On other occasions, such matters were settled without violence, as happened with Antonio Gil Ibarvo, María Padilla, and her lover.

In conclusion, women in the Spanish empire had many rights not enjoyed by females elsewhere. To again quote María Gertrudis de la Peña, they could and did expect to receive "mercy, justice, and goodwill" from royal officials.

Women also had to answer for their actions and live with "orderliness." They enjoyed the benefits of Castilian/Spanish law but faced the burdens as well. This was true whether the laws were transplanted from Spain to America or whether they were written on the East Texas frontier. It was also true whether the females were Spanish, French, *castas*, Native Americans, or African Americans.

SOURCES

Materials used in preparing this chapter are described below. You can find more information about these sources in the Bibliography at the end of the book.

Books

The best information on women and the law in colonial Texas is found in Donald E. Chipman and Harriett Denise Joseph's chapter "Colonial Women" in *Notable Men and Women of Spanish Texas*. Also important is Charles R. Cutter's *The Legal Culture of Northern New Spain, 1700–1810*.

Quotes

Quotes in this chapter are from the following sources: Heath Dillard, *Daughters of the Reconquest: Women in Castilian Town Society, 1100–1300*; A Criminal Code for Nacogdoches, 1783, Robert Bruce Blake Research Collection, Center for American History, Austin, volume 45. Quotes are also from the following documents from the Béxar Archives Translations: Last Will and Testament of María Melián, December 3, 1740, Reel 2; Contract for Sale of Lot by Pedro de Regalado, June 25, 1745, Reel 2; Petition of Antonia Lusgardia Hernández to Governor Manuel de Sandoval, August 9, 1735, Reel 2; Decree of Governor Manuel de Sandoval [August 1735], Reel 2; Writ from María Gertrudis de la Peña to Governor Domingo Cabello [January 25, 1785], Reel 6; Testimony of María Gertrudis de la Peña, February 7, 1785, Reel 6; Order Issued by Governor Domingo Cabello, March 3, 1785, Reel 6; Deposition of Matías Treviño, August 21, 1744, Reel 3; Deposition of Rosa Guerra, August 21, 1744, Reel 3; Summons Issued for Gertrudis Barrón, April 23, 1772, Reel 7; Summons to Priest of Mission Concepción to Deliver Gertrudis Barrón, April 24, 1772, Reel 7; Defense of Juan de Sosa by Joaquín de Orendáin, May 19, 1772, Reel 7; Summation of Proceedings by Domingo de Valcarcel, February 25, 1773, Reel 7; Petition of Gil Ibarvo to Governor Angel Martos, July 2, 1766, Reel 4.

Additional Information

Written records relating to women in colonial Texas, such as lawsuits, estate settlements, wills, and petitions, are contained in the Béxar Archives at Austin and the Béxar Archives Translations (microfilm holdings in various libraries). Also useful is Jean A. Stuntz's "The Persistence of Castilian Law in Frontier Texas: The Legal Status of Women" (master's thesis, University of North Texas, 1996).

Afterword

These men and women deserve attention for their own life stories. For example, readers of all ages have been moved by the story of Cabeza de Vaca and the hardships he faced. To be sure, the history of Spanish Texas is larger than any single life. Recognizing this, we have presented multiple biographies that span the entire colonial period—from explorers to key figures in Texas's independence from Spain in 1821. We have looked at important explorers and settlers in all parts of the future Lone Star State. You have read about Coronado in the west and north, José de Escandón in the south, and Antonio Gil Ibarvo (along with many others) in the east.

By studying explorers, missionaries, French Indian agents, Spanish military officers, crown agents, governors, rebel leaders, and colonial women we have tried to add color and interest to the rich subject that is Texas history. We have chosen these people for their human interest and because they played important roles.

Cabeza de Vaca and Alonso de León were early explorers and pathfinders. An important part of Texas's religious history is the role played by missionaries such as Fathers Francisco Hidalgo and Antonio Margil. María de Agreda, the famous Lady in Blue, adds mystery to the missionaries' actual work among the Indians. Military captains such as the Marqués de Aguayo and Pedro de Rivera made Texas first stronger and then weaker. Forty years later, suggestions by the Marqués de Rubí changed the face of East Texas and the lives of its settlers. In the meantime, Felipe de Rábago's sinful behavior and bad example for his men most likely led to a double murder and the failure of three missions in central Texas. Despite turning his life around, Rábago's record at San Sabá was not much better. Frenchmen Louis St. Denis and Athanase de Mézières are good examples of early multiculturalism. St. Denis's wife, Manuela Sánchez, is the first really important woman on the Texas scene. Domingo Cabello, although he did not like Texas, managed to sign a peace treaty with the Comanches. His efforts brought Spain peace with the most powerful and feared Indians in Texas. In the late colonial period, Bernardo Gutiérrez and Joaquín de Arredondo are two men who were almost exact opposites in their goals. As a group, these men and women represent truly interesting personalities.

But what about colonial women who are not so well known? Because Texas was a dangerous frontier province of New Spain, having hundreds of soldiers stationed at various presidios meant that men outnumbered women in Spanish Texas. Men did the fighting and were more likely to die young. While they were absent, women (at times widows) had to be leaders of families and protectors of children. By looking at what we have called faceless and nameless females, we have managed to give some of them names and make them better known. Their story adds balance to histories that have given almost total attention to explorers, conquistadors, soldiers, missionaries, and governors. These Spanish, French, *mestiza, mulata,* and Native American women are the true mothers of Texas.

Bibliography

ARCHIVAL MATERIALS

Archivo General de Indias (Seville)

Béxar Archives (Austin)

Béxar Archives Translations (Microfilm)

Catholic Archives of Texas, Austin

Robert Bruce Blake Research Collection, 75 volumes (1958–1959), Center for American History, Austin

Robert Bruce Blake Research Collection, Supplement, 18 volumes (1969–1970), Center for American History, Austin

University of Texas Archives, Center for American History, Austin

BOOKS

Alessio Robles, Vito. *Coahuila y Texas en la época colonial.* Mexico City: Editorial Cultura, 1938.

Almaráz, Félix D., Jr. *Tragic Cavalier: Governor Manuel Salcedo of Texas, 1803–1813.* Austin: University of Texas Press, 1971.

Arnold, J. Barto III, and Robert S. Weddle. *The Nautical Archeology of Padre Island: The Spanish Shipwrecks of 1554.* New York: Academic Press, 1978.

Arricivita, Juan Domingo. *Crónica seráfica y apostólica del colegio de propaganda fide de la Santa Cruz de Querétaro en la Nueva España.* Part 2. Mexico City: Don Felipe de Zúñiga y Ontiveros, 1792.

Bolton, Herbert E., ed. and trans. *Athanase de Mézières and the Louisiana-Texas Frontier, 1768–1780.* 2 vols. Cleveland: Arthur H. Clark, 1914.

Bolton, Herbert E. *Coronado: Knight of Pueblos and Plains.* Albuquerque: University of New Mexico Press, 1964.

Bolton, Herbert E., ed. *Spanish Exploration in the Southwest, 1542–1706.* Reprint. New York: Barnes and Noble, 1963.

Brinckerhoff, Sidney B., and Odie B. Faulk. *Lancers for the King: A Study of the Frontier Military System of Northern New Spain, with a Translation of the Royal Regulations of 1772.* Phoenix: Arizona Historical Foundation, 1965.

Castañeda, Carlos E. *Our Catholic Heritage in Texas, 1519–1936.* 7 vols. Austin: Von Boeckmann–Jones, 1936–1958.

Chipman, Donald E. *Spanish Texas, 1519–1821.* Reprint. Austin: University of Texas Press, 1994.

Chipman, Donald E., and Harriett Denise Joseph. *Notable Men and Women of Spanish Texas.* Austin: University of Texas Press, 1999.

Colahan, Clark. *The Visions of Sor María de Agreda: Writing Knowledge and Power.* Tucson: University of Arizona Press, 1994.

Cutter, Charles R. *The Legal Culture of Northern New Spain, 1700–1810.* Albuquerque: University of New Mexico Press, 1995.

Davies, R. Trevor. *Spain in Decline.* New York: St. Martin's Press, 1965.

Day, A. Grove. *Coronado's Quest: The Discovery of the Southwestern States.* Berkeley: University of California Press, 1940.

De la Teja, Jesús F. *San Antonio de Béxar: A Community on New Spain's Northern Frontier.* Albuquerque: University of New Mexico Press, 1995.

Dillard, Heath. *Daughters of the Reconquest: Women in Castilian Town Society, 1100–1300.* Cambridge: Cambridge University Press, 1984.

Espinosa, Isidro Félix de. *El peregrino septentrional atlante: Delineado en la exemplaríssima vida del Venerable Padre F. Antonio Margil de Jesús.* Mexico City: Joseph Bernardo de Hogal, 1737.

Estado general de las fundaciones hechas por D. José de Escandón en la colonia de Nuevo Santander. 2 vols. Mexico City: Talleres Gráficos de la Nación, 1929, 1930.

Faulk, Odie B. *The Last Years of Spanish Texas, 1778–1821.* The Hague: Mouton, 1964.

Favata, Martin A., and José B. Fernández. *The Account: Alvar Núñez Cabeza de Vaca's "Relación."* Houston: Arte Público, 1993.

Foster, William C. *Spanish Expeditions into Texas, 1689–1768.* Austin: University of Texas Press, 1995.

Garrett, Julia K. *Green Flag over Texas: A Story of the Last Years of Spain in Texas.* New York: Cordova Press, 1939.

Gómez Canedo, Lino, ed. *Primeras exploraciones y poblamiento de Texas (1686–1694).* Monterrey: Publicaciones del Instituto Tecnológico y Estudios Superiores de Monterrey, 1968.

Greenleaf, Richard E. *The Mexican Inquisition of the Sixteenth Century.* Albuquerque: University of New Mexico Press, 1969.

Hill, Lawrence F. *José de Escandón and the Founding of Nuevo Santander: A Study in Spanish Colonization.* Columbus: Ohio State University Press, 1926.

Jackson, Jack, ed., and William C. Foster, annot. *Imaginary Kingdom: Texas as Seen by the Rivera and Rubí Military Expeditions, 1727 and 1767.* Austin: Texas State Historical Association, 1995.

Joutel, Henri. *Joutel's Journal of La Salle's Last Voyage.* Reprint. Chicago: Caxton Club, 1896.

Kamen, Henry. *The Spanish Inquisition.* New York: New American Library, 1966.

Kavanagh, Thomas W. *Comanche Political History: An Ethnohistorical Perspective, 1706–1875.* Lincoln: University of Nebraska Press, 1996.

Kendrick, T. D. *Mary of Agreda: The Life and Legend of a Spanish Nun.* London: Routledge and Kegan Paul, 1967.

Keyes, Frances Parkinson. *I, the King.* New York: Fawcett World Library, 1967.

Kinnaird, Lawrence, ed. *Spain in the Mississippi Valley, 1765–1794: Translations of Materials from the Spanish Archives in the Bancroft Library.* 3 vols. Washington, D.C.: U.S. Government Printing Office, 1946–1949.

Leutenegger, Benedict, trans., and Marion A. Habig, ed. *Nothingness Itself: Selected Writings of Ven. Fr. Antonio Margil, 1690–1724.* Chicago: Franciscan Herald Press, 1976.

Miller, Hubert J. *José de Escandón: Colonizer of Nuevo Santander.* Edinburg, Tex.: New Santander Press, 1980.

Morfi, Juan Agustín. *History of Texas, 1673–1779.* Translated and edited by Carlos E. Castañeda. 2 vols. Albuquerque: Quivira Society, 1935.

Morris, John M. *El Llano Estacado: Exploration and Imagination on the High Plains of Texas and New Mexico, 1536–1860.* Austin: Texas State Historical Association, 1997.

Naylor, Thomas H., and Charles W. Polzer, comps. and eds. *Pedro de*

Rivera and the Military Regulations for Northern New Spain, 1724–1729: A Documentary History of His Frontier Inspection and the "Reglamento de 1729." Tucson: University of Arizona Press, 1988.

Oberste, William H. *The Restless Friar: Venerable Fray Antonio Margil de Jesús.* Austin: Von Boeckmann–Jones, 1970.

Ríos, Eduardo Enrique. *Life of Fray Antonio Margil, O.F.M.* Translated by Benedict Leutenegger. Washington, D.C.: Academy of American Franciscan History, 1959.

Santos, Richard G., trans. *Aguayo Expedition into Texas, 1721.* Austin: Jenkins Publishing, 1981.

Schwarz, Ted. *Forgotten Battlefield of the First Texas Revolution: The Battle of the Medina, August 18, 1813.* Edited and annotated by Robert H. Thonhoff. Austin: Eakin Press, 1985.

Simpson, Lesley B., ed. *The San Sabá Papers: A Documentary Account of the Founding and Destruction of the San Sabá Mission.* San Francisco: John Howell Books, 1959.

Starnes, Gary B. *The San Gabriel Missions, 1746–1756.* Madrid: Ministry of Foreign Affairs, Government of Spain, 1969.

Weber, David J. *The Mexican Frontier, 1821–1846: The American Southwest under Mexico.* Albuquerque: University of New Mexico Press, 1982.

Weddle, Robert S. *Changing Tides: Twilight and Dawn in the Spanish Sea, 1763–1803.* College Station: Texas A&M University Press, 1995.

Weddle, Robert S. *The French Thorn: Rival Explorers in the Spanish Sea, 1682–1762.* College Station: Texas A&M University Press, 1991.

Weddle, Robert S. *San Juan Bautista: Gateway to Spanish Texas.* Austin: University of Texas Press, 1968.

Weddle, Robert S. *The San Sabá Mission: Spanish Pivot in Texas.* Austin: University of Texas Press, 1964.

Weddle, Robert S. *Wilderness Manhunt: The Spanish Search for La Salle.* Austin: University of Texas Press, 1973.

Weddle, Robert S., Mary Christine Morkovsky, and Patricia Galloway, trans. and eds. *Three Primary Documents: La Salle, the Mississippi, and the Gulf.* College Station: Texas A&M University Press, 1987.

Wilkinson, J. B. *Laredo and the Rio Grande Frontier.* Austin: Jenkins Publishing, 1975.

ARTICLES

Adorno, Rolena. "The Negotiation of Fear in Cabeza de Vaca's *Naufragios." Representations* 33 (Winter 1991): 163–199.

Allen, Henry E. "The Parrilla Expedition to the Red River in 1759." *Southwestern Historical Quarterly* 43 (July 1939): 53–71.

Benson, Nettie Lee, ed. and trans. "A Governor's Report on Texas in 1809." *Southwestern Historical Quarterly* 71 (April 1968): 603–615.

Buckley, Eleanor C. "The Aguayo Expedition into Texas and Louisiana, 1719–1722." *Quarterly of the Texas State Historical Association* 15 (July 1911): 1–65.

Campbell, Randolph B. "Touchstone Corner." *Touchstone* 14 (1995): iv–vii.

Campbell, Randolph B., ed. *Texas History Documents: Volume 1 to 1877*. New York: Worth Publishers, 1997.

Chipman, Donald E. "In Search of Cabeza de Vaca's Route across Texas: An Historiographical Survey." *Southwestern Historical Quarterly* 91 (October 1987): 127–148.

Forrestal, Peter P., trans. "The Venerable Padre Fray Antonio Margil de Jesús." *Preliminary Studies of the Catholic Historical Society* 2 (April 1932): 5–34.

Garrett, Kathryn. "The First Constitution of Texas, April 17, 1813." *Southwestern Historical Quarterly* 40 (April 1937): 290–308.

Gronet, Richard W. "The United States and the Invasion of Texas." *The Americas* 25 (January 1969): 281–306.

Gumbinger, Cuthbert. "The Tercentenary of Mother Agreda's *Mystical City of God." The Age of Mary: An Exclusively Marian Magazine* (January–February 1958): 16–21.

Hackett, Charles W. "The Marquis of San Miguel de Aguayo and His Recovery of Texas from the French, 1719–1723." *Southwestern Historical Quarterly* 49 (October 1945): 193–214.

Haggard, J. Villasana. "The Counter-Revolution of Béxar, 1811." *Southwestern Historical Quarterly* 43 (October 1939): 222–235.

Haggard, J. Villasana, translator. "Spain's Indian Policy in Texas." *Southwestern Historical Quarterly* 44 (October 1940): 232–244.

John, Elizabeth A. H., ed., and Adán Benavides Jr., trans. "Inside the Comanchería, 1785: The Diary of Pedro Vial and Francisco Xavier Chaves." *Southwestern Historical Quarterly* 98 (July 1994): 27–56.

Lemée, Patricia R. "Manuela Sánchez Navarro." *Natchitoches Genealogist* 20 (October 1995): 17–21.

Lemée, Patricia R. "Tios and Tantes: Familial and Political Relationships of Natchitoches and the Spanish Colonial Frontier." *Southwestern Historical Quarterly* 101 (January 1998): 341–358.

Madden, Joseph Mary. "A Brief Biography of Venerable Mary of Agreda."
The Age of Mary: An Exclusively Marian Magazine (January–
February 1958): 91–98.

West, Elizabeth Howard, trans. and ed. "Diary of José Bernardo
Gutiérrez de Lara, 1811–1812, I, II." *American Historical Review* 34
(October 1928): 55–77; 34 (January 1929): 281–294.

PUBLISHED DOCUMENTS

Agreda, Venerable María de. Letter, 1631. In *The Age of Mary: An
Exclusively Marian Magazine* (January–February 1958): 127–128.

Benavides, Alonso de. Letter from Spain, 1631. In *The Age of Mary: An
Exclusively Marian Magazine* (January–February 1958): 126–127.

Campbell, Randolph B., ed. *Texas History Documents: Volume 1 to
1877.* New York: Worth Publishers, 1997.

UNPUBLISHED WORKS

Benavides, Alonso de. Memorial of Father Alonso de Benavides Regarding the Conversions of New Mexico, February 12, 1634. Catholic
Archives of Texas, Austin.

Faulk, Odie B. "Texas during the Administration of Governor Domingo
Cabello y Robles, 1778–1786." Master's thesis, Texas Technological
College, 1960.

Klier, Betje B. "Théodore Pavie." Unpublished manuscript in the possession of the authors.

Stuntz, Jean A. "The Persistence of Castilian Law in Frontier Texas: The
Legal Status of Women." Master's thesis, University of North Texas,
1996.

Index

Acoma (Sky City), 21
adultery, 233–239
Agreda (village), 32
Agreda, María Jesús de (Lady in
   Blue), 94, 211; birth and youth,
   32–33; bilocations, 32, 34–38;
   joins Order of Discalced Nuns,
   33–34; and Father Benavides, 36–
   37; and Inquisition, 38–41; and
   Philip IV, 41–42; death and assessment, 40, 43–44, 241
agriculture, Indian, 23, 55, 57, 116
agriculture, Spanish, 99
Aguayo, José Ramón de Azlor y Virto
   de Vera, Second Marqués de San
   Miguel de, 107, 227; agrees to mission at San Antonio, 100; offers
   services to viceroy, 108–109;
   crosses Río Grande, 109; to East
   Texas, 109–112; re-establishes
   missions, 113, 180; builds mission
   and presidio at Matagorda Bay,
   113; reconstructs presidios, 113–
   114; returns to Monclova, 114;
   death and assessment, 114, 117
Aguayo, Marquesa de San Miguel de,
   107
Aguirre, Pedro de, 77
Alamo. See San Antonio de Valero,
   Mission
Alarcón, Martín de, 219

Alazán, battle of, 204
Albuquerque, 22
Alhaja, Martín, 2
Almaráz, Félix D. Jr., 207
Altamira, Marqués de (auditor de
   guerra), 141
Altamira, Villa, 140
Alvarado, Hernando de, 21
Alvarez Barreiro, Francisco, 115
Alvarez de Toledo, José, 204, 205
Andrés (Indian), 123, 124
Andry, Luis Antonio, 166, 167
Angelina River, 80
Apache Indians (general), 24, 112,
   117, 126, 151, 155, 156, 159, 161,
   187; and De Mézières, 160, 220
Apachería, 125, 126
Arana, Catalina, 32, 33
Arizona, 21
Arkansas River, 27
Arocha, Antonia de, 223
Arredondo, Joaquín de, 223; birth
   and military career, 202; and
   Hidalgo revolt, 203; to battle of
   Medina, 204–205; executions by,
   206–207; leaves Texas, 207, 208;
   approves of Moses Austin's re-
   quest, 209; last years and death,
   207–210
Atlantic Ocean, 2, 18, 29, 44
Attoyac River, 162

Austin, Moses, 209
Avavare Indians, 10, 11
Aztecs, 17

Barbier, Gabriel Minime, Sieur, 214
Barbier, Madame, 214
Barrón, Gertrudis, 234, 235, 236
Benavides, Father Alonso de, 36, 37, 43
Benites, María, 222
Bernardino (Tejas chieftain), 72, 77
Béxar, Villa. *See* San Antonio (town)
Bidais Indians, 119, 155, 156
Bienville, Jean-Baptiste Le Moyne, Sieur de, 78, 79
Bigotes (Indian, sixteenth-century), 22, 23, 27
Bigotes (Indian, eighteenth-century), 154, 155
Blondel, Philippe, 105, 106, 107
Boca de Leones, 97, 98
Bonaparte, Joseph, 195
Bonaparte, Napoleon, 195
Boneo y Morales, Justo, 230
Bousquet, Juan Bautista, 171
Brazil, 13
Brazos River, 112, 207
Bréman, Eustache, 63, 216
Bryan–College Station, Texas, 110
Bucareli, Villa. *See* Nuestra Señora del Pilar de Bucareli
Bucareli y Ursúa, Antonio María de, 156, 187–188, 192
buffalo, 7, 10, 24, 25, 29, 51, 62, 110

Cabello y Robles, Domingo, 165, 232, 233; birth and early military career, 166; early problems as governor, 166–168; views of Indians, 168; and Comanches, 169–174; treaty with Comanches, 174; complaints about Texas, 175–176; troubles with ranchers, 176–178; departs San Antonio, 178; reassignment in Cuba, 178; last years and assessment, 178–179, 242
Cabeza de Vaca, Alvar Núñez: origin of name, 1–2; birth, 2; as soldier, 2; member of Narváez expedition, 2–4; on Malhado, 4–5; as ethnog-

rapher, 5–6, 8–9, 10–11; as trader, 6–7; as physician, 6, 11–12; as slave of Indians, 6, 8–9; from South Texas to Mexico City, 10–13; to Spain and South America, 12–15; banished from Indies, 15; death and assessment, 15, 241
Cacique (Indian), 22
Caddo Indians. *See* Hasinai Confederation
Cadillac, Antoine de La Mothe, Sieur de, 82–83, 84, 86
Cahinnio Indians, 154
Caldera, Mission, 120
California, 29
Calleja, Félix María, 203, 204
Calvillo, María del Carmen, 223
Calvillo, Ygnacio, 223
Camargo, Villa de, 140, 142, 232, 233
Cameron County, 147
Camino Real, 110
Canary Islanders, 219, 220, 228
Canary Islands, 219, 220
Candelaria, Mission. *See* Nuestra Señora de la Candelaria
cannibalism, 6
Cantú, Carlos, 140
Captain Iron Shirt (Indian), 171
Captain Shaved Head (Indian), 171
Captain Squint-Eye (Indian), 37
Carabajal, Cristóbal, 219
Caribbean Sea, 2
Carib Indians, 166
Castañeda, Pedro, 24, 25
cattle, 177, 178, 188
cattle brands, 177
Ceballos, Juan José, 120, 121, 122, 124, 129, 132
Cerda, Antonia de la, 217
Charles III, 150, 151, 152, 153, 158, 185, 188
Charles IV, 195
Charles V (emperor), 29
Chávez, Francisco Xavier, 171, 172, 173
Chiapas, 93, 96
chickens, 110
Chicken War, 100, 106, 107, 108, 110, 113, 117, 180

Chihuahua (province), 161
Chihuahua, Villa de, 196, 197
Chirinos, Andrés, 236, 237
Christians (general), 2, 5
Cíbolo Indians, 63
Claiborne, William C. C., 198, 200, 202, 204
Clement X (pope), 43
Coahuila (province), 94, 97, 108, 113, 124, 132, 196, 197, 204
Cocay (Indian), 152
Coco Indians, 119, 122, 123, 124, 129
College of Nuestra Señora de Guadalupe de Zacatecas, 96
College of Santa Cruz de Querétaro, 93
Columbus, Christopher, 1, 2, 17, 39, 40, 226
Comanche Indians, 125, 130, 131, 155, 159, 160, 162, 187, 188; enter Texas, 117; attack San Sabá, 127–128, 132; and De Mézières, 153–154, 156, 161; and Cabello, 165, 169, 171–174, 179; treaty with, 174, 242; and Rubí, 184
Comecrudo Indians, 137, 141
Concepción, Mission (Nuestra Señora de la Purísima Concepción), 199
Coronado. See Vázquez de Coronado, Francisco
Coronel, Francisco, 32
Costa del Seno Mexicano, 135, 148
Croix, Teodoro de: as commandant general, 159, 177, 178; and war councils, 159–161; and De Mézières, 162–163
Cruillas, Joaquín de Montserrat, Marqués de, 129
Cruz, Tomás de la, 166, 167
Cuba, 3, 166, 178
Culiacán, 29
Curbelo, María Ana, 222, 223

Davenport, Samuel, 198
deer, 110
De la Teja, Jesús, 220
Delgado, Antonio, 200
Delgado, Leonor, 222, 223

Delgado, Lucas, 228
Delgado Meleano, Mariana, 220
De Mézières, Athanase, 170, 175, 178; birth, education, and exile, 149–150; marriages and children, 150, 154, 163; as Indian agent, 150–157; visits Europe, 157; death of family members, 158–159; to San Antonio, 160; expedition to Red River, 160; named interim governor of Texas, 161; accidents and illnesses, 162; to Nacogdoches and San Antonio, 162; recommendations to Croix, 162–163; death and assessment, 163, 164, 242
De Mézières, Louis Christophe Claude, 149
Discalced Nuns, 33, 34, 43
dogs, 24
Díaz de Bustamante, José Ramón, 203
Dolores, Father Francisco Mariano de los, 125, 126
Dolores, Nuestra Señora de, 141

Eastern Interior Provinces, 203
El Cañón missions. See Nuestra Señora de la Candelaria; Nuestra Señora de la Candelaria del Cañón; San Lorenzo de Santa Cruz
El Dorado, 17
Elizondo, Ignacio, 202, 204, 205, 207
El Lobanillo, 186, 188, 192
El Morro (Havana), 237
El Paso, Texas, 12
El Señor de la Yedra, 166
Escandón, Josefa, 144
Escandón, Manuel de, 135, 147
Escandón y Elguera, José de: early life and military assignments, 134–135; and Sierra Gorda, 135; marriages, 135; explores Costa del Seno Mexicano, 136–138; settlement of Costa, 138–142; assignment of lands, 142–143; appointed Count of Sierra Gorda, 140; opposition to, 134, 140–141; inspections of his colonies, 143–145; charges against and defense,

145–147; death and assessment, 134, 147–148, 241
Espinosa, Father Isidro Félix de, 77, 102
Estevanico (Stephen), 8, 13, 18
Europe (general), 2

Fazende, Pelagie, 150
Ferdinand VI, 119, 140
Ferdinand VII, 195, 196
Flores, Gil, 187
Flores de Abrego, Juan José, 223
Flores y Valdés, Josefa de, 229, 231, 239
Flores y Valdés, Rosa, 229
Florida, 2, 3, 29
foods (of Indians), 9, 53
Franciscans (general), 35, 36, 69, 75, 91, 110, 116, 120, 121, 124, 125, 129, 132

Galve, Elvira, 216
Galve, Gaspar de Sandoval Silva y Mendoza, Conde de, 216
Galveston Island, 1, 4, 8
Gálvez, Bernardo de, 159, 161, 177
Ganzabal, Father José, 122, 123, 124, 129, 132
García, Father José Joaquín, 192
Garcitas Creek, 113
Garza Falcón, Blas María de la, 137
Garza Falcón, Miguel de la, 137
Gavino de la Trinidad, Juan, 223
Geronimo, Little (Geronimillo), 49
gifts (for Indians), 54, 112, 141, 152, 153, 161, 163, 168, 169, 171, 172, 174, 213
Gil Ibarvo, Antonio: birth, 185; as illegal trader, 186; and East Texas evacuation, 186–187; to Mexico City, 187–188; as founder of Nacogdoches and official, 188–189; and illegal trade, 189; and criminal codes, 189; and Juan José Peña, 189–191; last years, 192; death and assessment, 192–193, 241; and adulterous wife, 236–237, 239
Gil Ibarvo, Mathieu Antonio, 185, 222

goats, 64
Gomes Mascorro y Garza, Mariana, 85
Gorgoritos (Indian), 155
Grand Canyon, 21
Gran Quivira, 21, 23, 25, 30
Great Plains, 21, 23, 26, 27, 29
Guadalupe River, 110, 125
Guatemala, 95
Guerra, Ana, 217, 218
Guerra, Juana, 219
Guerra, Rosa, 233, 239
Guerrero, Coahuila, 217
Guersec (Indian), 171
Gulf Coast, 1, 4
Gulf of California, 181
Gutiérrez, Bernardo, 194, 205, 241; birth and family, 195–196; and United States, 197–198; expedition to Texas, 198–199; and independence of Texas, 200–202; removed as leader, 204–205; last years and death, 207–210
Gutiérrez, Father José Antonio, 197
Gutiérrez, Martín, 122–123, 124
Gutiérrez, Santiago, 197
Gutiérrez-Magee Expedition, 198
Guzmán, Nuño de, 13

Hasinai Confederation, 154, 214
Havana, 209, 211
Hernández, Antonia Lusgardia, 231
Hernández Ibarvo, Juana, 185
Herrera, María Guadalupe de, 191
Herrera, Simón de, 199, 200
Hidalgo, Father Francisco: birth and youth, 69; early missionary work, 69–71; and East Texas Indians, 71–72; leaves Texas, 73; assigned to northern Mexico, 76–77; plots return to East Texas, 77–78, 80, 82; missionary in East Texas, 85, 90, 241; leaves East Texas, 100, 107
Hidalgo County, 147
Hidalgo y Costilla, Miguel, 196, 197, 202, 203
Holy Inquisition, 38–41, 43
Honduras, 166
horses, 23, 29, 65, 67, 68, 108, 113, 169, 177

Huastec Indians, 140

Iberville, Pierre Le Moyne, Sieur d', 78
Ignacio (Béxar child), 231
Incas, 17
infanticide, 9
Inquisition, 38–41, 43
insects, 9, 64, 65, 110, 115
Isla de Malhado (Isle of Misfortune), 4, 5, 6
Isleta, New Mexico, 32
Italy, 2
Iturbide, Agustín de, 207, 208, 209

Jackson, Andrew, 208
Jarry, Jean, 49
Jaumave Indians, 146
Jews and Judaism, 39
Jicarilla Apaches, 169
Jiménez, Father Diego, 130
Joseph María (Indian), 167, 168
Joutel, Henri, 213, 214
Jumano Indians, 32, 34, 38, 63

Kadohadacho Indians, 67, 79, 152, 156
Kansas, 17, 21, 27, 30
Karankawa Indians, 4, 5, 48, 51, 53, 81, 165, 166, 167, 168, 184, 213, 214, 216
Kichai Indians, 153, 154, 162

La Bahía, 113, 116, 117, 137, 183, 184, 198, 199, 208
La Belle, 213
Lady in Blue. *See* Agreda, María Jesús de
Lafora, Nicolás de, 181, 182, 183, 184, 186
La Nana Creek, 100, 103
Laredo, Villa de, 141
La Relación (The Account), 8
La Rochelle, 79
La Salle, René Robert Cavelier, Sieur de, 109, 113, 115, 212, 213; colony of, 46–48, 51, 214; death, 51, 53
Las Casas, Juan Bautista de, 196, 197
Las Porciones Society, 147

Leal, José, 228
Leal Goraz, Juan, 229
León, Alonso de (the younger), 214, 216; importance of, 46; birth and parents, 46–47; in Spain, 47; early explorations, 47; 1st and 2nd searches for French colony, 48; as governor of Coahuila, 49; distrust of Indians, 49; executes Little Geronimo, 49; 3rd and 4th searches for French colony, 49–51; explores Matagorda Bay, 51–52; reports on Tejas Indians, 52, 57; differences with Massanet, 52–53; helps found Mission San Francisco de los Tejas, 54–55; ransoms French children, 55–56; death and assessment, 58–60, 241
Liñán, Francisco de, 230
Lipan Apaches, 125, 127, 133, 159, 160, 173, 174, 181, 184, 199; missions for, 126, 130–132
livestock, 62, 98, 99, 107, 108, 109, 110, 126, 142, 177
Llano Estacado, 25
Llera y Bayas, Josefa, 135
Longoria, María Antonia, 217
López, Father Diego, 34, 36, 37
López de Cárdenas, García, 21
López de la Cámara Alta, Agustín, 141
Los Adaes. *See* Nuestra Señora del Pilar de los Adaes
Los Ojos de Padre Margil, 100
Louisiana, 112, 113, 150
Louis XIV, 78
Luis (slave), 230
Luisa (Indian), 123

Madison, James, 198
Magee, Augustus W., 198, 199, 201
Malacosa (Bad Thing), 10–11
Mancilla, Father Sebastián, 34
Manso y Zúñiga, Archbishop Francisco, 34
Margil, Juan, 90
Margil de Jesús, Father Antonio: birth and youth, 90–92; arrives in New Spain, 92; helps found college at Querétaro, 92; and Central

America, 93–96; and miracles, 94, 95, 100; founds college at Zacatecas, 96; and Nayarit Indians, 96–97; and East Texas missions, 99–100; founds Mission San José, 100–101; returns to Zacatecas, 102; illnesses and death, 102–103; designated venerable, 103; efforts to beatify and sanctify, 103; assessment, 103–104, 241
Mariame Indians, 8, 9
Martínez, Antonio, 207, 209
Martínez, Francisco, 62, 63, 65, 68, 79
Martos y Navarette, Angel de, 237
Massanet, Father Damián: on search for La Salle's fort, 51; learns of Hasinais, 52; disputes with León, 55; founds Mission San Francisco de los Tejas, 55; proposes missions for Texas, 57–58; disputes with Terán, 62, 64, 67; at Red River, 67; remains in East Texas, 72; leaves East Texas, 72–73
Matagorda Bay, 56, 65, 67, 68, 109, 113, 114, 166, 167, 212, 213
Mateo (Indian), 167, 168
Mauget, Marie de, 149
Maya Indians, 93, 94, 96
medicine (surgery), 6, 10, 11, 162
Medina, Vicenta, 222
Medina River, battle of, 205, 206, 207, 209
Melián, María, 228, 239
Mena, Marcos, 212
Menard, Texas, 126
Menchaca, Diego, 234, 235, 236
Menchaca, José, 197
Menchaca, Luis Antonio, 235
Mendoza, Antonio de, 17, 18, 29, 30
Mexico City, 13, 17, 20, 21, 29, 30
Mississippi River, 4
Mobile, 82–83, 85
Molina, Father Miguel de, 127
Monclova, war council at, 68, 73, 114, 117, 128, 159
Monroe, James, 198
Monterrey, 197, 208
Moral, Guadalupe del, 203

Morelos y Pavón, José María, 196, 198
Mosquito Indians, 166
mules, 65, 67, 113, 169
Muslims (general), 2, 18
Mystical City of God, 38, 40, 41

Nacogdoches, 103, 161, 162, 187–192, 198, 207, 222, 237, 238
Nadador Indians, 109
Narváez, Pánfilo de, 3
Natchitoches (town), 81, 85, 86, 101, 105, 106, 112, 150, 151, 152, 153, 154, 155, 156, 158, 161, 162, 188, 197, 198, 204, 205, 208, 218, 222
Natchitoches (villages), 81, 82
Nations of the North. *See* Norteños
Native Americans (general), 1, 11, 15, 37, 155, 158, 159, 163, 165, 166, 168, 169, 170, 172, 181, 184, 205, 212
Navarro, Angel, 232, 233
Navasota River, 68, 111
Neches River, 80
New Christians, 39
New England Journal of Medicine, 11
New Mexico, 17, 18, 21, 23, 25, 27, 29, 32, 34, 36, 44
New Orleans, 198, 200, 208
New World, 2
Nicaragua, 95, 96, 166, 175
Niza, Father Marcos de, 17–18, 19, 20, 21
Nocona, Texas, 128
Norteños, 151, 152, 153, 154, 156, 158, 160, 161, 171
North Africa, 2, 15
North America, 3, 30
Notre Dame Cathedral (Paris), 3
Nueces River, 140, 147
Nuestra Señora de Guadalupe de los Nacogdoches (missionary college), 96
Nuestra Señora de la Candelaria, Mission, 122, 123, 124
Nuestra Señora de la Candelaria del Cañón (El Cañón mission), 130–131, 132
Nuestra Señora de la Purísima Concepción, Mission, 199

Nuestra Señora del Espíritu Santo de Zúñiga, Mission, 183
Nuestra Señora de los Dolores (settlement), 141
Nuestra Señora del Pilar de Bucareli (settlement), 188
Nuestra Señora del Pilar de los Adaes (presidio), 101, 106, 107, 112, 113, 115, 116, 117, 137, 153, 180, 181, 183, 187, 237
Nueva Vizcaya (province), 204
Nuevo León (province), 47, 204
Nuevo Santander (province), 137, 138, 140–147, 197, 203
Nuevo Santander, Villa de, 140, 141
Núñez Morillo, Josefa, 231
Núñez Morillo, Miguel, 230, 231

Ocean Springs, Mississippi, 78
Oklahoma, 17, 27
Old Christians, 39
Olivares, Antonio de San Buenaventura y, 76, 77
Orcoquiza Indians, 119
O'Reilly, Alejandro, 150, 151, 152, 154
Orobio Basterra, Joaquín, 137–138
Ortiz Parrilla, Diego: at San Sabá, 126–128; and Red River Campaign, 128
Osorio y Llamas, José, 144
oxen, 95

Pacific Ocean, 12, 13, 29
Padilla, Father Juan, 27
Padilla, María, 185, 236, 237, 239
Padre Island, 211, 212
Palacio, Juan Fernando, 144
Pame Indians, 141, 145
Panhandle (Texas), 21, 24, 28
Pánuco River, 212
Paraguay, 13
Paris, France, 3
Paso de Francia, 77
Paso Tomás, 188
Pecos River, 24, 28
Pedrajo, Dominga de, 135
Peña, José de la (informer), 156–157
Peña, Juan José, 189, 190, 191
Peña, María Gertrudis de la, 232, 233, 239

Peña del Castillo, Mission, 139
Pensacola, 3
Perea, Father Esteban de, 34
Perry, Henry, 204
Peru, 17, 30
Philip IV, 38, 41–42, 44
Pinilla, Father Miguel, 121, 122, 123, 124
pirates, 47, 92
plants (indigenous), 8, 9, 10, 15
Poor Clares Order. See Discalced Nuns
Presidio, Texas, 12
Presidio de los Tejas, 106, 113, 115, 116
presidios (general), 58, 82, 114, 116, 117, 119, 121, 182
Prudhomme, Marie-Madeleine, 222
Pueblo Indians, 22, 23, 25, 28

Queen Isabella, 39
Querétaro, 69, 73, 76, 77, 81, 92, 93, 94, 99, 102, 120, 121, 122, 135, 137, 138
Quivoz, Father Cristóbal, 37

Rábago y Terán, Felipe de: early life, 119; and women, 120; quarrels with missionaries, 121–122; relations with Cocos, 122; suspicion of murders, 122–124; imprisonment, 124; release and return to command, 128–130; and San Sabá, 129–132; death and assessment, 132–133, 241–242
Ragged Castaways, 1, 10, 11, 12, 13, 17
Rambin, Marie, 222
Ramón, Antonia, 229
Ramón, Diego, 76, 77, 81, 82, 83, 86, 98, 99
Ramón, Domingo, 84, 85, 106, 109, 113, 180, 217
rancherías, Indian, 130
ranching, 178, 181, 222–223
Rancho de las Cabras, 223
Real Presidio de San Sabá. See San Luis de las Amarillas
Reconquest (Spanish), 2
Red River, 27, 66–67, 101, 158
Regalado de Treviño, Pedro de, 229

religion (general), 33, 37, 75
Republican Army of the North, 198–206, 209
Republic of the Río Grande, 208
Resendi, María Bárbara, 146
Revilla, Villa de, 197, 203, 208
Reyes, María Alexandra de los, 229
Reynosa, Villa de, 140
Río de las Palmas (Río Soto la Marina), 137, 138
Río Grande, 1, 11, 12, 22, 23, 25, 26, 27, 28, 29, 109, 113, 137, 197, 212
Rio Grande City, Texas, 147
Río Soto la Marina. *See* Río de las Palmas
Río Verde (settlement), 146
Ripperdá, Juan María Vicencio, Barón de, 152, 153, 154, 155, 156, 158, 159, 161, 185, 186, 187, 188
Rivera y Villalón, Pedro de: character of, 114; as presidio inspector, 114–116, 181; and changes in presidios' manpower, 116; relocates three East Texas missions to San Antonio, 116–117; assessment, 117, 241
Rockdale, Texas, 119
Rodríguez Robayna, María, 220
Ros, Esperanza, 62
Rubí, Cayetano María Pignatelli Corbera y San Climent, Marqués de, 180, 186; parents, birth, youth, and character, 181; at Los Adaes, 181; visitation of presidios, 181–184; suggests reorganization of presidios, 184; recommends new Indian policy, 184–185; influences reorganization of presidios, 185; assessment, 181, 241

Sabine River, 67, 76, 198
Saint Anthony (convent), 32, 34
Salado Creek, 199, 200, 203, 204
Salas, Father Juan, 34, 36, 37
Salazar, Father Diego de, 76
Salcedo, Manuel María de, 196–200, 202, 207
Salinas Varona, Gregorio de, 62, 71, 72, 73, 75
Saltillo, 209, 229, 232

San Antonio (town), 63, 109, 111, 113, 114, 116, 121, 126, 165, 175, 200, 204, 220, 228, 237
San Antonio de Béxar (presidio), 113, 183, 184, 204, 205, 206, 208
San Antonio de Padilla, 139
San Antonio de Valero, Mission, 76, 100, 113, 116, 219, 233, 234
San Antonio River, 100
San Augustine, Texas, 103
Sánchez, Josefa, 217
Sánchez, Tomás, 141
Sánchez Navarro, Manuela, 82, 83; marriage, 84, 217; genealogy, 84–85; children, 86, 218; reunion with St. Denis, 86; death, 218
Sandoval, Manuel de, 231
San Fernando de Béxar. *See* San Antonio (town)
San Fernando de Güemes, 139
San Francisco de los Neches, Mission, 85
San Francisco de los Patos (hacienda), 108, 117
San Francisco de los Tejas, Mission, 63, 64, 68, 71, 72, 82, 217, 218
San Francisco Xavier de Gigedo, Presidio, 120, 124, 126
San Francisco Xavier de Nájera, Mission, 113
San Gabriel River, 119, 120
San José de San Miguel de Aguayo, Mission, 100–101, 113, 114
San Juan Bautista, Mission, 76, 77, 84, 98, 99, 113, 130, 217
San Juan Bautista, Presidio, 77, 81, 109, 184, 217
San Lorenzo, Mission (in Coahuila), 125
San Lorenzo de Santa Cruz, Mission, 130–131, 132
San Luis de Cadodachos, 153
San Luis de las Amarillas, Presidio, 126, 129–130, 182
San Luis Potosí, 132, 197, 203, 209
San Marcos, Texas, 125
San Marcos River, 207
San Miguel, Juana de, 217
San Miguel de los Adaes, Mission, 105

San Pedro Creek, 112
San Sabá. *See* San Luis de las Amarillas
San Saba River, 125, 126
Santa Cruz de San Sabá, Mission, 126, 128
Santa María, Fray Vicente de, 144
Santa María de Llera (settlement), 139
Santa María de los Dolores, Mission, 76
Santa María y Silva, Father Miguel de, 153, 154
Santiesteban, Father José de, 127
Santísimo Nombre de María, Mission, 64, 67
Santos, Anna de los, 228
San Xavier de Gigedo, Presidio, 122
San Xavier missions, 119, 120, 121, 122, 125
scurvy, 132
Seven Cities of Cíbola, 18, 19, 20, 22, 30
Seven Years' War, 150, 151
Shaler, William, 198, 199, 200, 202, 204, 205
Siena, Fray Bernardino de, 36
Sierra Gorda, 135, 138, 140
Sierra Morena (Spain), 2
Simon, Pierre, 216
slaves (of Europeans), 166, 230
slaves (of Indians), 6, 7
smallpox, 159, 164, 170
snakes, 9, 110
Sosa, Juan de, 234, 235, 236
Soto la Marina (settlement), 140
Soto la Marina, Spain, 134
South America, 3, 13, 14
Southwest Texas, 35
Spanish War for Independence, 195
Starr County, 147
St. Denis, Louis Juchereau de: birth and education, 78–79; with Iberville, 79; and Red River expedition, 79–80; searches for Hidalgo, 80–81; at San Juan Bautista, 82, 86; to Mexico City, 83, 86; marriage, 84, 217, 218, 227; expedition to East Texas, 85, 180; to Mobile and return, 85–86; to Natchitoches and reunion with wife, 86–87; as commandant, 86; death, 86–88; assessment, 86, 242
Stephen (Estevanico), 8, 13, 18

Talon, Isabelle Planteau, 57, 213, 214
Talon, Jean-Baptiste, 56, 60, 63, 79
Talon, Lucien, 56–57, 58, 213
Talon, Marie-Elizabeth, 56, 213
Talon, Marie-Madeleine, 55, 57, 58, 216, 217
Talon, Pierre, 54–55, 58, 79, 81, 82–83, 214, 216
Talon, Robert, 55, 57, 58, 81, 82–83, 213
Tamaulipas, 147, 208
Tampa Bay, 3
Tampico, 203, 212
Taovaya Indians, 153, 155, 160, 171, 172, 173
Tawakoni Indians, 153, 154, 162
Tejas Indians, 64, 71, 81, 83, 99, 110, 111, 112
Tello, Antonio, 233, 234
Terán de los Ríos, Domingo: first governor of Texas, 61; expedition of 1691, 61–65; to Matagorda Bay and return, 65–66; expedition to Red River, 66–68; leaves Texas, 68; assessment, 69
Terreros, Father Alonso Giraldo de, 125, 126, 127
Terreros, Pedro Romero de, 125
Texas Surgical Society, 11
Texita (Indian), 187
Tienda de Cuervo, José, 141
Tinhioüen (Indian), 152
Tonkawa Indians, 119, 155, 162, 199
Tonti, Henri de, 78
Treviño, Matías, 233, 234
Treaty of Paris (1783), 171
trees, 112
Trinity River, 111
Turk (Indian), 21, 22, 23, 27
turkeys, 23, 110

United States, 29
Unzaga, Luis de, 153, 154, 155, 156, 157
Uribe, María Josefa de, 197

Uribe, María Rosa de, 197
Urrutia, Joaquín de, 229
Urrutia, José de, 229, 230, 239
Urrutia, Juana de, 229
Urrutia, Pedro de, 229
Ute Indians, 169

Valencia, Spain, 90
Vázquez Borrego, Juan José, 140, 141
Vázquez de Coronado, Francisco, 17;
   appointed captain, 19; wife
   Beatriz, 19, 30; march to Cíbola,
   19–20; early explorations, 20–22;
   on Río Grande, 22–23; march to
   Quivira, 24–27; orders Turk's exe-
   cution, 27; return to Río Grande
   and Mexico City, 27–29; assess-
   ment, 29–30, 241; death, 30
Veracruz (city and port), 4, 92, 211
Vergara, Rita, 222
Vial, Pedro, 171, 172, 173
Vidales, Antonia, 217
Virgin Mary, 38

weather, 4, 23, 24, 65–67, 68, 99–100,
   108, 110, 124, 127, 141, 161, 187
Weddle, Robert S., 73

West Texas, 24, 32, 37
Wichita Indians, 27, 170, 171
wildflowers, 110
witches, 96
women: first non-Indian women in
   Texas, 85, 217–218; treatment of,
   207; and shipwrecks of 1554, 212;
   and La Salle's colony, 212–216; at
   Villa de Béxar, 219; Canary Islanders, 219–221; as settlers and
   ranchers, 222–224; on frontiers of
   Spain, 226–227; and Spanish law,
   227–233, 237–239; responsibilities of, 233–237, 239, 242
World War II, 44

Ximénez, María Antonia, 217
Ximénez de Valdez, Ana María, 217

Yatasi Indians, 152
Ygollo, Mission, 142
Yguaze Indians, 9
Yscani Indians, 153, 154
Yucatán, 93, 135

Zacatecas, 96, 97, 98, 99, 102, 103
Zuñi Indians, 18, 19